Christian Eco-Spirituality

"Parry makes a compelling case for a dynamic, Christian ecological spirituality that can enrich and transform individuals and communities. His writing is lucid, backed by brilliant scholarship, and uses humor alongside developing provocative and profound insights. Wisest book I have read in decades."

—**Charles Taliaferro**
Emeritus Overby Distinguished Professor, St. Olaf College

"I'm so grateful to Robin Parry for writing *Christian Eco-Spirituality*. He brings his deep-rooted theological understanding into conversation with his formational experiences leading worship in the cathedral gardens and has produced a truly beautiful book that is inspiring and refreshing. Whether you're wanting to discover what the Christian faith and ecology have to do with each other, or you've been living this stuff out for years, this is a book to be read slowly, savored, and lived out."

—**Ruth Valerio**
Eco-activist and Programmes, Partnerships & Advocacy Director, Embrace the Middle East

"The depth of Robin Parry's academic and practical experience shines through in this compelling combination of a wisdom-centered and ecologically attentive reading of the story of the Bible with extensive creative advice about how churches and individuals can faithfully inhabit this story. A delightful book brimming with theological insight and practical hope."

—**Jonathan A. Moo**
Bruner-Welch Endowed Chair in Theology, Professor of New Testament and Environmental Studies, Whitworth University

"There is an entire world to draw into our Christian worship and discipleship—quite literally—a world we may have been overlooking. The Revd Robin Parry, overseer of wild worship in the sanctuary garden by the towering Worcester Cathedral, offers this carefully written, thoughtful guide to enacting Christian eco-spirituality and understanding why it matters. I really like this book! Open your eyes and hands to the divine Word and Wisdom expressed in the creation of God."

—**Esther Lightcap Meek**
Professor of Philosophy *Emerita* at Geneva College

"Bzzzzzzz. Sweet! Bzzzzz."

—**Bees from the Sacred Garden**

"Robin Parry's truly original *Christian Eco-Spirituality* is a comprehensive and readable survey of the subject. The first part presents the theological basis of eco-spirituality through the lens of Sophia-wisdom, and the second part explores its practical outworking, including topics such as forest church and eco-anxiety. Highly recommended."

—**Martin J. Hodson**
Environmental biologist and Principal Tutor for Christian Rural and Environmental Studies (www.cres.org.uk)

"A tour de force of the landscape of Christian eco-spirituality which deftly moves through biblical and theological reflection so as to root worship within lives lived holistically as a part of God's creation, not apart from it, at a time of ecological crisis."

—**Graham Usher**
Bishop of Norwich and the Church of England's Lead Bishop for Environment

"This book on Christian eco-spirituality will surprise you. It is written by someone who, by his own confession, has never been a passionate tree-hugger, but a passionate theologian, yet who has been organically opened to creation by paying attention to Jesus Christ. Robin is energetic, funny, and invites us to walk in the way of Wisdom—Wisdom who is none other than Christ, the one who walked among us as a human being. For Jesus' flesh not only connects Christ to all humanity, but to all biological life, down to its very roots. Working as the 'eco-priest' at Worcester Cathedral, Robin pairs theological precision with practical ways for us to be formed by Christ as we live in our natural habitats. (Don't miss the A to Z of Wild Worship!)"

—**Julie Canlis (PhD)**
Author of *A Theology of the Ordinary* and *Calvin's Ladder*

"Refreshing!"
—**Sister Water**

"Smoking!"
—**Brother Fire**

"Cool!"
—**Sister Snow**

"Out of this world!"
—**The constellation of Orion**

Christian Eco-Spirituality

An Outline

ROBIN A. PARRY

CASCADE Books • Eugene, Oregon

CHRISTIAN ECO-SPIRITUALITY
An Outline

Copyright © 2025 Robin A. Parry. All rights reserved. Except for brief quotations in critical publications or reviews, no part of this book may be reproduced in any manner without prior written permission from the publisher. Write: Permissions, Wipf and Stock Publishers, 199 W. 8th Ave., Suite 3, Eugene, OR 97401.

Cascade Books
An Imprint of Wipf and Stock Publishers
199 W. 8th Ave., Suite 3
Eugene, OR 97401

www.wipfandstock.com

PAPERBACK ISBN: 979-8-3852-2415-9
HARDCOVER ISBN: 979-8-3852-2416-6
EBOOK ISBN: 979-8-3852-2417-3

Cataloguing-in-Publication data:

Names: Parry, Robin A., author.
Title: Christian eco-spirituality : an outline / by Robin A. Parry.
Description: Eugene, OR: Cascade Books, 2025 | Includes bibliographical references.
Identifiers: ISBN 979-8-3852-2415-9 (paperback) | ISBN 979-8-3852-2416-6 (hardcover) | ISBN 979-8-3852-2417-3 (ebook)
Subjects: LCSH: Ecotheology. | Nature—Religious aspects—Christianity. | Spirituality. | Human ecology—Religious aspects—Christianity. | Ecology—Religious aspects—Christianity.
Classification: BT695.5 P377 2025 (print) | BT695.5 (ebook)

VERSION NUMBER 100925

Scripture quotations taken from:

The Holy Bible, New International Version® NIV® Copyright © 1973, 1978, 1984, 2011 by Biblica, Inc. Used with permission. All rights reserved worldwide.

The ESV®Bible (The Holy Bible, English Standard Version®), copyright© 2001 by Crossway Bibles, a publishing ministry of Good News Publishers. Used by permission. All rights reserved.

New Revised Standard Version Updated Edition. Copyright © 2021 National Council of Churches of Christ in the United States of America. Used by permission. All rights reserved worldwide.

Cover image by Jane Skingley. https://www.janeskingley.com Reproduced by kind permission.

All images by Hannah Parry are reproduced with permission.

The hare image at the start of each chapter is James Seymour (1702–52) – A Hare Running, with Ears Pricked – B2001.2.1192 – Yale Center for British Art.jpg. Reproduced under creative commons license.

The extended quotation from The Deep Waters course is reproduced with permission from Green Christian. https://greenchristian.org.uk/

To the Benedictine Sisters and Brothers at Mucknell Abbey,
Worcestershire

To Monty, my mews,
"For he is the servant of the Living God,
duly and daily serving him."

To the team who enable Worship in the Garden, Sacred Garden, and
The Sophia Course to happen—with gratitude and affection.

To Sabrina, the River Severn, with gratitude and apologies.

"The sun rises every morning.... Now, to put the matter in a popular phrase, it might be true that the sun rises regularly because he never gets tired of rising. His routine might be due, not to a lifelessness, but to a rush of life. The thing I mean can be seen, for instance, in children, when they find some game or joke that they specially enjoy. A child kicks his legs rhythmically through excess, not absence, of life. Because children have abounding vitality, because they are in spirit fierce and free, therefore they want things repeated and unchanged. They always say, 'Do it again'; and the grown-up person does it again until he is nearly dead. For grown-up people are not strong enough to exult in monotony. But perhaps God is strong enough to exult in monotony. It is possible that God says every morning, 'Do it again' to the sun, and every evening, 'Do it again' to the moon. It may not be automatic necessity that makes all daisies alike; it may be that God makes every daisy separately, but has never got tired of making them. It may be that He has the eternal appetite of infancy; for we have sinned and grown old, and our Father is younger than we. The repetition in Nature may not be a mere recurrence; it may be a theatrical *encore*."

—G. K. Chesterton, *Orthodoxy*

"Words make worlds. In English, we 'it' rivers, trees, mountains, oceans, birds, and animals: a mode of address that reduces them to the statues of stuff, and distinguishes them from human persons. In English, pronouns for natural features are 'which' or 'that', not 'who': the river *that* flows; the forest *that* grows. I prefer to speak of rivers *who* flow and forests *who* grow."

—Robert Macfarlane, *Is a River Alive?*

Contents

Detailed Outline | ix
Acknowledgments | xv
A Note on the Divine Name | xvii

Introduction | 1

Part I: A Wise Story to Inhabit

1. Meet Woman Wisdom: An Ancient-Future Vision of God and Creation | 13
2. Wisdom's Choir: Creation as Festival | 27
3. The Wise Image: Humanity and Creation | 44
4. The Leviathan in the Room: The Dark Side of Wisdom's Creation | 60
5. Nothing Really Matters: Creation Out of Nothing | 76
6. Wisdom Made Text: Israel and the Eco-Spirituality of Torah | 88
7. Sophia's Shalom: Social Justice and Ecology | 107
8. Wisdom Made Flesh: Jesus-Sophia Among Us | 116
9. Saving Wisdom: The Cosmic Implications of Christ's Death and Resurrection | 125
10. The Spirit of Wisdom: Pentecost and Eco-Spirituality | 133

Conclusion to Part I | 147

Part II: Inhabiting The Story

A Wise Worship

11. The A to Z of Wild Worship | 153
12. Between Denial and Despair: Worship and Eco-Anxiety | 196

B Wise Living

13 Monastic Eco-Wisdom | 217
14 Philo-Sophia: The Way of Wisdom and Lifelong Learning | 228
15 Conclusion: Baptism and the Art of Living Gently on the Earth | 242

Appendix: The Sound of Silence | 251

Sources Cited | 265

Detailed Outline

Introduction
    Christian (Eco-)Spirituality
    Worship
    Confessions of a Reforming Sinner
    The Shape of Things to Come

Part I. A Wise Story to Inhabit

1. Meet Woman Wisdom: An Ancient-Future Vision of God and Creation
    Woman Wisdom in Proverbs
    What Is Wisdom in Proverbs 8:22–31?
        A Goddess?
        A Divine Attribute Personified?
        More Than a Personification (Wisdom as a Hypostasis)?
    Woman Wisdom in Second Temple Judaism
        Wisdom's Pre-Existence and Her Relationship with God
        Wisdom's Role in the Creation of the World
        Wisdom's Role in Providence
    Conclusion: A Wisdom Worldview

2. Wisdom's Choir: Creation as Festival
    Ordered Chaos (Genesis 1)
    Where the Wild Things Are
        "How manifold are your works" (Psalm 104)
        Wild God (Job 38–42)
    The Choir of Creation
        God's in the House: Creation as Temple
        "Let everything that has breath . . ." (Psalm 148)

3. The Wise Image: Humanity and Creation
   A Toxic Christian Legacy? (Genesis 1)
   Image and Dominion
     The Image of God
     Ruling and Subduing
        "rule"
        "subdue"
     Final Reflections on Humanity and Genesis 1
   Dust with a Destiny (Genesis 2)
   Humanity as a Microcosm of Creation

4. The Leviathan in the Room: The Dark Side of Wisdom's Creation
   A Dead-End Solution
   Does the Bible Teach That the Created Order Was Once a Paradise?
   Creation Has a Place for the Dark and the Deep
   Creation as Aimed at a Telos
   Natural Evils and the God of Love
     Knowing What We Don't Know
     A Warning Not to Exaggerate
        Extinctions
        Pain
     One: The Primary Response
     Two: God Can Bring Good Out of Suffering
     Three: The Suffering God
     Four: All's Well That Ends Well

5. Nothing Really Matters: Creation out of Nothing
   Ex Nihilo
   Divine Transcendence
   Divine Immanence
   Divine and Creaturely Action

6. Wisdom Made Text: Israel and the Eco-Spirituality of Torah
   Moses and the Wise Torah
   The Torah and Ecology
     Israel as an Agricultural Community
     Living Fruitfully in the Land
        The land is God's
        The land is a gift
        The land must be respected
        The earth/land is engaged with as a "personal agent"
     Animals
   Ecological Entanglement in the Prophets

7. Wisdom's Shalom: Social Justice and Ecology
   The Just God
   The Shalomic Vision
   The Just Nation
   Wisdom and Justice
   Justice and the Environment

8. Wisdom Made Flesh: Jesus-Sophia Among Us
   More Than a Sage (Matthew's Gospel)
   Jesus as Creator (Saint Paul)
   Wisdom Made Flesh and Blood (John's Gospel)
   The Eco-Spirituality of Incarnation

9. Saving Wisdom: The Cosmic Implications of Christ's Death and Resurrection
   The Cosmic Death of Jesus
   The Cosmic Resurrection of Jesus
   The Death and Resurrection of Creation in Christ

10. The Spirit of Wisdom: Pentecost and Eco-Spirituality
    The Spirit of Wisdom and the Trinity
    Excursus: Relationality in Creation and the Trinity
    The Spirit in Creation
    Pentecost and the Christ-Community
        Acts of Faithful Eco-Witness
        Eco-Prophets in the Spirit
            Saints
    The Spirit and Eco-Spirituality

SUMMARY of Part I (in a diagram)

Part II. Inhabiting the Story
Wise Worship

11. The A to Z of Wild Worship
    Y is for YHWH-Centric
    F is for Formation
    R is for Revelation
    T is for Tradition
    D is for Divine Presence
    P is for Place
    N is for Nature's Rhythms
    W is for Weather

B is for Bodies
L is for Liturgy
E is for Eucharist
G is for Gratitude
K is for Keeping (Guarding)
S is for Silence
C is for Creativity
M is for Music
J is for Journey
V is for Veritas
I is for Integration
X is for Mystery
U is for Unicorn
H is for Hospitality
O is for Outside-In
Q is for Questions of Practicality

12. Between Denial and Despair: Worship and Eco-Anxiety
The Rise of Eco-Anxiety
Unhelpful Responses to Our Ecological Crises
- Denial: The Fool
- Despair: The Hare
- Ignoring: The Ostrich

Worship as a Christian Path Between Denial and Despair
- Honesty: Confession, Intercession, Lament
  - Confession
  - Intercession
  - Lament
- Hope: Gospel-Shaped Living

Prophetic Acts of Hope (Jeremiah)

Wise Living

13. Monastic Eco-Wisdom
Monasticism and Ecology
Monasticism for the Rest of Us
- Asceticism
- Simplicity
- A Rule of Life

14. Philo-Sophia: The Way of Wisdom and Lifelong Learning
Philosophy as a Way of Life

The Pursuit of Wisdom as a Way of Life
    Traditional, Communal Wisdom
    Revelation and Wisdom
    Experience and Wisdom
All Wisdom Is God's Wisdom
The Ecological Implications
    Learning from Our Own Story
    Learning from Beyond Our Tradition
        Science
        Non-Christian Spiritual Traditions
    Remaining Open to Correction

15. Conclusion: Baptism and the Art of Living Gently on the Earth
    Go in Peace . . .
    Living Out Our Baptism
    Living Gently on the Earth
        Sin and the Environment
        Environmental Sin and Baptism
            Take off . . .
            Put on . . .
        Environmental Mission and Baptism
    And the Blessing . . .

Appendix: The Sound of Silence
    Biblical Silence
    Silence and the Classical Synthesis
    The Story of Christian Silence
    Silence: Individual and Communal
        Silence in Individual Spirituality
        Silence in Communal Spirituality

Acknowledgments

I would like to express my gratitude for the wonderful support I have received for my quirky eco-spirituality ministry from the dean and other clergy colleagues at Worcester Cathedral, and the cathedral's chapter, eco-group, congregation, and staff. I would also like to acknowledge the unwavering and enthusiastic support from Bishop John Inge, who was bishop of Worcester at the time I was appointed. Most especially I would like to thank my core group of co-laborers in the different strands of the eco-ministry: Staffan, Liz, Rachel, Stephanie, Dave, Caroline, and Carol, my wife. Indeed, without Carol's forest-school skills and unfailing support I could not have done any of this. I'd also like to thank my daughter Hannah for the beautiful doll she made of St. Melangell, a biblical cosmos image, a cosmic temple image, a two-hare picture, and the little hare Trinity symbol for the chapter openings. (The three-hares symbol is ancient and appears in various contexts around the world. Among them it appears in quite a few old churches in Devon, where it might possibly serve as a symbol of God,[1] which is how I employ it here.) I am also very grateful to the artist Jane Skingley (https://www.janeskingley.com) for permission to use one of her beautiful paintings—an image that has adorned the wall over our table for many years—on the cover. Additionally, praise is due to the wonderful team at Cascade Books, especially: Rodney Clapp, my editor; Ian Creeger, my typesetter; Shannon Carter, my cover designer; and Jesselyn Clapp, my proofreader. You excel. Finally, I thank all those who come regularly to our worship and spirituality events, for all their enthusiasm and encouragement.

P.S., Monty, the three-legged cat, tells me that I have to thank him too. Yes, sir! You are the gentle king of silkiness. Thanks for being so sweet.

---

1. Interpretation of the three-hares symbol in its medieval Christian contexts involves educated guesswork. A plausible alternative interpretation is found in Greeves et al., *Three Hares*, ch. 4.

A Note on the Divine Name

READERS WILL FIND THAT I render the Divine Name of God from the Hebrew Bible as YHWH (יהוה). These are the four consonants that compose the Name. Since the Second Temple period Jews have considered the Divine Name to be so holy that it cannot be spoken. Thus, since that time, whenever the Name appears in the Scriptures, pious Jews substitute an alternative for it when reading aloud (e.g., *Adonai* [meaning Lord] or *HaShem* [meaning "The Name"]). Jesus and the authors of the New Testament documents were devout Jews, and they too followed this practice, which is why the many clear references to YHWH in the New Testament always find work-arounds to avoid using the Name.[2] For instance, Jesus taught his disciples to pray "Father, hallowed by your Name"—the Name in question is YHWH, but it is deliberately not spoken. I consider this practice to be very healthy, for it preserves a sense of the deep, impenetrable mystery of God. It habituates us against domesticating the Divine.

Modern English Bible translations usually opt for the word LORD in capital letters as a substitute for YHWH. The reason I have not done so most of the time is that "Lord" is a title and "YHWH" is a name. I want readers to see the Name *as* a name. For that reason, I have modified the English Bible translations I use to refer to YHWH rather than "the LORD."

Of course, without the vowels one cannot easily say YHWH aloud—and that is the point. If you wish to say something, then say "the Lord" or "HaShem" or "the Name." My personal preference is "Yehovah." Yehovah is what is actually written in Hebrew Bibles. It is not a real word, not a word that is intended to be used. Rather, it is the consonants of the Name (YHWH) with the vowels of the title Adonai (Lord) written into it. (I know it doesn't look like it is, but trust me, it is.) This is to remind readers that when they *see* the Name YHWH while reading the text, they are to *say* Adonai. Well, I *say* Yehovah. Some people groan at that because Yehovah is not

---

2. On this, see Soulen, *Divine Name(s)*, ch. 1.

xvii

the Name. Absolutely. *That's the whole point*. It's a way to gesture towards the Name without saying it. And if that is not your cup of tea, try "Yah." That is a shortened version of the Name, which includes a vowel. It is allowed to be said (e.g., *hallelu-Yah*, Praise Yah).

Introduction

DOES CHRISTIANITY HAVE ANYTHING positive to contribute to the world at this time of ecological crisis? Obviously, churches can add bodies on the ground to swell protests and Christians can lobby politicians and banks and businesses; and they can help with conservation work and do their bit in terms of sustainable living. All that is good. But is there nothing *distinctive* that Christians can contribute to environmentalism beyond "human resources," responsible citizenship, and consumer power?

This book argues that what Christianity has to offer is a distinctive *spirituality*, one that provides a rich rationale for creation care, principles to guide it, and the resources to empower, equip, and form people to walk that pathway with resilience.

For Christians, positive environmental living must never simply be the panic response of people who don't want to die. Not wanting to die is good, obviously. And taking necessary action to avoid it is also good. Yet for Jesus-followers, living gently on the earth has got to be *much more* than that. I argue in what follows that being "eco" is a part of what Christian discipleship looks like. It's one aspect of walking the walk and inhabiting the biblical stories about God and creation. It is, in short, a matter of living the gospel, of embodying its narrative in our own lives. For the Christian, being creation-attuned is simply part of what a *faith-full* and *spiritual* life looks like. This book explores that idea.

1. Christian (Eco-)Spirituality

Let's take a step back. What is spirituality? And what is Christian spirituality? Befuddlingly, the word "spirituality" seems to be used in a plethora of ways, usually very fuzzy ones. It has something to do with our deep values and the meanings we see in life and try to live by, perhaps even with what we consider "sacred," but it is a watery word that can be poured into vessels of many shapes and sizes, blended with many ingredients, and sometimes evaporated into shapeless, shifting clouds of vagueness. The problem is that a word that can mean almost anything means almost nothing. For that reason, some Christian thinkers argue that it's a word better abandoned. I disagree. It resonates too well, with me and with many other people. It "feels" like it fits what I think about when I think of Christianity (perhaps because the word originated in Christian usage before it was applied more broadly). However, for it to be useful to us we need to spell out a little more clearly what we might have in mind when we speak of *Christian* spirituality.

To that end, let me offer my rough working understanding. Here's the short version: *"Christian spirituality is living out our baptism in the power of the Holy Spirit."* Everything I have to say is nothing more (nor less) than that. We'll return to that in our conclusion. But perhaps that is a wee bit too short and cryptic for now, so allow me to offer a more expanded version. You may think the following is a bit dense and clunky (you'd be right!), and you may find that you're not sure what on earth I am talking about. You might also worry about material you think should be included but appears not to be, like the cross and resurrection or repentance or prayer or baptism or the Eucharist and so on and so forth. Bear with. I can assure you that all those apparently absent ideas *are* included, but they are only revealed as the ideas below are slowly unpacked. I trust that my definition will make a lot more sense by the time you've reached the end of the book. With that in mind, here it is:

> *Christian spirituality is the gift of having our human lives united to Christ by the Spirit, enabling us to ascend ever deeper into God (and thus also into richer connection with the rest of creation). This life of union with Jesus involves our whole person—body, soul, and spirit—living in community with other creatures (human and nonhuman) and the loving Triune Creator. As such it is a life marked by a mutually enriching interplay and integration of Christian beliefs (about the Trinity and creation), values, virtues, principles, actions, and spiritual practices. It is a life of*

cooperating with the Spirit's inner work in our journey toward shalom, Christlikeness, and final union with God.[1]

OK. You can breathe again now. I think of this book as a meandering unpacking of that definition, so I won't attempt to explain it now. However, I would like to make a few important preliminary observations.

First, any *Christian* understanding of Christian spirituality will see it not merely as a description of what *human beings* think and do but as the activity of *God* in the individual and communal lives of humans. I do not expect someone describing Christian spirituality from the "outside" to see it in those terms, but Christians must see it that way.

Second, Christians believe that the God who is working among and within us, the God of the gospel, is not some generic "one God" of monotheism but the three-in-one Creator and Redeemer. A Christian account of spirituality will therefore be woven around the work of the three persons of the Trinity in the life of creation. This is, after all, a *spirit*uality. For a Christian that means it concerns spirit, both the human spirit and God's Spirit.[2] And for followers of Jesus, this Spirit is the Spirit *of God* and *of Christ*. No Christian conception of the Holy Ghost can be divorced from the work of God in Christ. In orthodox Christian thought, *every* movement of God towards and within creation and *every* movement of creation towards and within God occurs *through Christ* and *in the Spirit*. As far as spirituality is concerned, we could say that it is the Spirit's work in drawing us deeper into God through union with Christ.

Third, there's a lot more to Christian spirituality than the "obvious" stuff—spiritual practices like prayer, worship, confession of sin, contemplation, devotional reading of Scripture, Eucharist, pilgrimage, and the like. Those things are very important, but spirituality is much broader, weaving together various threads into a single garment. It involves spiritual practices, yes, but also beliefs, values, virtues, principles, behaviors, and patterns of relating with others in healthy ways (including social, economic, and political relations).

Fourth, these threads are mutually supportive and mutually informing. For instance, take belief. Beliefs matter—a lot. As Norman Wirzba observes, "the way we name and narrate the world determines how we are going to

---

1. With gratitude to the Facebook hivemind for help in refining this. Remaining errors are all my own.

2. To speak of the human spirit is to gesture towards the most inward and mysterious aspects of our life and identity—our *core*. Christian spirituality then can be understood in terms of the activity of God's Holy Spirit in the human spirit.

live within it."³ Beliefs have legs, they go places, they do things. Beliefs can lead people to heal or to hurt, to lift up or to tear down. Consequently, I make no apology for a long section of the book devoted to sketching a biblical and theological story within which Christians can live and move.⁴ That story tells us about God, about the cosmos, and about ourselves in relation to them. It explains *why* living in tune with creation matters for Christianity.

It should also be obvious that *ethics* is not distinct from spirituality. As Alasdair MacIntyre observed, "I can only answer the question 'What am I to do?' if I can answer the prior question 'Of what story or stories do I find myself a part?'"⁵ Values (like the goodness of creatures), virtues (like compassion), and principles (like "do not lie") "make sense" within a story we tell about God and the world. Change the story and you can change the ethics.⁶ For instance, in ancient Rome the weak and vulnerable were generally despised because classical stories of the world valorized strength and honor. Christianity was pivotal in changing that ethic in Western culture because it told a story of the world in which the Creator became a human and cared for and helped those who were weak. Out of love, God was prepared to become weak and dishonored for the sake of others.⁷ The different story supported a different set of values and principles, one in which the vulnerable were to be protected, cared for, and empowered. Change the story, change the ethic. (The extent to which Jesus' followers fail to live by Christian ethics is the extent to which they fail to truly inhabit the gospel.) Questions of social justice and political engagement are also, in this picture, aspects of Christian spirituality—of lives that indwell the Christian narrative. Similarly, devotional practices of prayer and worship need to reflect the beliefs and values of the Christ-community and to help participants inhabit that story in increasingly rich ways. So our beliefs, our ethics, our daily habits of life, our prayer (in its many forms) are supposed to work together in *a virtuous spiral of transformation* through which the Spirit moves us closer to the likeness of Jesus.

---

3. Wirzba, *From Nature to Creation*, 18. (The original was in italics.)

4. For what I consider to be the best all-in-one-place guide to biblical teaching on creation and ecology, see Moo and Moo, *Creation Care*.

5. MacIntyre, *After Virtue*, 216.

6. When the worldview supporting a widespread ethic changes, cultural inertia can keep the ethic in place for a while. Once the lack of support for the ethic becomes clearer people often seek alternative foundations for it. Failure to find them can lead to gradual shifts in a society's ethical views as values and principles morph to fit the new story (or stories) of the world.

7. On this claim, see Holland, *Dominion*.

Let me stress the "mutually supportive" and "mutually informing" aspect of the threads in the garment of Christian spirituality. Some people treat beliefs as the foundation on which everything else is built. To switch metaphors, Christian values, virtues, principles, and practices *"reflect"* Christian beliefs. And there is a lot of truth in that. They do. Or at least, they should. What we *seek* is a deep coherence and resonance between our beliefs and our values and practices. But the traffic is not one-way. It can run in the other direction too: a life of prayer or hospitality or justice-seeking, say, will in turn help to clarify, challenge, and inform one's beliefs. I believe that theology, prayer, ethics, and lifestyle should all be in constant round-table conversation—a conversation that is lively and brings change, for us and for those we interact with. In a nutshell: it's messy.

Fifth, it should be clear by now that Christian spirituality is not focused purely on the immaterial, with little concern about grubby things like bodies or actions or the physical world. Such an airy-fairy "spirituality" is OK for ghosts but would be a disaster for environmental responsibility, for obvious reasons. As we shall see in this book, such a view would be the *complete antithesis* of Christian spirituality. In Scripture human beings are conceived as *essentially embodied* creatures and biblical anthropologies are very holistic, seeing humans as psychosomatic unities. Any spirituality that wants to take our spirits seriously *has to take our bodies seriously too*, along with the spiritual-material earth we inhabit.

OK. That's all well and good, but what about Christian *eco*-spirituality? Is it some trendy "woke" version to keep "lefty progressives" happy? Or some quasi-pagan nature worship with Jesus-dust sprinkled on top? In brief: No. (See! I can be brief!)

"Alright then," I hear you say, "what's your working definition of Christian eco-spirituality?" Oh! Oh! Oh! I know that one! You already have it. It's *the same* as my generic definition of Christian spirituality. As we'll see in the following pages, the Christian story is *inherently* creation-affirming. To avoid that aspect of it you'd have to tell another story—a diluted gospel that has forgotten some of its own central characters and plot. To speak of eco-spirituality in this context is simply to bring into more prominent *focus* the creation attunement *already contained* in my definition. This book seeks to sketch the contours of that focus.

One (surprising?) implication of my argument in the following chapters is that eco-spirituality is not *first and foremost* something we should encourage because of the current ecological emergencies, though they are indeed a reason to encourage it. My contention is that creation-attuned spirituality is a mode of *ordinary* Christian spirituality and it's something we should be doing *irrespective* of any ecological crises. It would be an utterly fitting mode of Christian life even if all was well with the earth. Indeed, if we had attended more carefully to the eco-spiritual aspects of the life of discipleship then I suspect that Christians and churches would have been prominent among the pioneers at the forefront of the environmental movement rather than running behind to catch up.[8] Still, better late than never!

2. Worship

> "Farewell, farewell! but this I tell,
> To thee, thou wedding guest!
> He prayeth well, who loveth well
> Both man and bird and beast.
>
> He prayeth best, who loveth best
> All things both great and small;
> For the dear God who loveth us
> He made and loveth all."
> —Samuel Taylor Coleridge[9]

I will give a lot of space to the issue of worship (chapter 11). Worship is the beating heart of Christian life. When we gather in worship, we reorientate ourselves toward the Divine, our true north, which in healthy worship should simultaneously help us to realign our relationships with others. Worship shapes us and helps us to follow Christ in the ordinary world, day by day, transforming our *whole* lives into offerings of devotion to God. Worship should inform our heads, awaken our hearts, and steel our wills. Important as it is for Christian intellectuals to think through biblical interpretation, ethics, and theology, if we do not consider how to bring to the surface the often-submerged creation themes and aspects of our worship, we are inadvertently implying that creation is not very important to God. We are sending the implicit signal that you can love God without loving your nonhuman neighbor. After all, if nonhumans were genuinely important, we'd find ways to "include" them in this most intimate and holy of spaces.

My belief is that participating in acts of creation-attuned[10] public worship is profoundly important in helping Christians connect their relationship with God to their relationship with the natural world around them. Worship engages the *whole* person and helps, over time, to form hearts that respond to the world in gospel-shaped ways.

---

8. I know that some were at the forefront of the movements for animal rights and conservation, but not nearly enough.

9. Coleridge, *The Rhyme of the Ancient Mariner* (1798).

10. Not creation-*focused* worship, for worship is *God*-focused.

The holistic way in which worship engages people is very important. Real change does not come about from simply having the "right ideas" and "all the facts." It isn't enough to know all about how the world works and how our actions affect it. Norman Wirzba is right when he comments, "as desirable as it may be to have information about the world, what we need are capacities that will help us to love the world."[11] That! *We need to fall in love.* I'd like to consider the idea that worship is one place in which we can learn to fall in love with creation by falling in love with the Creator. In this book I shall explore the idea that patterns of worship can help foster such love.

What I am advocating for here is a slow spirituality, not a one-off-event spirituality. Having an annual animal-blessing service or a special outdoor service is all well and good, but it isn't going to cut the mustard. There are no quick fixes here. This reformation calls for "a long obedience in the same direction."[12] The good news is that all the core resources we need to fund it are found in Scripture, the tradition, and in creation itself. It's a matter of uncovering them, polishing them up, and putting them to work. This text offers a few suggestions in that direction.

3. Confessions of a Reforming Sinner

I confess that I feel something of a fraud writing this book, an interloper. I have not been a "nature lover" for most of my life. I was never into bird watching or wild camping or horses or gardening (though I did like geology). I have always loved looking at the natural world and being in it, but I was never much interested in knowing all about it. So biology and horticulture and the like held little appeal. I couldn't name most trees and flowers, I had little clue which fruit and veg were in season at any particular time, and I didn't know the life cycles of most animals. I liked looking at the sky but found astronomy dull. You get the general picture. To a very large extent I have been glancing at the world but not really looking.

I've known many people who have been at work in the areas of biology, ecology, conservation, and "green activism" for decades. And I've admired them. I believed that what they were doing was important, but it wasn't the focus of my own thinking or living, beyond token acts of recycling and reducing waste. And eco-spirituality was not something I was looking for. Indeed, it wasn't even something I'd thought about much. However, it was on the prowl. I heard the occasional crack of a twig, sometimes saw the

---

11. Wirzba, *From Nature to Creation*, 3.

12. Credit to Eugene Peterson, who appropriated this wonderful phrase from Friedrich Nietzsche.

bushes move, had that uncanny feeling that I was being watched, and even caught glimpses of it silhouetted on the horizon. I was being hunted. Then one day, just as I was getting used to this low-level surveillance, it pounced! It was unexpected and hit me like a freight train. I knew more or less immediately that eco-spirituality was something that God was calling me to help encourage. And I had a fairly clear picture in my mind, right from that moment, of the direction of travel. A new path lay before me, and I felt I needed to pursue it. And that's what I have done, albeit in a fumbling and bumbling fashion.

So I'm starting off from a low base. People sometimes imagine that I'm some wise eco-priest who knows all about plants and animals and spent years tending to sick birds and campaigning against the pollution of rivers, the destruction of forests, and the fossil fuel industry. Would that I was. But I am not. (Ask my wife, who will happily spill the beans about my ignorance.) I know many people who are far ahead of me on the green-brick road, people I feel are far better placed than I am to speak with knowledge and integrity about these matters. In other words, you are reading a book by a man who doesn't know what he's talking about. (That sentence is a gift to all those reviewers who hate the book. You're welcome!) Well, perhaps I'm putting it a little too starkly, but I am serious. Maybe a better analogy is one of the blind men who came to Jesus for healing (Mark 8:22–26). After Jesus' first intervention, the man's vision was partly restored. He couldn't see clearly, but he could see "people like trees walking." Well, that's me. I don't see clearly, and I still have a long way to go on my journey towards clarity, but I do see *something*, something worth sharing. This book is that something. It's not the last word. It's not even the first word. But it is *a* word. And I believe that it's a word worth hearing. It's a seed, full of hopeful potential. How it will grow, in my own life and the lives of others, I do not yet know. How my own understandings and practices will change as I move deeper into wisdom, I do not know. But the seed that I have, I plant, and I entrust it to God. May it bear some fruit.

4. The Shape of Things to Come

Finally, a word about the shape of this book. Part I explores the biblical and theological foundations for eco-spirituality. It is, in essence, the story-shaped eco-theology that informs my own attempts to live more gently on the earth, the rationale for doing what I do (or try to do). Part II is directed more towards the practical side of things: How should this vision affect our worship, and how can our worship affect us? How can eco-spirituality help us to better navigate life in a world of environmental crises? What practical lessons for living gently on the earth can we learn from Christian monastic traditions? What basic orientations of the mind towards wisdom and learning does eco-spirituality energize?

The goal in Part II is not to solve all the practical challenges we face—it hardly even begins to address them. Rather, the goal is to help foster a spirituality, a God-orientated way of being in the world, that will play a constructive role in forming (and informing) people who are better able to deal with such practical challenges. In a nutshell: it's about learning to walk the path of wisdom.

Now it's time to take a break.
Go hug a tree, then come back for Part I. 🌳

A warning: Part I begins with what may feel an unnecessary, long discussion of a character in the book of Proverbs. Go with it. She matters. In fact, she is at the heart of everything I have to say.

A permission: you may want to get straight into the practical material and jump to Part II. That's fine. I get it. However, you will need to come back to read Part I after that or the conceptual supports for the practices I am recommending will remain unclear.

PART I

A Wise Story to Inhabit

I

Meet Woman Wisdom

An Ancient-Future Vision of God and Creation

1. Woman Wisdom in Proverbs

IMAGINE A TOWN IN ancient Israel centuries before the time of Jesus. The book of Proverbs paints a scene for us in which a woman stands calling out to those who will listen. She is not timid or shy, she is out to grab the attention of those around her. She doesn't whisper or mumble, she cries out at the top of her voice; not in the house, not in the fields, but in public spaces in the town, where the people are. She wants to be heard. We are reminded of Israel's prophets disturbing the peace with their intrusive messages from YHWH. Yet this woman is no ordinary woman. This woman is God's Wisdom (Hebrew: *ḥokmâ*; Greek: *sophia*), personified as a human being.

> Wisdom cries out in the street;
>   in the squares she raises her voice.
> At the busiest corner she cries out;
>   at the entrance of the city gates she speaks:
> "How long, O simple ones, will you love being simple?
> How long will scoffers delight in their scoffing
>   and fools hate knowledge?
> Give heed to my reproof;

I will pour out my thoughts to you;
   I will make my words known to you."
(Prov 1:20–23)

Foolishly, many ignore her. Not the brightest move, for there is a price to pay for rejecting Wisdom (1:24–33).

Woman Wisdom speaks again in Proverbs 8. Now she stands on the heights, at the crossroads, at the entrances to towns, calling to travelers, again exhorting all who will hear (8:4–11). Those who attend to her good advice will prosper in what they do (8:12–21).

At this point, Wisdom's speech takes a very unexpected turn. Thus far Wisdom has been speaking with authority and making some grand claims about the importance of her words. Now she sets out the basis for her authority to speak in this way, why people ought to listen to her. It turns out that she is qualified to speak about how to live well in creation because *she was with God when he created the world*. So she understands the cosmos, and delights in it, and consequently can guide the simple to live well in it. Suddenly, Wisdom is no longer a mere prophet-like figure. She is something *much more* than that!

I. *Wisdom pre-existed God's work of creation*
²² YHWH acquired me as [the] beginning of his work,
   the most ancient of his acts of old.
²³ Ages ago I was set up,¹
   from [the] beginning, from [the] ancient times of [the] earth.
²⁴ When there were no depths, I was brought forth,
   when there were no springs abounding with water.
²⁵ Before [the] mountains had been shaped,
   before [the] hills, I was brought forth,
²⁶ before he had made [the] earth with its countryside,
   or [the] first of [the] dust of [the] world.

II. *Wisdom was with God during the work of creation*
²⁷ When he established [the] heavens, I was there;
   when he marked out a circle on [the] face of [the] deep,
²⁸ when he made firm [the] skies above,
   when he established [the] springs of [the] deep,
²⁹ when he assigned to the sea its limit,
   so that [the] waters might not transgress his command,
   when he marked out the foundations of [the] earth,
³⁰ then I was beside him, an artisan.

---

1. Or "poured out."

III. Wisdom, God, and creation now
   And I was [his] delight day after day,
     rejoicing before him always,
   ³¹ rejoicing concerning his inhabited world
   and delighting [in] the children of humanity.

(8:22–31, my translation)

The passage has two core messages. First, Wisdom was "brought forth" before God made the world (vv. 22–26). Second, Wisdom was "with" God during the work of creation (vv. 27–31). Clearly, then, Wisdom knows of what she speaks and only a fool would ignore her.

Perhaps we should not be so surprised about this change of direction in Wisdom's speech, because earlier in the book of Proverbs God's Wisdom was declared to be the *means by which* God made the world.

   YHWH
   by wisdom founded the earth;
   by understanding he established the heavens;
   by his knowledge the deeps broke open,
     and the clouds drop down the dew.²
   (Prov 3:19–20)

Here divine wisdom, understanding (i.e., practical competence), and knowledge are roughly synonymous, while the earth, the heavens, and the deeps are a threefold way of representing the whole cosmos (cf. 8:27–31; Exod 20:4). There is a good case for saying that 8:22–31 is intended to expand on these verses in chapter 3, further exploring Wisdom in relation to creation.³ Even if the emphasis in chapter 8 is on Wisdom's being *with* God, it would be very surprising if Wisdom were nothing more than a passive observer in creation, playing no role at all in the formation of the wisely ordered cosmos. If that were so, what would be the point of her presence?

Let's look a little more closely at the first two parts of this section of Wisdom's speech. In the first part she declares that she was "acquired" (v. 22), "set up"/"established" (v. 23), and "brought forth" (vv. 24, 25) (meaning, "born") before God made the world. And in fact, the Hebrew verb *qānāh* in 8:22, which means "acquired" or "possessed,"⁴ can also mean, by exten-

---

2. Wisdom is presented as a woman in 3:13–18, the verses immediately preceding 3:19–20. So the divine Wisdom of 3:19 by which God made the world *is* Woman Wisdom, not merely an abstract attribute of God.

3. Lenzi, "Proverbs 8:22–31."

4. Fifty-nine out of eighty-one occurrences of *qnh* in the Hebrew Bible mean "acquire" (about 75 percent). In Proverbs *qnh* is used fourteen times and, setting 8:22 aside, *all* of them are used to mean "acquire." So I take that to be the meaning in 8:22.

sion, "born" or "begotten." It seems that readers are quite possibly supposed to detect more than one layer of meaning here. In the first instance, God is presented as the model Sage for the readers to imitate. He "acquired" (*qānāh*) Wisdom, just as the readers of Proverbs are called to "acquire" (*qānāh*) Wisdom (1:5; 4:5, 7; 16:16; 23:23); he acts wisely as they are called to; he delights in Wisdom and loves her, just as they must. But then with the two instances of the birth terminology ("brought forth") readers are invited to look back and understand *qānāh* with its extended meaning of "to beget." YHWH is presented as both Wisdom's father (who begets her) and mother (who gives birth to her). She is the daughter of God.

At first sight, this seems somewhat strange. If one took this metaphorical language literally then one would say that originally Wisdom did not exist and then God brought her into being. This would be a very odd claim for Proverbs to make because it would mean that once upon a time God wasn't wise. Then God decided to bring his Wisdom into being, after which God was wise. Furthermore, YHWH's decision to create Wisdom was not a wise decision, for YHWH wasn't wise when he made it! That makes no sense, for the God of Israel is *inherently* wise.

For a critique of the translation "created" in 8:22, see Thomas, "אל קנה ארץ." Now the Greek translation of 8:22 does use the verb *ktizō* ("to create"). This choice generated considerable theological debate in the fourth-century church, which considered Woman Wisdom to be Christ. Did Proverbs teach that Christ was created? The orthodox consensus against the Arians was that Christ/Wisdom was not created, though exegetes differed in the way they understood *ktizō* in LXX Proverbs 8. Athanasius argued that it spoke of Christ *in his humanity* (not his divinity) while, by contrast, in 8:25 the Greek uses a present tense in the expression "he [God] *begets* me [Wisdom]," which Athanasius took to speak of Christ's eternal generation as the Divine Son. By contrast, Origen thought that "Wisdom was created as the beginning of his ways" *in the sense that* "she contained within herself either the beginnings, or forms or species of all creation" (*De Princ.* I.2.2). She was the principle according to which the world was made. For different patristic interpretations, see Dowling, "Proverbs 8:22–31 in the Christology of the Early Fathers." The Greek translation of Proverbs 8:22 influenced the Greek translation of Sirach, which also spoke of Woman Wisdom as "created" (1:4, 9; 24:9). However, things are not as straightforward there as they seem. The "creation" of Wisdom is distinct from the creation of the cosmos. Wisdom is "created" before the ages and before the beginning of the world. She is not a part of the created world, at least not in the same manner of everything else. Note too that a few verses later Wisdom is also said to be "created with" (*syn + ktizō*) faithful people in the womb (Sir 1:14), and yet clearly Wisdom does not come into existence with each of the instances of her being "created." It is as though the planting of the seed of her presence in each righteous person can be spoken of as her "creation" by God, even though she was active prior to those moments. In the same way, her "creation" "in the beginning" seems connected to her presence and work *in the world*. The wisdom writers are primarily concerned with the role of God's Wisdom in the cosmos, so talk of the "creation" (*ktizō*) of Wisdom in Sirach 1:4 and 9 may simply be a way to speak of her activity in God's creation *from its first moments*. Be that as it may, it is unlikely that the Hebrew text of Proverbs 8:22 speaks of Wisdom's creation.

I suggest, following some second-century exegetes, that we are looking at an implicit distinction between *inherent* Wisdom and *expressed* Wisdom. This is easier to make clear if we consider another concept closely linked with Sophia in the wisdom traditions and in the subsequent Christian tradition: word (Hebrew: *dābār*; Greek: *logos*). A word or idea can exist in the mind of someone—that is the *inherent* word. A word can also be spoken out, to do its work—that is the *expressed* word. And when it is so expressed it does not cease to be inherent. In the same way, we can consider wisdom both as an inherent quality of a person and as it is expressed outwardly in action. God is inherently wise, eternally. God's Wisdom is inseparable from God and consequently has no beginning or end. However, Proverbs is interested in discussing God's Wisdom *in relation to creation*; that is to say, Wisdom *expressed*. Wisdom is the essential *presupposition* of the creation of the world and so the emphasis of the opening verses is on Wisdom pre-existing God's act of creating that world. That's because Wisdom has to be already present for the world to be made through Wisdom. When God moves to create the world, God first reaches out with his inherent Wisdom to set things up for the creative acts. This is pictured metaphorically as Wisdom being acquired, begotten, born, and installed in office ("set up"), ready for what will follow. Perhaps this is also why the very first thing Wisdom says is: "I was acquired/begotten/born *as the beginning* of his work." She is "sent out" from God (to deploy another metaphor) so she can serve as the beginning of God's creative acts.[5]

In the second section of this part of the speech, Wisdom emphasizes her presence as God created the various realms of the cosmos. In vv. 27–28 there is a twofold movement from above to below: the heavens above to the churning deep below (8:27); the skies above to the underwater springs of the deep below (8:28). That covers the vertical range of the ancient cosmos. Then comes the horizontal plane in v. 29, as God tames the primeval chaotic sea and marks out limits for it, enabling the emergence of land, followed up by the stabilizing of the whole earth on its foundations.[6]

---

5. This understanding is strengthened when we appreciate that talk of being born or begotten appears able to serve as a technical metaphor for the formal installation of someone in office. Thus, in Psalm 2:6 the new king is "installed" (*nsk*, the same word used of Wisdom in Prov 8:23) by God, who says to the monarch, "You are my son, today I have *begotten* you." Yet Psalm 2 is not about literally bringing the king into existence. It is about installing him ready to exercise his rule. So too with Wisdom. Proverbs 8 does not concern her literal coming into existence. It describes her being set in place as the prior condition of the work of creation.

6. You would not be mistaken for hearing echoes of the same ancient ideas that are so beautifully crystallized in Genesis 1.

"I was there" when God did all that, says Wisdom (Prov 8:27). Throughout all these things "I was beside him as an artisan (*ămôn*)" (8:30).[7] And the outcome of her presence is that "wisdom is built into the very fabric and foundations of all God's work."[8] For "Wisdom is the skill, plan, and knowledge God uses to secure and order the cosmos."[9]

With the building project of creation completed, there is ongoing rejoicing: YHWH delighting in his Wisdom and Wisdom delighting in creation (8:30–31).

2. What Is Wisdom in Proverbs 8:22–31?

a) A Goddess?

Many biblical scholars believe that in Proverbs 8:22–31 Wisdom is being presented in ways influenced by the goddesses of the ancient Near East. Parallels have been drawn with Inanna in Sumeria, Ishtar in Mesopotamia, Astarte and Anath in Syria and Canaan, and Isis, Mut, and Ma'at in Egypt. Consider, for instance, Ma'at. She was there at the beginning of creation. In Egyptian cosmology the world was divinely ordered and the goddess Ma'at, daughter of the sun god Ra, was herself that cosmic order. She is thus associated with morality, truth, and justice, which characterize her structuring of the cosmos. Good living was living in accord with the world-ordering of Ma'at. Similarly, in Proverbs the cosmos is structured according to Wisdom—indeed, she is the blueprint for the order of the universe—and wise living is living according to the structures of that order. She too is associated with goodness, truth, and justice.

---

7. The meaning of the Hebrew word *ămôn* is disputed. It might mean "an artisan" or perhaps "a sage," an advisor at God's side as he creates. (Other suggestions have also been made.) We can't be sure. Whatever it means, it places Wisdom alongside God in the creation of the world.

8. Murphy, *Proverbs*, 117–18. As such, some have suggested that the figure of Wisdom is in fact *the wise order of creation*, which God built into the cosmos from the very foundations up. In other words, Wisdom is a glittering aspect *of creation* rather than of God. However, this distances God too much from Wisdom. Wisdom is an aspect of creation, yes, but *only because she is first an aspect of the God who created*.

9. Bowen, "God and Wisdom," 8.

Meet Woman Wisdom 19

The goddess Ma'at[10]

A few scholars think that in Proverbs 1–9 we have the echo of what was once a goddess worshipped in Israel alongside YHWH, perhaps his wife. It is impossible to know the evolving prehistory of the concept before it erupts into the text we have, so one cannot rule out this possibility. However, even if this was her origin, then unlike the surrounding polytheistic traditions, in which Wisdom would simply have joined the pantheon of deities, in Proverbs something very different has happened.

In biblical thought, including in Proverbs, only *one* God was worshiped. There is no evidence that Wisdom was considered a second deity alongside YHWH in biblical religion.[11] She had no temple, no priests, and received no worship. And she was not considered by the editors of Proverbs to be a competitor to YHWH. For them, Wisdom is not the goddess alongside Israel's god, even though she is presented in ways that daringly allude to the figure of a goddess. Rather, she is *YHWH's own Wisdom*. YHWH cannot be thought of apart from his Wisdom and she cannot be thought of

---

10. Goddess Ma'at or Maat of Ancient Egypt—reconstructed by TYalaA. Reproduced under Wiki Commons license.

11. This is not to deny that popular religion in ancient Israel often involved the worship of other gods and goddesses alongside YHWH. Both the biblical texts and archaeological evidence make clear that this happened.

apart from him. We might say that she participates in the identity of the one God of Israel.[12]

b) A Divine Attribute Personified?

Many scholars argue that the language is clearly poetic and that an abstract attribute of God (his wisdom) is personified as a prophetic woman or, in 8:22–31, a goddess alongside YHWH. But, they argue, it would be a mistake to understand it as more than a mere literary device. As R. B. Y. Scott puts it, "the personification of wisdom in chapter viii is indeed poetic only and not ontological."[13]

c) More Than a Personification (Wisdom as a Hypostasis)?

However, some scholars argue that 8:22–31 goes beyond personification. Obviously, the presentation of Wisdom as a woman standing in public spaces calling out to people is metaphorical imagery. But 8:22–31 takes things further. Helmer Ringgren suggested Wisdom was "a quasi-personification of certain attributes proper to God, occupying an intermediate position between personalities and abstract beings."[14] Wisdom is presented in a way that seems more than mere personification and she takes on some real existence, albeit not independent existence. Richard Davidson notes:

> Wisdom in Proverbs assumes the very prerogatives elsewhere reserved for [YHWH] alone in the Hebrew Bible: giver of life and death (Prov 8:35–36);[15] source of legitimate government (8:15–16);[16] the One who is to be sought after, found, and called (1:28; 8:17);[17] the one who loves and is to be loved (8:17);[18] the giver of wealth (8:18–21)[19] and security (1:33);[20] and perhaps

---

12. I borrow the phrase "to participate in the divine identity" from Richard Bauckham's work on Christology.

13. Scott, *Proverbs, Ecclesiastes*, 71. Numerous scholars take this route.

14. Ringgren, *Word and Wisdom*, 8.

15. Cf. Num 11:16–17; 1 Sam 2:10; 10:1; 1 Kgs 3:4–15; 10:9; Ps 2:7.

16. Cf. 2 Chr 15:2; Hos 5:6; Amos 5:4–6; 8:12; Ezek 8:18; Deut 1:45; 4:29; Judg 10:11–12; Job 35:12; Pss 22:3; 28:1; Isa 1:15; Jer 11:11, 14; 14:12; Mic 3:4; Zech 7:13.

17. Cf. 2 Chr 15:2; Hos 5:6; Amos 5:4–6; 8:12; Ezek 8:18; Deut 1:45; 4:29; Judg 10:11–12; Job 35:12; Pss 22:3; 28:1; Isa 1:15; Jer 11:11, 14; 14:12; Mic 3:4; Zech 7:13.

18. Cf. 1 Kgs 3:3; 1 Sam 2:30; 2 Sam 12:23; Neh 13:26; Isa 48:14.

19. Cf. 1 Kgs 3:13; 1 Chr 29:12; 2 Chr 1:12; 17:5.

20. Cf. Lev 25:18, 19; Jer 32:37, etc.

most significantly, a source of revelation (Prov 8:6–10, 19, 32, 34; 30:3–5).[21] In Prov 9:1 (cf. 7:6), Wisdom builds herself a temple "as befits a deity of her status."

In Prov 8, specifically v. 12, Wisdom uses the common rhetorical self-asseverating form of "divine self-praise" ("I am Wisdom") regularly reserved elsewhere in Scripture and in the ancient Near East for deity: "I am [YHWH] your God"; "I am Ishtar of Arbela"; "I am Isis the divine." Biblical parallels to this "divine self-praise" with the same grammatical structure can be found in Ezek 12:25; 35:12; Zech 10:6; Mal 3:6. Based upon these precise grammatical parallels, I agree with scholars who argue that the better translation of Prov 8:12 is "I am Wisdom . . ." not "I, wisdom . . ." and that this is a form of "divine self-praise." From the perspective of genre analysis, I concur with Silvia Schroer that Wisdom "in the book of Proverbs is a divine figure . . . [who] speaks like a deity, or like the God of Israel."[22]

Wisdom is presented in Proverbs in a paradoxical way that simultaneously *distinguishes her from* and *identifies her with* God. We might, if we were cheeky, describe their relationship after the pattern of John's Gospel: in the beginning was Wisdom, and Wisdom was *with* God and Wisdom *was* God (John 1:1).

It is hard to say for sure whether Proverbs merely personifies a divine attribute or goes further. There is a case to be made either way. There is little doubt, however, that by the time we get to the later part of the Second Temple period, Woman Wisdom is much more than a personification, she is a full-blown divine reality. And, as we shall see later in the book, that understanding influenced various New Testament theologies.

3. Woman Wisdom in Second Temple Judaism

The bombshell of Proverbs 8:22–31 left its mark on several later Jewish writers in works written between the second century BC and the first century AD. Here I simply identify some key ideas about her in their writings.

---

21. Cf. Prov 29:18; Pss 19:10; 119:1–2.

22. Davidson, "Proverbs 8 and the Place of Christ," 42–43. The quotation is from Silvia Schroer, *Wisdom Has Built Her House*, 27.

a) Wisdom's Pre-Existence and Her Relationship with God

The Wisdom of Jesus Ben Sirach (sometimes known as Ecclesiasticus), a text written by a Jerusalem sage sometime between 196 and 175 BCE, is our earliest. The writer, clearly leaning on Proverbs, explains that *God alone* is wise (Sir 1:8) and that his Wisdom precedes creation and is active in creation from its first moments (1:4, cf. 1:9; 24:9).

The Wisdom of Solomon—a book written by a Jewish wise man (adopting the persona of Solomon) in Alexandria, Egypt sometime in the second or first century BCE—similarly teaches that Wisdom precedes the creation of the world. As divine Wisdom, she is "with God" (Wis 9:9) and "living with God" (8:3). Their relationship is intimate. She is "unique" (*monogenēs*), indicating a relation to God unlike that of any creature (7:22). Indeed, she lives in "the holy heavens" alongside God (9:10), where "she sits by [God's] throne" (9:4). God sends her out from heaven on a mission in creation (9:10, cf. 1 En. 42). Wisdom herself is highly valued by God: "The Lord of all loves her" (Wis 8:3b, cf. Prov 8:30).

If that was not elevated enough, the Wisdom of Solomon contains what is the most exalted picture of Woman Wisdom in all Jewish literature. We find Wisdom described with twenty-one epithets (7 x 3, symbolizing perfection):

> There is in her a spirit that is intelligent, holy,
> unique, manifold, subtle,
> agile, clear, unpolluted,
> distinct, invulnerable, loving the good, keen,
> irresistible, beneficent, humane,
> steadfast, sure, free from anxiety,
> all-powerful, overseeing all,
> and penetrating through all spirits
> that are intelligent, pure, and altogether subtle.
> For wisdom is more mobile than any motion;
> because of her pureness she pervades and penetrates all things.
> For she is a breath of the power of God
> and a pure emanation of the glory of the Almighty;
> therefore nothing defiled gains entrance into her.
> For she is a reflection of eternal light,
> a spotless mirror of the working of God,
> and an image of his goodness.
> Although she is but one, she can do all things,
> and while remaining in herself, she renews all things;
> in every generation she passes into holy souls
> and makes them friends of God and prophets,

for God loves nothing so much as the person who lives with
wisdom.
She is more beautiful than the sun
and excels every constellation of the stars.
Compared with the light she is found to be more radiant,
for it is succeeded by the night,
but against wisdom evil does not prevail. (Wis 7:22–30)

This passage is dense with philosophical (especially Platonic and stoic) and theological ideas, which we do not have the space to explore. What I'd like to draw your attention to are some more metaphors that seek to communicate the idea that Wisdom originates in God himself. She is:

- a breath (*atmis*, mist, vapor, smoke) of the power of God (7:25a); as smoke rises from a fire or breath comes out from a person, so Wisdom "comes out" from God.

- a pure emanation (*aporroia*) of the glory of the Almighty (7:25b).[23] In 7:25 Wisdom's outflowing from God is expressed in the present tense, describing her mode of existence as an eternal effluence from God. Wisdom exists as an emanation from God, ever flowing out from God, an expression and extension of God's own self. And she intermediates between the transcendent God and the cosmos.

- a reflection of eternal light, a spotless mirror of the working of God, and an image of his goodness (7:26); the invisible God cannot be seen but he can be glimpsed in Wisdom for she is the perfect representation of God's light, God's workings, and God's goodness. In her we see God.

This goes some way to explaining the ways in which Wisdom seems to be interchangeable with God in certain respects. Consider, for instance, Solomon's prayer for Wisdom in Wisdom of Solomon 7:15–22. The prayer is topped and tailed by a reference to the one who taught Solomon: "For it is *he* [God] who gave me unerring knowledge of what exists, . . . for *wisdom*, the fashioner of all things, taught me" (vv. 17, 22). So who taught Solomon about the structure of the world? Was it God? Yes. Was it Wisdom? Yes. So closely are they associated that you can't get so much as a nanofiber between them.

Wisdom is described with attributes that seem to belong to God alone. She is holy, all-powerful (Wis 7:23), can do all things (7:27), oversees all

---

23. The philosophical concept of emanation is drawn from Middle Platonism, in which the Prime God generates a "Second God" (Intellect), not through an act of creation, but by means of its own mind eternally thinking on its own thoughts.

(7:23), she fills the world and holds all things together (1:7), and renews all things (7:27, cf. Ps 104:30).

Or consider how the same book goes on to speak of *God's* acts in Israel's history, such as delivering Israel from slavery in Egypt, *as Wisdom's acts* (10:1—12:27; 15:18—19:21). What Wisdom is saying, God is saying. What Wisdom is doing, God is doing.

Our author is trying to find a way to speak of something very hard to express. There is only one God, yet this God's Wisdom can be thought of as in *some* sense alongside God while simultaneously being indistinguishable from God. The one God speaks and acts in the world *through her*.

b) Wisdom's Role in the Creation of the World

The biblical idea that God created the world through his Wisdom (Ps 104:24; Prov 3:19–20) is stressed in Wisdom of Solomon: not only was she *present* when God made the world (Wis 9:9), but God *"by [means of] wisdom formed humankind"* (9:2). As such, she is "an associate in his works" (8:4). Indeed, Wisdom herself is "the fashioner of all things" (7:22; 8:6), and even "the active cause of all things" (8:5). This is to stress her active role in creation as the means *through which* God created the world. "Accordingly, all things have been designed by wisdom such that all things, in their created-crafted being, reflect wisdom. One might elaborate this thought: God has woven wisdom throughout the design of creation such that the cosmos, like a hologram, reflects the wisdom of God in every part of the whole."[24]

As the one who was with God during the creation of the world (9:9) and through whom he made it, Wisdom is she who can reveal the structures and meaning of that world to those who seek her. Thus, Solomon declares:

> For it is he [God] who gave me unerring knowledge of what exists,
> to know the structure of the world and the activity of the elements,
> the beginning and end and middle of times,
> the alternations of the solstices and the changes of the seasons,
> the cycles of the year and the constellations of the stars,
> the natures of animals and the tempers of wild animals,
> the powers of spirits and the thoughts of human beings,
> the varieties of plants and the virtues of roots;
> I learned both what is secret and what is manifest,
> *for Wisdom, the fashioner of all things, taught me.*
> (Wis 7:17–22)

---

24. Belousek, "God the Creator in the Wisdom of Solomon," 15.

c) Wisdom's Role in Providence

Wisdom is not simply the means by which God fashioned the world but is also central to the way God remains engaged with and governs creation. Ben Sirach speaks of how God has poured her out on *all* his works, especially on living things, and most especially those who love her (i.e., the seekers of Wisdom) (Sir 1:9–10). There seems to be a sense in which all things share in God's Wisdom to some extent, but animate things do so more than inanimate, and wise people even more so.

Wisdom is ubiquitous. She lives in the heights, in heaven, in the abyss, in the sea, and in the earth (24:4–6). There is *nowhere* in creation where Wisdom is not present. This omnipresence is connected to her role in governing God's world. The Wisdom of Solomon puts it this way: "She reaches mightily from one end of the earth to the other and she orders all things well" (Wis 8:8). As we have seen, it also says: Wisdom is "all-powerful, overseeing all, and penetrating through all spirits that are intelligent, pure, and altogether subtle. . . . For wisdom is more mobile than any motion; because of her pureness *she pervades and penetrates all things*" (7:23b–24). Wisdom indwells everything created. She is everywhere, sees everything, and is all-powerful.

4. Conclusion: A Wisdom Worldview

To gather all this together, we can say that in the wisdom traditions of ancient Israel, to speak of Wisdom is to say something about God and something about creation.

- About God it says: YHWH is inherently and eternally wise, the source of all wisdom.
- About creation it says: the cosmos is a work of divine Sophia, and as crafted by Sophia, it displays divine wisdom in both its grand contours and in its details.

Wisdom is "in" the world, structuring it, ordering it, permeating it, infusing it. Through her God is active within the world. Yet she is not an object in the world like a mountain or a river or a sheep or a rock. She indwells all things but simultaneously transcends all things.

Human wisdom is the learned art of discerning her holy presence in creation and then walking in her ways. We might picture all this in the following diagram.

Having sketched the theology of Holy Wisdom in some detail, for it will be the theological hub at the center of the eco-theological wheel developed in this book, let us turn our gaze upon some more traditional biblical texts and themes regarding creation.

2

Wisdom's Choir

Creation as Festival

1. Ordered Chaos (Genesis 1)

ON CHRISTMAS EVE 1968, the first humans to travel to the moon made a broadcast from space to the people on earth—a broadcast that was heard by around a billion people across sixty-four countries. It began, "We are now approaching lunar sunrise, and for all the people back on earth, the crew of Apollo 8 has a message that we would like to send to you." They then proceeded to read the first ten verses of the Book of Genesis: "In the beginning God created the heavens and the earth . . . ."[1] This biblical text is unquestionably the most famous creation story in the world. And how awe-inspiring to read it in orbit! Its ancient author(s) and original audiences could never have imagined such a thing!

In some ways, however, reading Genesis 1 from space can be somewhat misleading. What the astronauts saw was not the earth as ancient Israelites imagined it. It is important to appreciate that Genesis 1 is ancient literature, not modern scientific literature. The cosmos as understood by the Bible's original authors and audiences was in some ways very different to the

---

1. Numerous popular music artists have used parts of the recording of the Apollo 8 reading of Genesis 1 in their music, including Michael Jackson and Mike Oldfield.

cosmos we understand today. For starters, the "heavens and the earth" as conceived by most biblical writers is, roughly speaking, a three-decker universe.² It is often pictured as something like the image below:

The Biblical Cosmos³

Notice the flat disc of the earth—on which we live. Yup, the biblical earth was indeed flat. Notice too, the underworld beneath. That is the realm of the dead (though this is not mentioned in Genesis 1). Be aware also that biblical cosmology did not conceive of a solar system (i.e., the earth as a planet orbiting the sun). Rather, the situation is the reverse of that—the sun, moon, and stars orbit a static earth in a geo-system. Even more surprising to us is the place of water. In an ancient Israelite cosmology, we are surrounded by water, not only in the seas, oceans, and rivers but also below the ground and, more surprisingly for us, above the sky, *beyond the sun, moon, and stars*. Think of the sky in Genesis 1 as a vast solid inverted bowl on which the sun, moon, and stars are fixed. This sky-dome (*rāqîaʿ*), or "firmament" (vv. 6–8), is there to keep the "waters above" (not to be confused with clouds) from crashing down and drowning us. Modern geography and cosmography do not look like this.

---

2. Ancient biblical cosmology is explored in a lot more depth in my book *The Biblical Cosmos*.

3. Copyright Hannah Parry.

It may be tempting, given its ancient cosmology, to think that Genesis 1 has little to teach us today. Nothing could be further from the truth! Often it is the very strangeness of the text that enables it to stop us in our tracks and crack open our imaginations, allowing God to speak afresh. Genesis 1 is full of critical insights that are essential to a Christian eco-spirituality. I will simply pick out a few for our consideration.

Genesis 1 concerns creation understood primarily as *an act of divine ordering*. The world begins in a state of disorder, inhospitable to life. It is nothing but pitch-black darkness and churning sea, "formless and empty" (*tōhû wābōhû*, v. 2). Step by step, over the first three days, God creates an orderly environment and then, on the following three days, God fills it. The whole structure of the passage communicates order.

FORMING	FILLING
Day One Light was created and a separation of light and dark (day and night) was instituted	*Day Four* Populating the night with the moon and stars; populating the day with the sun
Day Two Separating the waters above (the sky-sea) from the waters below (the seas) by means of the sky-dome (*rāqîaʿ*)	*Day Five* Populating the waters below with living creatures of many kinds; populating the sky (this side of the sky-dome) with birds
Day Three The sea is gathered and separated from the dry land. The land produces rich and diverse vegetation.	*Day Six* Populating the land with wild and domestic animals of many kinds; creating humanity in the divine image.
Day Seven Sabbath "rest"	

There is a very clear point being made, even in the shape of the text. God addresses the issue of the earth being "formless" and thus "empty" by forming it—so it can sustain life—and then filling it. The world we inhabit is a *cosmos*, not a chaos. It has divinely granted pattern, structure, and order. Notice the acts of separation on Days One to Three. Notice how Day One corresponds to Day Four, Day Two to Day Five, and Day Three to Day Six. But this is no claustrophobic "order" that suffocates, it is an enabling order that facilitates fecundity, vibrancy, and life.

Getting caught up obsessing over whether this is "literally" true—in the sense of whether the world was created over six twenty-four-hour periods—is a dreary exercise in missing the point. Christian theologians have pointed out for centuries, long before the rise of modern science, that it would be odd to read the text in such a way. After all, light (Day One) is created before the sun (Day Four). In fact, so too are day and night and evening and morning! These oddities are little clues indicating that we should read less woodenly. Genesis 1 speaks truth about God and the world, but truth is not as brittle or two-dimensional as some moderns take it to be. Yes, as creationists[4] point out, the seven days are indeed seven twenty-four-hour periods (after all, they each have evening and morning), but they are being used as *a literary device* to present a theological vision of God's creation. The truth of that vision does not depend on the literal truth of, say, the claim that the sun was made on a Wednesday (Day Four) nor on the literal truth of the claim that vegetation was created on a Tuesday (Day Three) before the sun even existed. Reading Genesis 1 as a quasi-scientific description of an event some six to ten thousand years ago is both inappropriate and unhelpful.[5] Moving on . . .

Genesis 1 tells us that God creates through authoritative divine speech: "Let there be . . ." (vv. 3, 6, 9, 14, 20, 24, 26). Contrary to what we find in various other ancient Near Eastern mythologies, in which the gods create the world through divine conflict and violence, there is no battling here. God does not have to defeat any dragons to bash the world into being. There is no sense of anxiety or doubt about the outcomes. "And God said, 'Let there be light,'" and there was light" (v. 3). God speaks . . . and it is. End of. Indeed, the sea monsters (*tannînim*) that in some other ancient Near Eastern myths needed defeating for the habitable world to exist only make an appearance in Genesis 1 as creatures that God crafts to live in the sea. They are part of the good world, not enemies to vanquish (v. 21).

And it *is* a good world. That's another point driven home over and over in Genesis 1, seven times in fact, the number symbolic of completion (vv. 4, 10, 12, 18, 21, 25, 31). Creation, with all its vast diversity of habitats and inhabitants, is good, and is valued by God as being good. Embracing the goodness of creation is a foundational plank in Christian eco-spirituality. It forms a bulwark against any attempts—even pious Christian ones—to denigrate the natural world.

And notice that this creation is not made good by God arbitrarily *declaring* it good. Yes, creation is good because God created it that way; it reflects the goodness of its Creator. However, God did not create some value-neutral world that was subsequently converted to being valuable by a

---

4. The term "creationists" refers not people who believe in creation (for all Christian believe in creation) but to people who interpret Genesis in a very literal way.

5. I do not intend to get distracted defending this claim, which seems to me to be bleedin' obvious, but for those who are interested there are plenty of helpful books and articles available.

further divine utterance, a "Let it be good!" Nope. God created a world that had value *in itself*. Genesis 1 tells us that God simply observed and recognized the *inherent* value of the world he had made: ". . . and God *saw* that it was good." Recognizing that creation's goodness is not dependent upon *us* is a further critical component in Christian eco-spirituality. We do not bestow meaning and purpose and value on the natural world. It is good irrespective of what we think of it. It is meaningful and purposeful quite independent of any meanings we project onto it or any usefulness it has to us. Its value is part of its very God-created core; it is something we seek to *discern* and *discover*, not something we invent. This matters because if the natural world only has the value that we project onto it then it is at our mercy, dependent on our wills and whims and self-serving lifestyle choices. There be dragons, for that path leads to a whole world of environmental abuses!

Now the goodness of the world in Genesis 1 does not mean that it is "perfect" or has reached its destination. As the rest of Scripture makes clear, creation was only just beginning its journey of growth and development. Its completeness in Genesis 1 does not mean it was intended to be static or unchanging. Rather, it was set up and ready to go—fit for the journey.

The culmination of the week of creation is the seventh day, on which God rests from the work. The idea is not that God is knackered and needs a break. The seventh day is set apart from the others and serves a different function in the story than Days One to Six. As Richard Bauckham observes, "the seventh day, radically different in kind from the others, relates directly to each of the six, and forms the vantage point from which the work of all six days may be seen, not as a sequence, but as a whole."[6] Sabbath, in part, is about Divine *delight* in beholding creation.

Another aspect of Genesis 1 is its celebratory vision of creation as abounding with a vast diversity of environments and life-forms. The firmament is awash with stars, the sea and the sky and the land are teeming with creatures of all shapes and sizes and species—all blessed by God and all told to be fruitful. This vibrant image of nature's fecundity as the divine will and a cause of divine satisfaction underpins the importance of diversity in general, and of biodiversity in particular. The seraphim in the prophet Isaiah's vision go even further, declaring that the vast array of life on earth is itself the very glory of God: "Holy, holy, holy is YHWH of Hosts; *the fullness of all the earth ($m^e l\bar{o}$' kol-$h\bar{a}$'$\bar{a}reṣ$) is his glory*" (Isa 6:3, my translation). And God loves it all, from the rock to the rock badger, from the sea to the sea lion, from the sun to the sunflower. As the author of the Wisdom of Solomon was later to write in a prayer, "For you love all things that exist, and detest none

---

6. Bauckham, *Bible and Ecology*, 15.

of the things that you have made, for you would not have made anything if you had hated it" (Wis 11:24).

And there's more. God invites what is created to participate in the act of creation. "Let the earth bring forth . . ." (v. 24); "Let the waters swarm with swarms of living creatures . . ." (v. 21). The earth and sea are to *act* in the story of creation, albeit in response to the divine action and divine invitation. Here we see that God is creating *through* their acts. God also calls the land to produce vegetation, "plants bearing seed according to their kinds and trees bearing fruit with seeds in it according to their kinds" (v. 12). These plants are enabled by God to be *self-perpetuating*, making seeds which make more plants, which make more seeds, in an ongoing development of the work of creation.

So Genesis 1 is a terrific passage to open the Bible with! It really sets things up for everything that follows. However, often discussions on creation in churches don't get much further than Genesis 1–2, which is something of a travesty given how much else Scripture has to say on the matter. For a more rounded picture, let's take a look at some other biblical creation texts.

2. Where the Wild Things Are

Ancient Israel was a farming community, so it is unsurprising that domesticated animals appear frequently in the Bible. However, there is also an appreciation of wildness in the pages of Scripture. Two texts that wonderfully illustrate this are Psalm 104 and Job 38–39.

a) "How manifold are your works" (Psalm 104)

Psalm 104 is a joyful celebration of the Creator and the delightful creation. It begins by looking up to consider the sky (vv. 1–4): the light, the clouds, the wind, the lightning. All these atmospheric phenomena are seen as simultaneously revealing and concealing God: he wraps himself in light, like a garment; he rides on the clouds scudding across the sky, like they are chariots; he speaks in the lightning. In all these things we perceive something of the divine presence and work, yet we never see God directly—only the radiance of God's concealing cloak, the flash of his passing chariot, the thunderous after-echo of his voice.

The psalm moves on to behold the earth in relation to water, much like Genesis 1. The waters retreat from the land, taking up residence in the places allotted to them (vv. 5–10). Once set within fitting limits, the waters play a constructive role in the flourishing ecosystems of the land:

> 10 You make springs gush forth in the valleys;
>   they flow between the hills;
> 11 they give drink to every beast of the field;
>   the wild donkeys quench their thirst.
> 12 Beside them the birds of the heavens dwell;
>   they sing among the branches.
> 13 From your lofty abode you water the mountains;
>   the earth is satisfied with the fruit of your work.

The focus is on divine provision *for* creation *through* creation. And that focus continues, with consideration of divine provision for human and animal needs and pleasures:

> 14 You cause the grass to grow for the livestock
>   and plants for humans to cultivate,
> that they may bring forth food from the earth
> 15   and wine to gladden the heart of people,
> oil to make their faces shine
>   and bread to strengthen human hearts.
> 16 The trees of YHWH are watered abundantly,
>   the cedars of Lebanon that he planted.
> 17 In them the birds build their nests;
>   the stork has her home in the fir trees.
> 18 The high mountains are for the wild goats;
>   the rocks are a refuge for the rock badgers.

Different kinds of habitat and provision for different kinds of creatures. The psalmist is clearly finding great delight in all this variety. And it's not only things that meet human needs that are in focus, like certain plants and animals. Habitats and creatures that have little or no "use" to humans are also a source of joy and praise.

Next, the natural cycles of created time are pondered:

> 19 He made the moon to mark the seasons;
>   the sun knows its time for setting.
> 20 You make darkness, and it is night,
>   when all the beasts of the forest creep about.
> 21 The young lions roar for their prey,
>   seeking their food from God.
> 22 When the sun rises, they steal away
>   and lie down in their dens.
> 23 Humans go out to their work
>   and to their labor until the evening.

It is not merely that different animals thrive in different habitats, but they also work to different temporal and seasonal patterns. Some, like humans, are creatures of the day. Others are creatures of the night. And that is not a cause of fear or revulsion but of wonder:

> 24 O YHWH, how manifold are your works!
> In wisdom have you made them all;
> the earth is full of your creatures.

Here is expressed sheer unadulterated joy at the mind-blowing variety of God's creatures. (And notice how it highlights Wisdom's role in creation.) The psalmist goes on to take the sea as an example—how vast and wide it is, and see how it "teems with creatures innumerable, living things both small and great" (v. 25), including the great Leviathan, which here is presented not as some chaos dragon for God to kill but as a creature formed by God "to play" (śaḥeq) in the sea (v. 26). Even big, scary, dangerous creatures are celebrated.

The singer then moves on to consider what we might call "the circle of life"—the pattern of life, death, and new life, of generations replacing generations:

> 27 These [creatures] all look to you,
> to give them their food in due season.
> 28 When you give it to them, they gather it up;
> when you open your hand, they are filled with good things.
> 29 When you hide your face, they are dismayed;
> when you take away their breath, they die
> and return to their dust.
> 30 When you send forth your Spirit, they are created,
> and you renew the face of the ground.

Here we see again God's provision *for* creation *through* creation. The food that God provides does not drop out of the sky or miraculously materialize out of thin air. Divine action was not conceived in such a way. The food God provides *is* the plants and animals that grow and live on the earth. The point is that everything that exists ultimately depends on and comes from God. As such, God is the one who provides food and the one who breathes life. God is also the one who withdraws the life-breath, and in this way God ever-renews the face of the earth. Both life and death are a part of the pattern of God's wise creation.

And it is not only the psalmist who celebrates the cosmos. He continues: "May the glory of YHWH endure forever; may YHWH rejoice in his works..." (v. 31). God celebrates this fiesta of creation.

b) Wild God (Job 38–42)

The vision of creation towards the end of the book of Job is somewhat different. To set the scene: Job is a righteous man who, although not one of God's chosen people, Israel, is a good man and a true worshipper of God. Yet despite his fidelity and goodness he experiences a series of terrible losses. Contrary to what Job's "comforters" claim, these sufferings are not a divine punishment for his sin, and Job rightly refuses to see them as such. He rages against God for the inexplicable torments he has experienced and eventually God appears to him from the midst of a terrifying storm (Job 38:1). What God does *not* do is explain the reasons for Job's griefs—they remain a mystery. Instead, God helps Job to realize just how much humans do not understand about the cosmos and the way it works. The world is beyond Job's ability to fully grasp and manipulate. The result is that Job learns the wisdom of owning his ignorance and being able to live with it.

There are two divine speeches to Job. The first one (38:1—40:5) begins with a set of rhetorical questions to Job intended to help him appreciate how little he understands about the universe. Were you there to see the beginnings of the world, when God laid its foundation and marked out its dimensions or when the sea was set within its limits? Do you command the dawn? Have you been to the depths of the sea or the ends of the earth or into the sky from whence comes the weather? Do you control the constellations? Do you provide food for the animals? Do you even know the patterns of pregnancy and birth amongst different wild animals? The answer to all these questions is, of course, no. Job lacks both understanding of and power over such things.

Having raised the issue of wild animals, God moves on to consider a range of wild animals about which Job knows little: the lion, the raven, the Nubian ibex, the wild donkey, the wild ox, the ostrich, the horse (which is not wild, but is powerful), and the hawk (38:39–40:2). It is God, not Job, who provides habitats and food for them. And God knows every detail of their lives whereas Job knows (and cares) little about them.

What is fascinating about this vision of creation is the clear pleasure God takes in these diverse animals. Each species has its own kind of life, its own habits and habitats, its own strengths and weaknesses, and God is interested in each flourishing in whatever way is fitting for it. God delights in the particular features of each creature. The hawk, for instance, soars with jaw-dropping elegance and its astonishing eyesight enables it to be an excellent predator. How is this so? Because divine wisdom made it that way (39:26–30). (Yes, Wisdom—there she is again.) And even creatures that display what we might call "sub-optimal design"—the kinds of creatures that a

New Atheist might say God would never create—are celebrated by God as his creations. The ostrich, for instance, displays what seem foolish behaviors "because God has made it forget wisdom" (39:17). Yet look how flaming fast it runs! "When it spreads its plumes aloft, it laughs at the horse and its rider" (39:18). God is here cheering on this "silly" ostrich.

Furthermore, these animals are valuable to God irrespective of their usefulness to humans. In fact, the animals under discussion are mostly wild and of little interest to humans, and they themselves are disinterested in human life, or even actively resistant to it. The wild donkey thus "scorns the tumult of the city; it does not hear the shouts of the driver. It ranges the mountains as its pasture..." (39:7–8a). It is completely indifferent to human civilization. And: "Is the wild ox willing to serve you? Will it spend the night in your crib?" No! God values these creatures *for their own lives*, not because of the use they have to us.

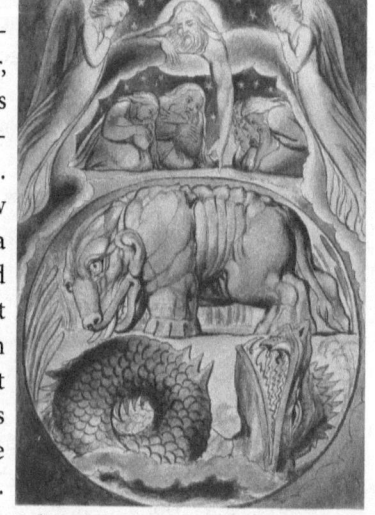

John Linnell (1792–1882), Behemoth and Leviathan[7]

Job gets the point. He ceases his complaints (40:3–5). God continues, however, with a second speech in which he introduces two fearsome mythic chaos beasts: Behemoth (40:15–24) and Leviathan (41:1–34). The point is that both represent the raw and dangerous power of God's creation—a power that is beyond human control and that must be treated with great respect. Yet both of these fearsome creatures are within God's control. Job again acknowledges that his ranting against YHWH arose from his ignorance and his misguided feeling that he knew better how things should be (42:1–6). Now he acknowledges that God has the requisite understanding and power to govern the cosmos and that he, Job, can accept his own finitude, his inability to understand why things have worked out as they have.

The book of Job offers a vision of creation in which divine wisdom and power are underpinning the very existence and the ongoing life of the world. It's a world ordered by God in which each kind of thing has its place and is valuable for being the kind of thing that it is. The world, as seen in Job, is not human-centric. Yet this is not a cause of lament but of humility in the face of grandeur and mystery. It's also a cause of celebration of God's

---

7. B1992.8.7(16)—Yale Center for British Art. Reproduced under Wiki Commons license.

wisdom refracted in all the myriad wonders of the world. There is something far more splendorous going on than we can imagine in our wildest dreams.

3. The Choir of Creation

The final thing to understand from this chapter is the way that creation is orientated towards its Source and as such can be thought of as characterized by worship. So before introducing the biblical image of all creatures praising God, I'd like to set the stage by introducing another cosmos-affirming idea, that the heavens and the earth are God's temple-palace.

a) God's in the House: Creation as Temple

> He built his sanctuary like the high heavens,
> like the earth, which he has founded forever.
> (Ps 78:69)

In the Bible the cosmos is imagined as a vast temple, a holy dwelling place for God. There is a lot that can be said here, but I will keep things brief.[8] The temple in ancient Israel, and its tabernacle precursor, was understood to be the most holy place on earth: the place set apart for YHWH to dwell among his people. It was composed of three zones that increased in holiness as one approached the center of the structure:

- The outer court (where any ritually clean Israelite could go to worship)
- The holy place (where only priests could go)
- The most holy place (where only the high priest could go, once a year)

---

8. For details on temples and some of the reasons for taking the temple in Jerusalem as a microcosm of the cosmos, see Parry, *Biblical Cosmos*, ch. 7.

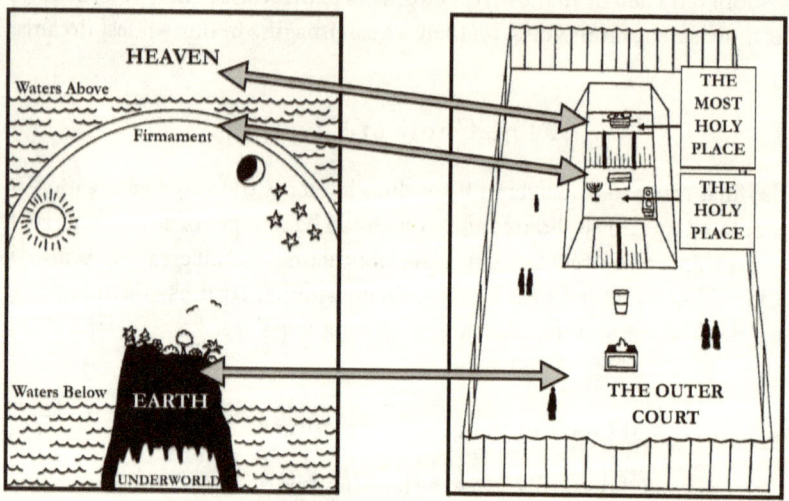

Temple and cosmos[9]

There is very good reason to think that this temple, as other ancient Near Eastern temples, was a symbolic representation of the universe.

- The outer court represents the land and sea (where we live)
- The holy place represents the sky
- The most holy place represents heaven, God's focal dwelling place

When priests moved around the ritual space of the temple, they were symbolically navigating the cosmos. On the Day of Atonement, when the high priest entered the most holy place, he was symbolically entering heaven. But if the temple is a mini-cosmos, that means *the cosmos itself is a temple*. That is why so many biblical creation texts use the language of constructing a building when they speak of creation: God measures up, lays foundations and beams, stretches out the heavens like a canopy.[10] All such building metaphors are part of picturing the cosmos as a sanctuary.

Ancient Near Eastern temple-building texts present the process as having two steps. First, *building* the house.[11] Second, *filling* the house. That is exactly what we see in Genesis 1. First God builds (Days One to Three)

---

9. Copyright Hannah Parry.
10. E.g., Isa 40:12, 22; Job 28:25; 38:4–6; Prov 3:19–20; 8:27–29; Ps 104:2–3, 5.
11. I owe this insight to Raymond Van Leeuwen, "Cosmos, Temple, House."

and then God fills (Days Four to Six). So even there, in Genesis 1, just below the surface, lies the idea of constructing a sanctuary.[12]

And this brings us back, once again, to Wisdom. For in the ancient Near East the process of temple construction was to be performed "with wisdom." Building without wisdom would lead to a house that could not stand. So the strong and recurring connection between God's Wisdom and creation in the Bible is not incidental but integral to the idea of the world as a temple.

This temple image is a way of speaking of God's closeness to and presence in the world. In Scripture, God's "otherness" is communicated through images of dwelling in heaven or "in unapproachable light" (1 Tim 6:16). But such important imagery is always balanced with imagery that says to us that God is not "far away," not "remote," not "absent." God is here, now, always: around, above, below, beside, within. To see the universe as a temple is to see the intimacy between Creator and creature as *integral* to the very idea of creating a world. It is to view the natural world as a *fitting* and *hospitable* home for God, welcoming divine indwelling with open arms.

The critical and beautiful tension between divine transcendence and divine immanence is wonderfully put in King Solomon's prayer at the dedication of the temple in Jerusalem. As he considers the idea that God would "inhabit" the temple he'd had built in Jerusalem, he exclaims: "But will God really dwell on earth? The heavens, even the highest heaven, cannot contain you. How much less this temple I have built! Yet . . ." (1 Kgs 8:27). How can it be that the One who is "beyond" can simultaneously be "within"? And yet . . . and yet it is so. Martin Luther captures the same paradox:

> God is substantially present everywhere, in and through all creatures, in all their parts and places, so that the world is full of God and He fills all, but without His being encompassed and surrounded by it. He is at the same time outside and above all creatures. These are all exceedingly incomprehensible matters . . . . For how can reason tolerate it that the Divine Majesty is so small that it can be substantially present in a grain, on a grain, through a grain, within and without, and that, although it is a single Majesty, it nevertheless is entirely in each grain separately . . . ? And that the same Majesty is so large that neither this world nor a thousand worlds can encompass it and say: "Behold, there it is!" His own divine essence can be in all creatures collectively and in each one individually more profoundly, more intimately, more present than the creature is in itself, yet it can

---

12. Which, incidentally, points us towards the idea that the climactic seventh day is, in part, about the Divine presence taking up residence in the palace of creation.

be encompassed nowhere and by no one. It encompasses all things and dwells in them all, but not one thing encompasses It and dwells in It.[13]

Cosmic temple talk is also a way to speak of the importance of the created world. Temples were sacred space, holy ground. They were to be treated with respect and reverence. If the holiness of the Jerusalem temple is a mere picture of the holiness of the cosmos, then that invites us to see the world around us differently and to inhabit that newly perceived world with awe and wonder. In a non-trivial sense, we stand on holy ground. As Wendell Berry observes: "There are no unsacred places; there are only sacred places and desecrated places."[14]

b) "Let everything that has breath . . ." (Psalms 148)

If creation is a temple, its creatures are the worshippers. In Scripture heaven and earth, the sun, moon, and stars, fields, and trees, the sea, floods, and coastlands are said to "declare" God's glory and "recount" God's ways and "sing" and "shout" and "give thanks" and "praise" and "clap" and "rejoice" and "be glad" and "exalt" (e.g., Pss 19:1–4; 96:11–14; 98:7–9).

Nowhere is this clearer than in Psalm 148. After calling on the celestial creatures—angels, sun, moon, stars, and the ocean beyond the firmament—to worship in vv. 1–6, it moves to the earthly realm:

> Praise YHWH from the earth,
>   you sea monsters and all deeps,
> fire and hail, snow and frost,
>   stormy wind fulfilling his command!
>
> Mountains and all hills,
>   fruit trees and all cedars!
> Wild animals and all cattle,
>   creeping things and flying birds!
>
> Kings of the earth and all peoples,
>   princes and all rulers of the earth!
> Young men and women alike,
>   old and young together!
>
> (Ps 148:1–12)

---

13. Luther, *WA*, XXIII, 134–36, cited in Santmire, "Supremely Natural God," 33.
14. Berry, "How to Be a Poet."

That covers sea creatures, weather, landscapes, insects, arachnids, and mollusks, birds—oh, and let's not forget humans: all joining together in a choir of creation.

What does it *mean* to speak of nonhuman creation worshipping God? We tend to view most of the cosmos as just inanimate "stuff," having no interests or inherent value. Its value is whatever value it has to living things, especially intelligent ones like us. And this has real-world impact on how we think about and relate to inanimate things like mountains. By contrast, animist cultures tend to think of all sorts of nonhuman creatures and aspects of nonhuman creation as "alive" and indeed as "persons" in some sense.[15] And that goes hand-in-hand with a different way of relating to their environments and the other creatures that share them. Can *we* think of so-called "inanimate" things as "alive" in some way? Even as "persons" in *some* sense? If so, in *what* way? In *what* sense?

To focus on the topic to hand, in what manner can a plant, animal, rock, or an environment worship?[16] Probably not in terms of their having conscious thoughts about God with propositional content nor of their intentionally relating to the Creator. It seems beyond unlikely that snails, say, consciously engage with God, and if we're speaking of a cactus or a hill . . . well, you get the idea.

As a result, biblical interpreters tend to think of the biblical language as inspirational poetry, yes, but as ultimately serving a merely *decorative* purpose. Now it is obvious that the language is operating in a poetic and metaphorical mode, but that does not mean that it is not simultaneously making truth-claims about the structures of reality, claims that are essential for Christian understanding of and engagement with nonhuman creatures. The praise of the sea is *not* the same as human praise, the mourning of the land is *not* the same as human mourning. Nonetheless, these metaphors do provide a true way of seeing.

I am reminded of the ancient notion of the music of the spheres. This is a metaphor, but it was intended to highlight a *very real* connection between the mathematical patterns one sees in music and those one sees in the movements of stars and planets. There is an ontological analogy between human

---

15. On animism and the Hebrew Bible, see Joerstad, *Bible and Environmental Ethics*.

16. Scripture presents God relating to environments, their parts, and the creatures that inhabit them as subjects to be engaged—never as mindless, lifeless "stuff." Speaking of an environment, say, or even Mother Earth as a whole, as if it was a subject, even a person, is a way to consider an environment *as an organic whole* that has integrity rather than as a mere assemblage of parts. And, sure, environments have fuzzy edges, but so do human persons. None of us are islands—not even islands are islands. And that poetic way of speaking has an ontological correlate. So personification is never just decorative—it provides new ways to see, new insight.

music and the celestial symphony. The stars make music, albeit according to their own mode of being. Thinking of both music and astral orbits as manifesting divine glory and as modes of response to the Creator is not an irrational leap, nor an unenlightening one.

In the Bible, we have seen already that God is presented as enjoying nonhuman creatures being and doing what they were created to be and do. We've also seen that nonhuman creation is often presented as *obedient* to God. But it is important to note that this obedience involves creatures doing things that are "natural" to them. It essentially involves them in being what they are. For instance, God commands the sea creatures to "Be fruitful and increase in number and fill the water in the seas, and let the birds increase on the earth" (Gen 1:22). They obey by being and doing what they were created to be and do. The sun and moon are commanded to "rule" the night and day by shining in the sky at the right places and right times. Their obedience is their being themselves by shining and following their God-ordained orbits. Similarly, the rain obeys by falling (or not falling) from the sky when God desires. The wind obeys by blowing when and as God desires. The sea obeys by crashing its waves and rivers by flooding (or not flooding). And so on. Creatures behaving according to their created natures *is* their obedience. It *is* their worship.

A rather touching reflection on how animals may be thought to worship is the poem "For I Will Consider My Cat Jeoffry," written by Christopher Smart in 1763. The poem opens thus:

> For I will consider my Cat Jeoffry.
> For he is the servant of the Living God
>   duly and daily serving him.
> For at the first glance of the glory of God in the East
>   he worships in his way.
> For this is done by wreathing his body seven
>   times round with elegant quickness.
> For then he leaps up to catch the musk,
>   which is the blessing of God upon his prayer.
> For he rolls upon prank to work it in.[17]

The cat worships by being a cat, *doing cat stuff*.

---

17. Meaning, the cat grabs some leaves from the musk plant and rolls around in them for fun. Having done this, Jeoffry engages in self-care: checking that his paws are clean, stretching, sharpening his claws, washing himself, and so on. During the night Jeoffry guards the house against the adversary. Smart continues by extolling the many strengths of his cat: his dextrous defence, speed, agility, and tenacity, his "mixture of gravity and waggery": "For there is nothing sweeter than his peace when at rest. For there is nothing brisker than his life when in motion."

Humans too are worshippers. We are *homo liturgicus*, created to *consciously* orientate our lives towards our divine Source, and this is what obedience and worship looks like *for us* (and other intelligent beings, whether angelic or alien). Our worship is consciously directed towards God, it has intentionality and intention. And unlike most other creatures, we have freedom to turn away from that calling—we are free to not worship, free to orientate our lives away from their divine Origin.

So, what we do when we worship is analogous to what nonhuman creatures do, but in us the *meaning* of this ontological structure in creation starts to manifest itself more clearly. Human worship *reveals* the glory of creation in a new mode. *This* is at least a part of the insight gained by construing nonhuman creatures as worshippers. And the fact that we must use heightened, poetic language to do so in no way diminishes the reality of which we speak. The language focuses it, heightens it, elevates it, and in so doing *reveals* it. Indeed, perhaps *only* poetry can articulate or crack open this reality for us to behold.

Having introduced humans into the picture, it is time to take a closer look at the place of humanity in the Christian story of creation.

3

The Wise Image

Humanity and Creation

1. A Toxic Christian Legacy? (Genesis 1)

It is sometimes claimed that Christianity is significantly to blame for our current environmental crises. At the heart of that accusation is a short text from the Bible that has had a massive impact on Christian cultures, both East and West: Genesis 1:26–28.

> [26] Then God said, "Let us make humans in our image, according to our likeness, and let them have dominion over the fish of the sea and over the birds of the air and over the cattle and over all the wild animals of the earth and over every creeping thing that creeps upon the earth."
>
> [27] So God created humanity in his image,
> in the image of God he created him;
> male and female he created them.
>
> [28] God blessed them, and God said to them, "Be fruitful and multiply and fill the earth and subdue it and have dominion over the fish of the sea and over the birds of the air and over every living thing that moves upon the earth."

The complaint is that in this passage humans alone are made as God's image, setting them above all other creatures. Then humanity is told to "subdue" the earth and "have dominion" over all other animals. This, it is alleged, is what underpins the idea that the earth is given to humans as their possession to use as they see fit. Given the huge cultural impact of Christianity, is it any wonder that we see the widespread exploitation of the natural world today? We think we have a God-given right to treat it however suits us. As Lynn White Jr. influentially argued in 1967, "we shall continue to have a worsening ecological crisis until we reject the Christian axiom that nature has no reason for existence save to serve man."[1]

There are some obvious reasons to pause before embracing this analysis, such as the fact that humans have been creating environmental damage from ancient times, and that includes many cultures with little or no exposure to Jewish or Christian thought. Or the fact that the environmental cataclysms of our day owe far more to very modern cultural, economic, and technological shifts than to the book of Genesis. At the very least, we need to take care not to overload Genesis with blame, using it as a scapegoat on which to place our own sins. Be that as it may, there is a legitimate worry here: Does this text do more to undermine than to support the kind of eco-spirituality required in our day? We need to take a look at what Genesis does and doesn't say about the human family and other animals.

2. Image and Dominion

There is no question that Genesis 1 gives a dignified place to humanity within the order of creation. However, before we explore that, it's worth keeping some perspective. We've already seen the positive value that the text places on *all* created things. And it's not a value that derives merely from the contribution of other creatures to human life. We should also notice that humans don't even get a day to themselves in Genesis 1 but share Day Six with all the other land animals, creepy crawlies included (Gen 1:24–28). Yes, God makes provision for the food that humans are to eat, but in the same breath God gives this food to the other animals as well (1:29–30). And yes, God does speak directly to humans (1:28–30), but throughout the chapter God also speaks directly to all the diverse creations, not needing human intermediaries to address them. It's also true that humans are given the command to fill the earth and are blessed by God, but so are other animals: "God blessed [the sea creatures] and said, 'Be fruitful and increase in number and fill the waters of the seas, and let the birds increase on the earth'"

---

1. White, "Roots of Our Ecological Crisis."

(1:22). Humans are declared "good" but so too are all God's creations. Even the command to humanity to "govern" is shared by the sun, moon, and stars (1:16–18). It's easy to miss these important commonalities and to be blinded by the glare of vv. 26–28. With that in mind, let's turn to the ideas that some find so troubling.

a) The Image of God

The ancient Near East was awash with temples to many and various deities, and at the heart of each temple lay a cultic statue, an image (Hebrew: *ṣelem*) of the god. This image was not the deity as such. After all, there were many statues of Baal, but there was only one Baal. There were loads of images of Osiris, but there was only one Osiris. Nevertheless, after the cult statue was dedicated and the spirit of the god had "activated" it, the image became the ritual representation of the god. To attack the image was to attack the deity. To pray to the image was to pray to the deity. Perhaps it may help us to understand if we think of it a little like the image of a person on our computer screen during a video call. The image on our screen is not the person, who may be hundreds of miles away. Nevertheless, we interact with that person through their visual and auditory representation via the computer. That image *functions as* the person in certain respects. We engage with them through it. Idols were thought to work a little bit like that.

Ancient Israel, however, was different from all its surrounding cultures. To the perplexity of other nations, the temple in Jerusalem had no cult statue in it. Israel was strictly forbidden from representing the living God by something so . . . static. A statue cannot see or hear or sense in any way at all; neither can it make decisions or speak or move or act (e.g., Isa 44:9–20). How can such an inactive thing represent the dynamic God of the exodus! Israel was therefore forbidden from having an image (*ṣelem*) of God. Except . . . hold your horses. The Creator *had* in fact authorized an image (*ṣelem*): human beings. Humans were created to be filled with the Spirit of God and to mediate specific aspects of divine presence in creation. They were the divinely authorized icon of God. Even though it is true that every creature mediates something of the Divine, in the Judaeo-Christian tradition no other creature is ever called an "image of God," not even angels. There's no doubt that this is an especially honorable position. And in this text it is specifically related to the idea of "governing." Humans are to image God by acting as God's royal representatives.

b) Ruling and Subduing

Humans are to "rule" (*rādâ*) over the other animals and to "subdue" (*kābaš*) the land. Let's consider these terms.

i. "Rule" (*rādâ*)

Rādâ is a word from the domain of ancient conceptions of royal authority, and it simply means "to have dominion" or "to govern." In certain contexts, it can have violent connotations, but those connotations are not essential to the word. It all depends on the context. So what of *this* context?

One interesting thing to observe is that in Genesis 1 human beings appear to be vegetarians. God gives them plants to eat, but the divine concession to allow meat eating comes much later, following the great flood (Gen 9:1–3). Whatever "ruling over" animals meant in Genesis 1, it did not involve killing them to eat. Human "rule" clearly has limits. How might we understand its nature?

A common image of a king in the ancient world, including Israel, was that of a shepherd. As a shepherd watched, guarded, and provided for the flock, so the monarch was to protect and provide for his or her (usually his) people. That was the ideal. Monarchs who used their position to enrich themselves and who neglected or exploited their people were considered to have abandoned their sacred duty. "[T]he Old Testament never authorizes kings to use their position to benefit themselves, and denounces them when they do so: rather they exist to benefit their subjects."[2] The ideal Israelite king was to be chosen from among the community, "one from among your brothers," who would govern as a sibling for the benefit of the whole family (Deut 17:14–20). The reality was that monarchs fell short of the ideal with depressing but predictable regularity, yet the ideal remained the standard against which they were measured and judged.

In Genesis 1, human "rule" is connected in the text with being created as the divine image. In the ancient Near East cult statues were not the only divine "images"—a monarch too served as the *ṣelem* of his patron deity. Genesis 1 radically democratizes that notion and declares *all humans without exception* to be created as icons of God. We are all called to represent aspects of God's rule over creation in the way we inhabit the world.

One vital question then concerns the nature of the God whose rule humans are to image. This God is one who seeks the blessing and flourishing of the world and its ultimate glorification. "Governing" then regards care for

---

2. Houston, *Justice for the Poor?*, 202.

creation, which is why many prefer nowadays to render the idea in terms of stewardship or custodianship, concepts suggesting tending creation on behalf of God. When humans image God well—with justice, mercy, compassion, and love—then human "rule" is a means by which God is acting in the world. That is what being an icon of God is all about. Humans govern as those commissioned by God from among the community of creation, siblings with other creatures, who are to pursue the welfare of the whole family. Human *mis*rule—in which we abuse creation in an attempt to enrich ourselves at the expense of the natural world—is not imaging God. It is, in fact, a sinful subversion of the image.

A second vital question concerns the aspects of divine rule that humans are to image. Obviously, the author of Genesis 1 did not think that humans were to reflect *every* aspect of God's rule, which is infinitely beyond our capacities: we lack the knowledge, the wisdom, and the power necessary for that.[3] The world is much too complicated for us to micromanage! The Bible is clear on many occasions that much of the divine rule of the cosmos *completely bypasses* humanity. Humans are subject to that rule, as are all other creatures. So the "dominion" delegated to humans is clearly circumscribed.

Throughout Christian history the text was understood as having limited application, applying to the daily activities of human life and culture: fishing, growing crops, rearing cattle, mining, logging, and so on (or it was read as an allegory in which the beasts that humans were to control were their own unruly passions). It was not until the seventeenth century, with the rise of modern science, that people started interpreting the Genesis passage as a command for humans to try to gain control over everything.[4] This, however, is pushing the dominion saying beyond—and arguably *against*—its intended scope. The authors of Genesis 1 could not even imagine a world in which human actions had the power to impact the earth the way that our actions can now. And their words cannot be used to justify such actions.[5]

---

3. Recognizing our ignorance and owning it is a key element in a wisdom orientation (Prov 3:5–6).

4. The historian Peter Harrison shows that Christians in the early church and Middle Ages did not interpret the dominion mandate in Genesis in ways that allowed the abuse of creation. The rise of modern science in the seventeenth century was the turning point when such an interpretation began to appear. See Harrison, "Subduing the Earth."

5. I ought to add an additional point here, to cover a base not mentioned in the main text (in a vain attempt not to make things complicated). While in my view Genesis 1–2 do not teach that the world used to be a flawless paradise, it is easy to see why they are often read that way. Those texts do "lean into" the *telos* of creation by anticipating the end in the way that the beginning is imagined. Thus, for instance, the "dominion"

ii. "Subdue" (kābaš)

While the verb *kābaš* can mean "to forcibly subdue," if used with enemies as its object, when it is used with land as its object (as here) it means "to take possession of," in the sense of "to live in," as we might "take possession" of a house when we buy it. It has no essentially violent connotations. It does not mean "to beat the land into submission to your will." Its most likely reference is simply to agriculture and the hard effort needed to farm the land well. And working the land *is* a lot of effort, but if done while cooperating with the flow of nature it enables the land to be more fruitful than it otherwise would be.

Humans are here authorized to use the land for their own survival and flourishing, but not at the expense of the land or of its nonhuman inhabitants. As the text explains:

> 29 Then God said, "I give you [humans] every seed-bearing plant on the face of the whole earth and every tree that has fruit with seed in it. They will be yours for food. 30 And to all the beasts of the earth and all the birds in the sky and all the creatures that move along the ground—everything that has the breath of life in it—I give every green plant for food." And it was so.

The land and the plants are to be shared by humans and beasts and bugs and birds. Use of the land need not be a zero-sum game. To the extent that it becomes such, Genesis 1 presents a challenging call to find a different approach.

Additionally, and importantly, the Bible does not anticipate or hope for humans transforming the whole landscape into farmland. Wild land is assumed to be a permanent feature and, as we have already seen, is valued by God for itself and for the creatures that inhabit it, irrespective of its relative uselessness to humans. There are texts in which, for instance, God tends to ecosystems that are uninhabited by human beings. Consider YHWH's rhetorical question to Job:

---

of Genesis 1 is, as I have said, rather mundane in its scope. However, it could be seen to anticipate a fuller, more cosmic destiny of humanity in Christ. Notice the way that Psalm 8 picks up on the "dominion" motif from Genesis 1 and then how Hebrews 2:5–9 says that this dominion is not a present reality for humans, but that it is a reality for the ascended Christ, our human representative in whom our human destiny is realized. So, the mundane dominion of Genesis 1 is read as an anticipatory picture of a fuller mode of human "dominion" in the age to come. What exactly that eschatological "rule" will be like is not yet clear, but that it will be *life-enhancing* and not life-degrading to creation's other inhabitants should go without saying. Furthermore, like the resurrection, it is not something humans can or should try to bring about. It serves rather as the promise of an eschatological destiny that lies in the hands of God.

> Who cuts a channel for the torrents of rain,
>   and a path for the thunderstorm,
> to water a land where no one lives,
>   an uninhabited desert,
> to satisfy a desolate wasteland
>   and make it sprout with grass? (Job 38:25–27)

Likewise, God transforms landscapes and cause them to flourish without any human assistance (e.g., Isa 41:17–19; 43:19–20).[6] And this might further suggest that some ways to manage nature should focus on leaving space for nature to manage itself. After all, it was created through God's Wisdom. So human wisdom works *with* nature, not against it.

c) Final Reflections on Humanity in Genesis 1

So there is no escaping the fact that Genesis 1 does set humans apart from other creatures in one particular respect. Some may feel that this is unhelpful, but I do not agree. There is no question that humans have incredible impact on our planet. Whether we like it or not, we have vast power for both good and harm. We must face "the inescapable dominance of the human race over the earth. This is simply a fact which cannot be wished away. . . . The ethical conclusion from this is surely not to entertain fantasies of a world without such dominance, but to accept the responsibility which that entails, of making conscious reflective decisions about any action affecting other living creatures and earth systems."[7] Genesis 1 does not serve to legitimize human abuse of the natural world—to the contrary, it should provide a bulwark against it. With great power comes great responsibility, and the responsibility to protect and care for the land we inhabit is elevated here to the level of a sacred duty. To ignore that duty is to reject not only the earth and its inhabitants but also God and even our own identity as God's image. In the end, nobody wins when humans swim against the flow of creation.

The notion of stewardship is, however, potentially problematic. It does need handling with some care for it can be open to certain distortions. It can be overextended in hubristic directions. It needs restraining by clarifying the limits of the claim and by setting it alongside other biblical images of human relations with the nonhuman world. But once the idea of "stewardship" is disconnected from the claim that humans are to control or micromanage (or even generally guide) the natural world—tasks that are both impossible and unnecessary—it can come into its own. Wise "ruling" is as much about

---

6. My thanks to Dr. Peter Atkins for this insight from his own work.
7. Houston, *Justice for the Poor*, 212.

discerning when to step back and let nature take its course (a key insight of "rewilding") as it is knowing when and how to step in and "manage" for the sake of the health of the ecosystems and to meet human needs.

One strength of the image of stewardship is that it says, "You humans do not own the world. You are to care for it and protect it on behalf of God. As creatures that need to live and flourish you must, of course, inhabit the natural world in ways that are to your benefit. Enjoy its rich resources, as all creatures do, and let it be a blessing to you. But do not do this to its detriment or at its expense. Be a blessing to it as it as it is to you."

An additional strength of the idea of stewardship is the pragmatic one that it provides a concept of caring responsibility and non-ownership that resonates with many non-Christian environmental activists, creating a bridge for cooperative action between Christians and others. One finds very similar ideas in Judaism, Islam, and other religions. And secular perspectives can get on board too. Economist Kate Raworth, for example, speaks of the importance of "smart stewardship" in rethinking our economies for the twenty-first century.[8] As Martin and Margot Hodson observe:

> Stewardship has many shortcomings but it continues to make an effective starting point for environmental action at all levels. It becomes a blind alley if it is seen as a destination and the only approach to environmental action. If it is seen more as a gateway leading to more holistic approaches, both Christian and secular, it can have a dynamic role for Christians as they take up environmental concern. It also enables a point of partnership with secular people and organizations as well as those of other faiths.[9]

3. Dust with a Destiny (Genesis 2)

Genesis contains a second creation story (Gen 2:4–25), which many scholars consider to be older than that found in Genesis 1:1—2:3. In this story, the focus is very much on the creation of humanity. The curtain rises (2:4–6) on an earth with no rain and no crops in the fields, for there was no one to tend them.[10] (Though presumably there was vegetation, for the earth was

---

8. Raworth, *Doughnut Economics*, 286.
9. Hodson and Hodson, *Ethics of Environmental Management*, 23.
10. The text does not say that there is no plant life at all. The Hebrew phrase "bush of the field" (*siaḥ haśśādeh*) refers to pasturage for animals while "plant of the field" (*'ēseb haśśādeh*) refers to field food crops of the kind humans cultivate. So the scenario is one in which there is as yet no agriculture.

watered by a stream that rose from underground.) So God creates a being to grow crops: "YHWH God formed the human from the dust of the ground and breathed into his nostrils the breath of life, and the human became a living being" (2:7).

This wonderful verse captures something of the paradox of human life: we are dust, but we are dust with a destiny. Some Christians complain about the theory of evolution, objecting that it is demeaning to humanity to suggest that we share ancestors with apes. But look at this text! We share a common ancestor with a mud pie! Humans are made from *soil!* As God later reminds the first couple, "You are dust . . ." (3:19). If there is a competition to encourage a little humility in humanity, I think Genesis has the edge over Darwin. Even the name of the species is intended to recall its humble origins: "YHWH God formed the human (*ādām*) from the dust of the ground (*ădāmâ*)." That's like saying God formed Rocky from the rock or Dusty from the dust or, more precisely, Human from the humus.

To speak of humans as made from the ground is to make a provocative point about the kinds of creature that we are. We are made of the same stuff as the earth itself. We are sons of the soil and daughters of the dust. We are biologically grounded (excuse the pun) in and connected to our environment. As such, the earth is essential to our very human identity. Not merely in the sense that it is necessary for our existence but also that it is literally integral to us and we, in turn, are one with it. This is a kick in the crotch to any "us-and-them" mentality we humans can be seduced by. We speak of "nature" and "the natural world" as though it's something distinct from us. We speak of animals as though they're something "other" than us. We are part of nature; we are animals; we are dust. This is all captured by Ragan Sutterfield when, in a bid for us to pay more attention to our fundamental connections with the ground, he writes, "Your body, each cell of your skin, each synapse of your brain, every wriggling sperm or quaking egg, the pigment of your retina was made of sunlight and earth, converted into proteins and sugars, made useful by plants and animal rumens and the microbes that team inside us all."[11] Thus, "through attention to the earth itself, we may discover the lost art of being human—Creatures born from clay, spirit-filled soil."[12] Remember—you are dust.

Yet at the same time God breathes into this earthling, and on receiving this breath he becomes a living being or soul (*nepeš ḥayyâ*). This is to see divine activity not simply in the processes that form bodies but also in the process by which nonliving matter becomes, mysteriously, alive (even if we

---

11. Sutterfield, *Art of Being a Creature*, 13.
12. Sutterfield, *Art of Being a Creature*, 4.

see these processes as two aspects of the same events). There is something astonishing about life, something more mysterious than the mundane definitions given at school in biology classes, helpful as they are. For Scripture, life is a divine gift, indeed it is the divine breath itself in creation.

> The soul is the body
> The body is the soul
> I look at you and it is always you
> Your soul is your body
>
> When I weep
> That is my body
> It is my soul
> You only have to ask
> And I will always say
>
> When I look at your body
> I love the soul of you
> Undying perfect shot
> Aimed before time
> God's hands all over you
>
> You only have to ask
> And my soul will receive
> I would rip up the floorboards to find you
> your body is your soul
>
> —Caitlin Gilson Smith[13]

We need to be a little careful here. Many believe that this episode in Genesis 2 distinguishes humans from other animals, making them unique. However, being "formed of the ground" is something that in Genesis is true of other animals too (2:19), as is having the "breath of life" and being a "living being/soul" (*nepeš ḥayyâ*) (1:30). The life-breath of *all* animals is as much breathed into them by God as is the case with Adam here (Ps 104:29–30).

What sets humans apart from other animals in Genesis 2 is the *task* to which God calls them. "YHWH God took the human and put him in the garden of Eden *to till it and keep it*" (2:15). God has bespoke tasks for other creatures, but the focus here is on the human vocation of gardening and cultivating. We could even say that we are one way in which God enables the earth to look after itself. We are soil tending the soil. All this requires a mindset shift away from seeing ourselves as "outside of" and somehow

---

13. Part I of "Imagine Utopia: The Sextet," in Scott and Smith, *Luminous Darkness*, 298. Used with permission.

"distinct from" the web of creation. We have a place within something much bigger.

In the story, God wants a creature to work the land and to that end God plants a garden (2:8–9), in Eden, perhaps as a place for the humans to learn. Turns out that God has green fingers too. And into this garden the earthling is placed (2:15). After that God seems to be in the habit of walking in the garden, in the cool of the day, communing with the plants and animals and with humanity as they in turn care for the habitat (3:8).

The focus on humans as agricultural creatures is understandable coming from ancient Israel, which was an agrarian society. Humans are to work/till/serve (*'ābad*) the ground but also to watch over (*šāmar*) it—that is, to guard it and protect it. There is *nothing* here to fund the idea that humans can do whatever the hell they want with the rest of the natural world. Such behavior is contrary to the sacred calling of "working and protecting." And I use the words "sacred calling" deliberately. Various scholars have observed that the story of Eden is full of allusions to the idea of temples, allusions the original audiences would notice.[14] (Yup, we're back to temples again.) The point is this: the garden is a temple; the humans are priests; tending the ground is their worship.

In the modern period, with its stark division between "nature" and "culture" (as if human cultural activities are somehow unnatural), there has been something of a romantic valorizing of wilderness, seen as a pristine landscape untouched by humans. This has gone hand in hand with a sometimes belittling attitude towards human modification of the landscape, as in agriculture. The problem here is that it "results in a view of nature in which people are only welcome as tourists and in which they cannot make a durable home."[15] Humans are creatures as much as any other creatures and need to live in and off the land. The question is how to do that *responsibly*. And it is precisely here that the biblical vision offers direction.

Located as it is immediately after the Genesis 1 creation story, this narrative serves to clarify and refine our understanding of what "the image of God" and "ruling" and "subduing" look like. It turns out they look like "working" and "protecting."

---

14. One of the first modern scholars to draw attention to this was Gordon Wenham in "Sanctuary Symbolism in the Garden of Eden." It has been widely, albeit not universally, adopted since.

15. Wirzba, *From Nature to Creation*, 39.

4. Humanity as a Microcosm of Creation

To end this chapter, I wish to step away from Genesis to consider an idea about humanity that is perhaps implicit in biblical texts and is made more explicit in subsequent Christian thought. Underpinning various biblical and subsequent Christian theological ideas about humanity is the notion that human beings can serve as *representatives of the whole creation* before God. This does seem to be a very grandiose claim, so it is understandable why some would find it objectionable!

Let me briefly explain the thinking here and what it does and does not mean. A range of different versions of the idea, of varying degrees of complexity (and some of them frankly bonkers), arose over time, but the most basic instinct underpinning the idea, crudely put, is something like this (which I am framing in terms influenced by Aristotle):

	Material beings	Living beings with a "nutritive soul"	Living beings with a "sensitive soul"	Living beings with a "rational soul"
Inanimate beings (e.g., rocks, clouds, rivers)	X	–	–	–
Plants	X	X	–	–
Nonhuman animals	X	X	X	–
Human animals	X	X	X	X
Heavenly beings	–	–	–	X

To explain: all earthly beings (in contrast to heavenly beings) are material creatures, whether alive or not. But many material things are living (in more traditional language, they are "souls" or are "ensouled").[16] Living beings come in many varieties, but there seems to be a clear distinction between plants, which are capable of feeding and growing and reproducing, and animals, which can do all those things but are also consciously aware of their environments and are capable of self-direction. Humans share all

---

16. We may wish to make space for speaking of nonliving creation as living in *some* sense, per the animist instinct, with which I have a lot of sympathy. But we still need to find a way of making the distinction that Aristotle (and every biologist ever) makes here between inanimate and animate creatures, between rocks and plants. I will leave that task as homework. ☺

these things in common with inanimate things, plants, and other animals. However, in addition, humans have a far more developed intellectual and imaginative capacity. They share this capacity with the nonmaterial heavenly beings. In that sense, humans have an awareness of both the transcendent heavenly dimension of the world and the earthly dimension, consciously manifesting the two sides of the coin of creation.

Obviously the sketch above is extremely crude and would need a lot of qualification. For instance, it is clear that many animals have varying capacities of intellectual processing ability, some having rudimentary language capacity, and that something that might be called proto-cognition is even found in some plants species. These discoveries are fascinating and important. Nonetheless, it seems undeniable that while there is no tidy dividing line between humans and other animals when it comes to intellect, human capacity for abstract thought and emotion and art and ethics *far exceeds* any other material creatures that we are aware of. And while, in my view, these capacities are not what constitutes the image of God in humanity, they are capacities that enable us to reflect God in certain ways.

Let me make a quick aside at this point. To link to our overarching framework of Divine Sophia, it is worthy of passing note that this distinguishing feature of humanity—our relatively high level of rational capability—is connected with wisdom. Indeed, it is why we named our subspecies homo *sapiens* (*wise* humans). Divine Wisdom is, of course, manifest in all created things, not simply in humans, but our intellective capabilities are one key means by which we can *discern* God's Wisdom in the world and live according to her ways. Reason, of course, is hardly foolproof! It can get twisted and can go horribly wrong for a range of reasons, spiraling into folly, and this is why developing healthy habits of thought and intellectual virtue is so important in training our minds to discern the mind of Sophia (see chapter 14).

OK, let's return to the idea of humans as representative of the rest of creation: the thinking is that humans can meaningfully play such a symbolic role in certain contexts precisely because they participate in the same aspects of being as other kinds of creature. Humans are pictured as being made from the earth. And at a chemical level we are composed of the same atoms and molecules as countless inanimate creatures. Yet we are "living souls" like the plants. And the Christian tradition is clear that humans are animals too—in Aristotelian terms, we could be said to share a sensitive soul with all other animals. And we even share something with the heavenly creatures that transcend materiality—namely, (relatively) complex thought. Thus, humans can be seen from one perspective as a kind of miniature cosmos, a symbolic microcosm of everything God created. On that basis, and in certain symbolic contexts, humans can meaningfully be understood to represent the whole universe.[17]

The reason that this is important for Christian eco-spirituality is that Jesus is able to represent all creation in his death and resurrection, and thereby to save all creation, *because he is a human being*. That is why, in Christian thought, his saving work has *cosmic* implications and not merely implications for humans (Col 1:15–20). Jesus, in his embodied humanity, is the true temple of God (John 2:18–22), filled with all the fullness of God (Col 2:9; John 1:14). And as ancient temples were seen as stylized models of the cosmos, so the embodied Jesus symbolizes the whole world. As such, his death and resurrection *is* the destruction and rebuilding of the temple, which *is* the death and resurrection of the whole universe! (We will explore this idea in more detail in chapter 9.)

However, one may still feel rather uncomfortable with this idea. So let me offer a few further clarifications and qualifications. First, the sense in which humanity represents other creatures in its capacity as microcosm is narrow. It is only in *certain ritual and symbolic contexts* and only in *certain respects* that humans are said to be representatives of the whole. We humans obviously cannot represent mountains or trees or bees or dolphins as if we were members of those classes of creature or as if they had elected to have us represent them, as one elects a politician. We are not bees. We cannot even *imagine* the world from a bee's perspective. The "what-it's-like-ness" of being a bee is beyond our comprehension. Appreciating our limits in this regard is part of the respect we need to learn towards the "otherness" of other creatures. In *many* ways they are *not* like us. We can stand up on behalf of bees, in defending some of their interests, and in that sense represent them, but even that kind of representation is circumscribed. The claim that humans are a microcosm is not saying that humans can represent other creatures in *any* capacity or *any* context. There are innumerable ways in which we cannot serve to represent them. What humans symbolically represent in their role as microcosm is very general—it is *the cosmos as a unified and ordered whole, composed of material, living, sentient, and intelligent beings*. That.

Second, the idea of humanity as microcosm does not in any sense suggest that humans *replace* other creatures. Quite the contrary, it connects our being with their being. Humans do not exist or act *instead of* other creatures

---

17. This idea is not merely found in strands of Christian thought but also in some Greek thought from at least the fifth century BC and it remained popular within the Platonic tradition, in both its pagan and Christian forms. It can also be found in Jewish Kabbalistic thought and much esoteric thought. It was popular amongst many Renaissance thinkers and was widespread until the early modern period in the West.

but—within certain contexts—*on behalf of* them. I'll illustrate this soon in relation to worship.

Third, the point of the microcosm idea is *not* that divine presence and activity in creation trickles down a "chain of being" from humans to other animals then to plants and finally to inanimate things, so that a plant, say, experiences God at several removes from the Divine Source. No. God is not part of any chain of being, not even at the top as some kind of "Supreme Being."[18] And God is *directly* present and active in all things, whether rivers or trees or giraffes. Now humans can (and should) mediate something of God's presence and activity to other creatures—that is what having "dominion" is all about—but equally, other creatures can mediate something of God's presence and activity to us. It is not a one-way street. This is a community of creation, and the divine life should flow back and forth in enriching the good of the whole. Thomas Aquinas (d. 1274) touches on this when he comments:

> The distinction and multitude of things come from the intention of the first agent, who is God. For he brought all things into being in order that his goodness might be communicated to creatures, and be represented to them; and because his goodness could not be adequately represented by any one creature alone, he produced many and diverse creatures, that what was wanting to one in the representation of the divine goodness might be supplied by another. For goodness, which in God is simple and uniform, in creatures is manifold and divided and hence the whole universe together participates [in] the divine goodness more perfectly, and represents it better than any single [kind of] creature whatever.[19]

This is also an important qualification to make concerning the restriction of "image of God" language to human beings in the Bible. *Every single creature* refracts God's light in distinctive ways—we can see traces of God's truth, goodness, and beauty in all things. So humanity's call to image God on the earth should not be taken to mean that God is not manifest in other important ways in nonhuman creatures.

Fourth, the idea does not sponsor harmful attitudes towards nonhuman creatures. It does not treat them as existing simply to meet our needs. Rather, it bestows value on them and symbolically ties our being to their being. They do not exist for us. If anything, we exist for them. (After all, in

---

18. I am not saying that the idea of a "chain of being" is unhelpful. I am merely saying that if it is the way things are, God is not part of it, but its transcendent cause.

19. Aquinas, *Summa theologiae* I.47.1.

Genesis 2, God created the human to meet a need in the earth, not the other way around.)

Let's bring this microcosm discussion back to its natural home, in worship. One element in the Christian tradition is that humans have a priestly calling in relation to the rest of the created order and, as part of that calling, they give voice to creation's praises. The rest of creation, of course, worships with or without humans. We are not needed for that to happen nor for God to find delight in it. However, when the psalmist, say, brings the whole chorus of creation into focus, that nonhuman worship is articulated in a way that brings out something of the meaning of the ontological contours of creation. This resonates with the ancient tradition of humanity as microcosm. As such, we play a representative, priestly role before God on behalf of nonhuman creatures. This idea, as it relates to worship, can be found in the early third-century *Apostolic Constitutions*: "The choir of stars moves us to wonder, declaring him that numbers them, and showing him that names them. The animals declare him that put life into them; the trees show him that makes them grow. All these creatures, being made by your word, show forth the greatness of your power. Therefore, every human being, through Christ, ought to send up a hymn from his very soul to you *in the name of the rest*, since you have given him power over them" (*Apostolic Constitutions* VII.35).[20] Here human "power over" creatures is explicated in terms of offering worship "in their name." Not *instead of* them, but *on their behalf* and attentive to their modes of being and thriving. Stars and trees and various kinds of animal all worship in their own way, and they do so irrespective of anything humans do. What we are is conduits that gather, and funnel, and articulate that worship. We write the songs that make the whole world sing, and in so doing we bring to the surface something of the *significance* and *value* of the structure of the being-in-the-world of nonhuman creatures. Perhaps we may also in some sense "complete" the worship of nonhuman creatures by incorporating and enfolding it within our own worship. As with a choir, without each other our worship is not whole.

All of this sounds very lovely, but perhaps it's all a bit too twee. After all, the world we live in is full of suffering and pain and death, so any creation spirituality has to take that seriously. Our next chapter will attempt to do that.

---

20. I am grateful to Elizabeth Theokritoff for drawing my attention to this quote in *Living in God's Creation*, 159–60.

4

The Leviathan in the Room

The Dark Side of Wisdom's Creation

> Who trusted God was love indeed
> And love Creation's final law —
> Tho' Nature, red in tooth and claw
> With ravine, shriek'd against his creed.
>
> —Alfred Lord Tennyson, *In Memorian A.H.H.*, Canto 56 (1849)

THERE'S A LEVIATHAN IN the room. The picture I've painted of creation can sound rather idyllic, but it's glaringly obvious that the natural world isn't simply "all things bright and beautiful." It's impossible to miss the vast amount of danger and suffering and death, both human and nonhuman. Ours is a world of "beauty and barbed wire," as the mathematician John Lennox puts it. How can it be the creation of the good God?

1. A Dead-End Solution

One tradition in Christian theology seeks to account for Lennox's "barbed wire" in terms of a fall from paradise. The idea is that once upon a time the world contained no pain, no horrors, no death. Creatures lived in harmony with one another and with God. "There was . . . nothing bad in that created world, no hunger, no struggle for existence, no suffering, and certainly no death of animal or human life in God's perfect creation."[1] But it all went to hell in a handbasket. Adam and Eve misused their God-given free will, sin entered stage left, and in its wake *all of creation* fractured. Pandora's box was opened and out flowed all the evils of the world; not only human corruption but also earthquakes, floods, diseases, animals predating other animals, and, of course, of death. (Except for plants, which were an exception to the "no death" rule—apparently their deaths don't count as deaths.)

There's just one problem this story. It's not true. Think about it. Take the situation before the fall. For starters, animals with bodies anything like the ones they currently have are susceptible to harm. What if an animal had slipped and fallen from a high cliff? Would it have bounced? Or would God have to catch it? Or take another hypothetical scenario: What happens if the animals don't eat? If they can't die, then . . . what? Or think about this: in Genesis 1 creatures are commanded to reproduce, but what would happen if they obeyed that command yet didn't die? Jon Garvey notes that the unchecked reproduction of the "vast biomass of creatures at the base of the food chain—such as insects on land and plankton at sea— . . . would make the earth uninhabitable within no more than a year or two."[2] That makes the command to "fill the earth" sound sadistic![3]

Now consider the situation after the fall. We are being asked to imagine that human sin led to a rapid change in the biology of the natural world. The act of Adam and Eve eating the fruit would have to cause new species, like parasites or viruses, to burst into existence. It would also have caused existing species to rapidly transform. Imagine the poor old vegetarian lions in Africa chomping away on delicious leaves and suddenly finding themselves changing for no explicable reason into carnivores.[4] This would not simply be a matter of a little dental work but would involve extensive changes to the biochemistry, anatomy, and physiology of the animals. Or picture creatures suddenly developing complex defensive mechanisms and behaviors, features only needed in a world with predation: hedgehogs find themselves with spines; chameleons dazzle with a newfound ability to camouflage; bombardier beetles develop complicated internal systems enabling them to spray scalding liquid out of their backside. (I know some people like that.) Adam and Eve, it seems, ate some *flipping potent fruit!*

---

1. Morris, "Fall, the Curse, and Evolution."
2. Garvey, *God's Good Earth*, 31.
3. Besides, if God's plan was to make a batch of immortal animals, then why not just create a fixed number and do away with reproduction altogether?
4. Or maybe the veggie lioness gave birth to a carnivorous cub—I bet that was a shock at dinnertime.

The laws of physics would need to change too. Hurricanes, for instance, result from the operation of the laws of thermodynamics in particular geographic and atmospheric conditions. For there to be no dangerous weather, the world would need to be a *very, very* different one to the one we inhabit.

The kind of changes in physics and biology needed to lead from the paradise some Christians postulate to the world we live in now are vast and systemic. Yet everything we know from the various sciences about the past of our cosmos, our planet, and the creatures that live on it speaks with one voice: long before there were any human beings to even think about sinning there were potentially lethal astronomical and geological events (asteroid collisions, volcanos, earthquakes), dangerous and devastating weather patterns (droughts, blizzards, hurricanes), diseases, predation, and death.

2. Does the Bible Teach That the Created Order Was Once a Paradise?

What may surprise some is that the Bible does not explicitly teach that the world was once a paradise. "Eh?" I hear you say. "Surely Genesis 1–2 portray an idyllic world without pain." There are big questions circling the interpretation of Genesis 1–3, but in this short space I offer just a few quick observations.

First, nothing in the Genesis origin stories—which are most fruitfully (a terrible pun) read in terms of their symbolism, not as history in any straightforward way—requires that human beings, let alone animals, were created immortal or could not experience pain and injury. Immortality was offered to Adam and Eve as a gift, symbolized by their access to the Tree of Life. That clearly suggests that humans were created mortal.[5] So long as they had ongoing access to the tree, they had access to life, but once cut off from it, death took its natural course.

On this interpretation of the story, we might say that the cutting off of humanity from access to the divine life turned death, which was already a reality in the world, into something deeply ambiguous. On the one hand, it is a natural part of creation, playing an important and positive role in the world. On the other, the withdrawal of access to the Tree of Life—an act of divine judgment—makes death simultaneously an enemy permanently blocking the road to the destiny for which God created us. This is why many Christians see Genesis 1–3 not as concerning the loss of perfection but as

---

5. And, in passing, it is worth noting that when God warned the humans that they would die if they ate from the fruit of the Tree of Knowledge, they did not respond, "Death? Ummmm . . . dunno what you're talking about."

about the loss of the opportunity to develop towards the destiny intended by God.

Second, although in the popular imagination the garden in Eden is the earth in its paradisical state, even in that story the garden is only *an enclave within* the world. Outside of the garden, where Adam and Eve are later cast, the world is the world as we know it.[6]

Third, even the garden, which does indeed speak of a state of divine provision and protection within the world, was not "perfect"—it contained its shrewd serpent and had opportunities for evil. Furthermore, the garden needed work and cultivation (Gen 2:15). It also needed "keeping," which implies a role in protecting it from possible hostile attack. And if we consider the creation mandate in Genesis 1:28, that humans are to "rule" and "subdue" creation, this implies effort and some struggle in human existence, even if there was no sin on the scene.

Fourth, what of the Tree of the Knowledge of Good and Evil? This was not, despite the claims of many, an inherently bad tree. Quite the contrary. The "knowledge of good and evil" is biblical language that indicates wisdom to discern the difference between right and wrong (1 Kgs 3:9). God has such wisdom (Gen 3:5, 22), of course, and the rest of Scripture leads us to presume that God intends to share the fruit of wisdom with humans in due course, at the right time and in the right way. The issue in the story is *how people seek to acquire* such insight, and the sin of eating the forbidden fruit represents the illicit attempt by humans to bypass God in the pursuit of such understanding. The "wisdom" acquired as a result is not true wisdom from above but a simulacrum, a wisdom "from below" (Jas 3:15), and their sin ironically led to a loss of both true wisdom and life.

It also brought various other hard, alienating consequences for humans in their relationship with God, with each other, and with the natural world around them (Gen 3:16–19). But none of those consequences require any structural changes in the physics, chemistry, or biology of the world.[7]

According to Irenaeus, a second-century church leader, Adam and Eve were not created perfect, but like infants, needing to grow and develop (*Against Heresies* 4.38.2). Their maturity and completion were to be the end-result of a process. Eden, then, is merely a starting place, not an ending

---

6. As an aside, it's a good job, because there are many plants and animals that thrive in environments very different to that in Eden. If the world was Eden-like everywhere such species could not exist.

7. On the doctrine of sin understood in the light of modern science, see especially Haarsma, *When Did Sin Begin?* Haarsma helpfully explores four different possible ways in which Christian theology of sin can be harmonized with modern scientific accounts of human origins.

place, and the fall is not the loss of perfection but a barrier blocking the road, making the journey impossible to complete. Impossible, that is, unless God does something about it. And, as we shall see, God is determined to bring the divine plan to its intended completion.

3. Creation Has a Place for the Dark and the Deep

Importantly, various biblical passages seem to assume that the way that the world works now is the way God created it to work. Let's go back to the very opening passage of the Bible—the influential story of God shaping and populating the cosmos over a period of six days. What's often missed by readers is the significance of the primeval state from which God started. "In the beginning, God created the heavens and the earth. The earth was without form and void, *and darkness was over the face of the deep*" (Gen 1:1–2). This is not a world. Nothing can live here. Indeed, there's isn't really a distinct "here," just the pitch dark, churning, unpredictable deep. Modern readers may not be attuned to such imagery, but an ancient Near Eastern audience would immediately "get it"—it's mythic imagery with deep cultural resonances. The sea was a common symbol of, amongst other things, a state of affairs inhospitable to thriving, indeed, to life. It is disorder. That's why ancient creation myths can involve the slaying or taming of a sea god.[8] Consider what God does with this darkness and "the deep" in Genesis 1. There's no battle. God doesn't slay any monsters. Rather, God effortlessly speaks commands that serve to order the world, transforming it from chaos to cosmos.

There is something in this story, however, that often goes unnoticed. What does Elohim (God) do with the darkness and "the deep"? He doesn't annihilate or banish them. Rather, he *puts them in their place*. The dark and the sea are not "evil" as such—they are dangerous, and they do need taming and restraining, but when they are rightly fitted into the cosmic web they function as a part of the creation that God declares "good." When they are properly placed, they can play a positive role in the creation order: the dark, with the moon and the stars, is integral to the rhythms of time (Gen 1:14–19), and there are animals that are native to the darkness (Ps 104:20); the sea too is now abundantly populated and bursting with life (Gen 1:20–23; Ps 104:24–26).

Yet in the mythic symbolism of the Bible both the sea and the dark remain dangerous elements within creation, and they need to be contained

---

8. On sea symbolism in the ancient Near East and the Bible, see Parry, *Biblical Cosmos*, ch. 2.

lest they cause harm. The great flood story in Genesis 6–9 reveals this clearly—it a symbolic act of "de-creation" in which the windows in the firmament are opened, allowing the waters above to come back down, threatening the separations of Day Two, and submerging the land, reversing the separations of Day Three. Human and animal life is blotted out as a result. Ancient biblical authors remained aware of the importance of God's ongoing restraining of these primeval powers (e.g., Ps 104:6–9). So the sea remains a mythic symbol of the wild, untamable, and dangerous dimensions of God's good world. These are forces that can be harnessed by God to play a constructive role in the story of life, but such forces must always be treated with respect.

This is symbolized in the visions of creation that YHWH speaks to Job from the whirlwind. The cosmos, as God presents it, is to a large degree veiled in mystery, inviting humility. It is wild, and largely indifferent to human beings. One significant focus in God's speeches are two watery chaos beasts—Behemoth and Leviathan (Job 40–41). These are mythic symbols representing the powerful, untamable, dangerous dimensions of the world—aspects of the cosmos that humans cannot control or contain but that God can and does. They are God's "pets" (cf. Gen 1:21; Pss 104:26; 148:7).

Meric Srokosz and Rebecca Watson helpfully capture this tension: "in biblical times 'chaos' was understood . . . as a fundamental aspect of the world. The earth itself was understood as founded on water and surrounded by water, above, below and all around. This was essential for life: the rains nourished the earth, and the waters beneath did the same by welling up as rivers and streams. At the same time, the sea that surrounded the earth was also understood as presenting a constant threat."[9]

This ancient symbolism still speaks to us. Nowadays we might think, for instance, of the plates composing the earth's crust, which can cause devastating earthquakes and tsunamis, but which also play a vital role in the provision of nutrients necessary for the emergence and sustenance of life. Similar things can be said about volcanos. Even cancer is complicated. The genetic processes that cause cancers and genetic diseases are *the exact same* genetic processes that enable the evolution of species, including our own. Without them we would not be here. All these, along with many other examples, are dangerous and potentially devastating aspects of the natural order that are harnessed to contribute to the flourishing of life.

The cycle of life, birth, and death is also a part of the natural patterns of the world that God made, patterns in which God is actively involved.

---

9. Srokosz and Watson, *Blue Planet, Blue God*, 138.

> All creatures look to you
> > to give them their food at the proper time.
> When you give it to them,
> > they gather it up;
> when you open your hand,
> > they are satisfied with good things.
> When you hide your face,
> > they are terrified;
> when you take away their breath,
> > they die and return to the dust.
> When you send your Spirit,
> > they are created,
> > and you renew the face of the ground.
> (Ps 104:27–30)

God is at work not only in giving life to creatures but also in taking away their breath and returning them to the dust; both life *and death* are the work of God. In fact, death is a critically important aspect in the ecosystems of our planet. Animals and plants need to die to make space for successive generations. And nature is a wonderful recycler. Nothing is wasted. The decomposing plants and animals become vital sustenance for other creatures, all part of a vast and complex web of life. Without death ecosystems would not work.

We should note too that God *in wisdom* created wild predators:

> Does the hawk take flight by your [Job's] wisdom
> > and spread its wings toward the south?
> Does the eagle soar at your command
> > and build its nest on high?
> It dwells on a cliff and stays there at night;
> > a rocky crag is its stronghold.
> From there it looks for food;
> > its eyes detect it from afar.
> Its young ones feast on blood,
> > and where the slain are, there it is.
> (Job 39:26–30)

There is no hint that such animals used to be vegetarian and that human sin had turned them to predation. In the Psalms too we see that God created and supports predator animals, like lions: "the lions roar for their prey and seek their food *from God*" (Ps 104:20). We may find wild nature uncomfortable, but according to Scripture, it is God's good creation. In the Bible divine activity is seen as present in both the bright and the dark sides of natural processes.

All of this is offering a vision of the world that is not sentimental but that recognizes the real blessings and curses it can bring to creatures. The "good" world of Genesis 1 is the world we still live in. It's good in a specific sense—not in the sense of being free from hardship but in the sense that it is *fit for purpose*.

But what is that purpose?

4. Creation as Aimed at a Telos

The world as created in Genesis 1 is complete in one sense—in the sense that it is made fit for life and then filled with life. However, according to a long Christian tradition, the universe is not a completed, static project. It is a dynamic world that is created to grow and develop and change. We might say that it is made aimed towards a destiny, directed towards an end (Greek: *telos*).

In the language of the Bible, the world comes into being "from God" and it is directed "to God" (Rom 11:36). God is both the origin and destiny of the cosmos, its Alpha and Omega. The ultimate goal, in biblical language, is "the summing up of all things in Christ, things in the heavens and things on the earth" (Eph 1:10), that God may fill everything. Consequently, the end is not something distinct from the beginning but what the beginning was always about.

The Bible gives only hints of the final destiny of creation. In symbolic images we are told that God himself will be its light and there will be no more sea (Rev 21:1, 23), because in the end darkness and chaos will no longer be features of the world. Death too will be vanquished forever (1 Cor 15:51–57). This is the "new creation" for which the pattern is the risen Jesus. His mortal body was transformed and transfigured in the resurrection, raised full of glory. So too with our bodies, and so too with the whole creation. This is the culmination of the work of God in the world across the ages upon ages of the world. St. Paul sums the vision up with these words, pregnant with meaning: "God will be all, in all" (1 Cor 15:28).[10]

According to St. Paul, God's project of creation as it related to humans was always a phased project. Phase one involved humans like Adam: earthly, fleshly, and mortal. Phase two involved humans imaged after the risen Christ: heavenly, spiritual, and immortal (1 Cor 15:44b–49). Thus, while death may be an integral part of the order of life in God's world, just as the dark and the sea are, that does not mean that death was ever intended to be a *permanent* part of creation nor that it remains in the final state.

---

10. Those are the words I want on my gravestone.

This climactic theological horizon frames every Christian attempt to make sense of the world we live in.

5. Natural Evils and the God of Love

All of this still leaves us with many agonizing real-life issues when facing the problem of suffering. It is one thing dealing with what we might call "human evils"—which often result from the freely chosen sinful acts of people, acts that God condemns and seeks to lead us away from. But what of suffering and death resulting from natural processes in the world, processes that do not depend on wretched human decisions? Illness? Disease? Accidents? Starvation?

Often, of course, such matters are profoundly bound up with human decisions, so that to a significant extent even they can be blamed on human actions. Human actions might directly or indirectly bring about natural catastrophes. To take an obvious example, think about the ways human activity directly leads to climate warming with the suffering it brings in its wake. Human action can also amplify the impact of natural events. Consider the shocking cases in recent years where we have seen mass destruction of buildings and consequent loss of life during earthquakes as a result of the corner-cutting decisions of building companies pursuing increased profits. Or the instances in which the impact of a drought on a population is massively exaggerated by military conflicts that hamper aid. These kinds of examples can be multiplied many times over. The line between suffering caused by human actions and "natural" events is very blurred. Nonetheless, a lot of suffering cannot be laid at our door. Why does God allow such things?

a) Knowing What We Don't Know

God has revealed some things to human beings, for which we are grateful, but there is much that has not been revealed (Deut 29:29; 1 Cor 13:12). That was the burden of God's reply to Job. Job could make no sense of why he'd suffered as he had—losing his wealth, his health, and his children, as a result of a combination of human-caused and natural events[11]—and he

---

11. I use the terms "nature" and "natural" with some hesitation because the implied contrast with "culture" (i.e., human activity) could be taken to suggest that humans stand *outside* "nature." We do not. Human "culture" is a *subset* of "nature"—a human using a hammer as a tool is as much a part of nature as a raven using a stone or twig as a tool. Human house building is as natural as ants making a nest. However, for pragmatic

raged against God at the sheer injustice of it. He refused to see it as a punishment for his sins, and the book as a whole endorses Job's stance. Yet when YHWH finally speaks to Job, what YHWH does *not* do is explain the suffering. Rather, God stresses the vastness of human ignorance about creation. Human beings, like Job, simply do not understand much at all about the cosmos and there is great wisdom in having the humility to recognize that. And this means learning to live without tidy answers to all our questions.

While suffering may well seem like a positive disproof of divine love or power or existence, we are simply not in the position to draw such a conclusion. It may be true that neither I nor my educated friends can imagine a good reason for God allowing the world to contain natural processes that inflict the injuries that they do inflict, and this may haunt us, but it is hardly a reliable ground for concluding that there is no such reason. After all, what basis do I have for thinking that if there really are good reasons for allowing the sufferings of the world, God would be sure to tell *me* what they are? The sober truth is that we don't know why God created a world in which suffering and death feature so largely.

However, that does not mean that there is nothing we can say that might help us to understand some of the possible factors at play. Before we consider them, let me offer a brief warning.

b) A Warning Not to Exaggerate

There is a danger that we underplay the problem of "natural evil," for it is a very real problem. However, there is an equal danger that we exaggerate the problem. Listening to some people speak about the natural world one might be forgiven for thinking that nature is some kind of horror show, a mass torture chamber in which countless animals live in constant terror and excruciating aguish. Drawing on the work of Jon Garvey, I offer just a few brief reflections regarding this.[12]

i. *Extinctions*

It is often said that something like 99.9 percent of the species that have ever existed are now extinct. This is suggested to be a source of great suffering

---

reasons, the term "natural" here follows the normal convention and indicates evils that arise from nonhuman causes. That distinction is an important one even if the terminology needs some refining.

12. The following observations are all drawn from Garvey, *God's Good Earth*, 119–80. I highly recommend the book.

and to display astonishing waste in the cosmos. Not something that a good God would do.

To start with, the oft-cited 99.9 percent figure is a guess postulated on Darwin's assumption that species change in very tiny steps in all directions at once, with only a lucky few offspring surviving. That assumption is not shared by more recent versions of evolution theory. So the 99.9 percent figure is very likely to be grossly overinflated.

Second, whatever the true number of extinctions is, we should not imagine that extinctions are painful or necessarily involve any suffering. A species becoming extinct means that its last members die without offspring. That need not be painful, and the dying creatures are almost certainly unaware that they are the last.

Third, that a species has become extinct does not mean that it was a "failure" or a "waste." Some of the extinct species were in fact very successful, existing on earth for millions of years until their environments were no longer able to sustain them. That they are no longer around does not mean that their existence was a waste. They made countless contributions to the world, contributions that outlast them. Their existence was valuable, both for its own sake and because our planet would literally not be what it is now without them.[13]

ii. Pain

Pain is a part of the world. In fact, pain plays a positive role, serving as a warning for animals to avoid certain things that could threaten them.

We need to be very careful not to project human experience of suffering onto the experiences of other creatures. Of course, we cannot even imagine what it's like to be a different kind of animal and we can't know how they experience pain, but if our experience of pain is facilitated by our complex brains and nervous systems and by higher cognitive beliefs (e.g., the belief that we will not live to see our children grow up increases our pain) and mental states (e.g., depressed people feel pain more than others) then we can say that many plants and animals that are injured or die do not experience pain in anything like the way that humans would in similar circumstances.[14]

---

13. These observations in no way serve to justify the very rapid and increasing rise in extinctions caused by human activity. In addition to the depletion such a shocking rate of biodiversity loss brings to creation, the number of extinctions is posing an increasing threat to our ecosystems and, in the end, to humanity itself.

14. Recent research suggests that plants and lower animals do experience sensation and pain in *some* sense and even something akin to cognition, but almost certainly in a very different sense than humans do.

The higher animals, with nervous systems and complex brains, can certainly experience pain and loss, but the vast majority of plants and animals in the world lack the biological features that underlie the experiences of deep pain. Perhaps less than 1 percent of species are capable of experiencing what we could call agony.

Consider the practice of parasites, like the infamous Ichneumonid wasp, laying eggs inside living hosts. The young parasites then eat their way out of the host as they grow. What a horror show! However, the host insects have few internal pain receptors and mostly carry on life as normal, unaware of the parasite within until it bursts out and the host quickly dies. While many things in nature are distasteful to us, we need to be very careful not to project human morality and feelings onto the natural world. Human ethics applies to humans, not to other creatures. The wasps are not behaving immorally nor are they causing untold misery. Furthermore, parasites make a very valuable contribution to ecosystems.

It is also the case that the natural world is not gratuitously pain-inducing. Predators, for instance, do not torture their prey. There is no benefit for them in doing so. The kills are usually swift and efficient. Many use venom to paralyze or anesthetize their prey.[15] Others kill with a blow or bite. And while it may look gruesome, the prey experiences fear and pain for only a very short time. Indeed, with the adrenaline in its system and the shock of the killing strike (or the anesthetic of the venom) it may well not feel much pain at all.[16]

Observation in the field also suggests that it is not true that prey species live their lives in a state of constant stress or fear. And that makes sense. After all, such a state is designed to trigger survival strategies in crisis situations and would be counterproductive if it was a constant state of mind.

The vision of creation as a horror show is a very recent one in Western culture and says more about the cultural lenses through which we are guided to view the world than it says about the world itself. The natural world does contain fear and pain, but if we think such to be its defining characteristics our vision is myopic.

---

15. The suffering caused to humans from snakebites are usually because humans are not their natural prey and are too large for the dose to kill.

16. It is suggested that God can't make his mind up which animals he supports because God both designs cheetahs to kill gazelles and simultaneously equips gazelles to escape from cheetahs. In the Bible, God both provides food for predators and supports prey. God is on the side of *both* kinds of species, for the good of *all*, with both species achieving a balance in their relationship. Jesus says that God cares for the sparrow and knows when each individual sparrow falls (i.e., dies) (Matt 10:29–31). He does not say that God stops the sparrows falling.

With that in mind, allow me to identify four brief Christian approaches to the problem.

c) One: The Primary Response

The primary Christian response to suffering caused by the workings of the natural world is not to find some way to explain it or to justify God in the face of it. The priority has always been to respond with compassion and care to those affected. It is to be the body of Christ bringing God's help and healing and comfort and hope. It is to weep with those who weep, to bind up the broken hearted, to strengthen the feeble knees, to set the oppressed free. This is not a trivial point. The agonizing question of why God has allowed calamity is a perfectly legitimate one, and is one worth pursuing answers to, but we can live without knowing those answers. However, the more primal responses of lament and compassion are not optional. They are what serving God's mission in the world looks like in such circumstances. The first question then is not "why did God will (or allow) this?" It is, "how would Christ have us respond to this?"

There has been much ink spilled in reflection on why God might allow a world containing the injuries and sufferings and tragedies caused by its normal workings. And there have been various kinds of answers proposed, each with its various strengths and weaknesses. Some, for instance, appeal to God having greater purposes that we cannot yet see but that put the immediate crisis into a bigger picture that sheds new light on it. Others argue that God does not directly will or cause the sufferings brought about by the workings of nature. Rather, they are the costly by-product of creating the kind of lawlike cosmos necessary for creatures with morally significant free will to be formed. And there are various other approaches. It is not my intention to explore and evaluate such ideas here. Suffice to say that, in my opinion, all of the responses, while having helpful things to offer, are ultimately unsatisfying answers to the question. I stand with Job in my ignorance.

d) Two: God Can Bring Good Out of Suffering

The Bible is clear that whatever the reasons God either "wills" (in some nuanced sense of the term) or at least "permits" harm, God can work in and through terrible events to bring about ultimately good purposes. Even wicked human choices, which are clearly against the will of God, can be used by YHWH for good ends. Take Joseph, sold by his brothers into slavery.

Their intentions were immoral and culpable. The deed was bad. And Joseph endured much suffering as a result. But it also led to a chain of events that saved the lives of many, including Joseph's own family. In retrospect Joseph came to see that, as he said to his brothers years later, "You intended to harm me, but God intended it for good to accomplish what is now being done, the saving of many lives" (Gen 50:12). It is just such a surprising pattern of bringing good from obvious bad that causes St. Paul to burst into praise: "Oh, the depth of the riches of the wisdom and knowledge of God! How unsearchable his judgments, and his paths beyond tracing out!" (Rom 11:33).

The supreme example of this reality is seen in the execution of Jesus. The Lord's arrest, trial, torture, and humiliating crucifixion were inexcusable deeds of injustice. The Bible never attempts to justify or excuse them. Yet Christians insist that God used even such a horror to be the doorway through which the salvation of the world could come. As Peter said to his audience, "You disowned the Holy and Righteous One and asked that a murderer be released to you. You killed the author of life, *but God* raised him from the dead" (Acts 3:14–15). The alchemical turning point that enables base metal to become gold is the "but God . . . ."

So a Christian spirituality will be looking for the "but God . . ." in the midst of sufferings. The church should be seeking to work with God's Spirit in bringing beauty from the ashes.

e) Three: The Suffering God

The Christian story of the incarnation of God is a story in which God becomes a creature, sharing in the bodily and mental life of a creature, and experiencing the sufferings of creaturely life. In this story God suffers in body and soul with creation, as a part of creation. As the church fathers put it, "one of the Trinity suffered in the flesh." Such a God does not stand aloof from the sufferings of the world, distant and indifferent, but is nailed to a cross alongside creatures in the midst of their own crucifixions. This does not *explain* the sufferings of the world, nor does it justify them, but that is not the point of such teaching. Rather, it is to offer comfort to those who suffer or who witness the suffering of others, that God stands alongside the broken, that God can understand such grief from the inside, that God cares. Furthermore, it is to offer hope that the end of creation's story will mirror Christ's. It will not end in a tomb, but with a resurrection.

f) Four: All's Well That Ends Well

Theodore Parker, the nineteenth-century social reformer, anticipating the abolition of slavery, said: "I do not pretend to understand the moral universe; the arc is a long one, my eye reaches but little ways; I cannot calculate the curve and complete the figure by the experience of sight; I can divine it by conscience. And from what I see I am sure it bends towards justice."[17] This was a sentiment echoed many years later by Martin Luther King Jr.

The biblical vision is one in which, to quote Lady Julian of Norwich, "all shall be well." This too is not to explain or to justify the sufferings of the present time. Nonetheless, it does make a big difference, for it contextualizes the world's present anguish in an eternal frame, which changes our perspective, even now in anticipation. As St. Paul—a man familiar with pain—comments, "For I consider that the sufferings of this present time are not worth comparing with the glory that is to be revealed in us" (Rom 8:18).

In the end, no creature will look back at its life and wish that it had never existed. Not even those who have experienced what Marilyn McCord Adams calls "horrendous evils"—evils that rip the heart of personal meaning from a creature's life. (Such evils are only able to be experienced by humans and perhaps to some extent other higher animals, or aliens.) Divine goodness requires that God brings good from horrendous evils for the benefit of the world as a whole. More than that, the good God must redeem *the individual sufferer* too. "*God would have to . . . defeat any horrendous evil in which [a person] participated by giving it a positive meaning through organic unity with a great enough good within the context of his/her life.*"[18] Adams means that God must ensure that the evil is situated in the context of, and organically related to, a life that, when looked at *as a whole*, is accepted by the person as a good life. And some evils are so life-ruining that only the infinite love of God is capable of weaving meaning back into lives shattered by them. It is only from the perspective of union with God in the new creation that victims of horrors can look back and see their lives as being a great good to them.

Given that the Christian vision of the telos is not limited to humans but is creation-wide and given that many nonhumans suffer in the story of the world, there is a good case for saying that God's goodness will not only rectify human sufferings in the new creation but also the pains of other creatures.[19]

---

17. Parker, *Ten Sermons of Religion*, 84–85.

18. Adams, *Horrendous Evils*, 31.

19. The case for "elephant heaven" has been argued at length by Christopher Southgate in *Groaning of Creation*.

"The natural world is both unspeakably beautiful and also a place of competition and violence. In this ambiguity, I believe it is the good news of Jesus that is decisive for Christians. In Wisdom made flesh, God is revealed as Love that embraces suffering creation, transforming it from within, promising liberation and fulfillment."[20]

The gospel hope is that the last word goes to the resurrection, not to suffering and death. And this hope is what enables resilience and endurance in the face of tragedy.

Having considered the biggest challenge to the Christian vision of creation, it is time to delve a little more into the philosophical heart of the vision.

---

20. Edwards, "Experience of Word and Spirit in the Natural World," 23.

5

Nothing Really Matters
Creation Out of Nothing

1. Ex Nihilo

ACCORDING TO JOHN'S GOSPEL, anything and everything that is not God is created (John 1:1–3). Reflecting that insight, the classical view taught by Christian theologians since the second century is that God created the world *ex nihilo*, out of nothing.[1]

It's very hard to think about . . . nothing. If I say that Bob made the desk out of wood, the wood is the stuff from which the desk is made. But when I say that God made the world out of nothing, the nothing isn't some weird "stuff" out of which God composed the world. It is *absolutely nothing at all!*[2] So the creation of the world is not like any act of making that takes place within the world. It is *utterly unique*.

---

1. For a helpful theological account of this doctrine, see especially McFarland, *From Nothing*. Some people have argued that the doctrine of creation out of nothing is not biblical. I make the case for its biblical credentials in a YouTube video called "Creation Out of Nothing," Part 5.

2. And when some scientists claim that physics can explain how the universe came into being from nothing (e.g., through appeal to theories like quantum vacuum fluctuation), the "nothing" they have in mind is *not* the *absolute* nothing theologians speak of. Thus, to say that physics can explain how something can come from nothing is

Just consider for a moment how creation is unlike other acts. To start with, when *we* create something, we take some material and change it. We move it from one state to another. For instance, we get some wood and carve it into a statue. When God creates the world *God changes nothing*. There is nothing to change. God creates *ex nihilo*.

In addition, when we make something, we do so *in time*. We first think of the idea, then we gather the materials and tools necessary, and then we create. God's act of creation isn't like that. There is no time *before* creation. St. Augustine says that when God made the cosmos, space and time were brought into being together. Time thus begins with creation. (Something modern physicists would have a lot of sympathy with.) So we can't think of God pondering whether to make the world, then, after a while, coming to a decision—I'll do it!—and after that doing the work of creating. Such a process takes time, and there is no time "before" creation. All of which is to say that creation isn't an event that occurs in time; it is, rather, that by which events in time come to be.

So the idea of creation out of nothing is a lot more mind-blowing than we may at first realize. When Christian theologians first proposed this idea, we can perhaps start to see why it was considered shocking. Other thinkers in the ancient world approached the question very differently. Some thought that the world was eternal. It's always been here. It simply exists and that's that. Others thought that while God shaped and forged the world, making it orderly and beautiful, the matter from which it was made is as eternal as God. And the matter imposed certain limits on what was possible for God. God did very well with the material available but was forced to accept compromises. (This, for some thinkers, explained the origins of evil—which they saw as linked to the weakness of the material world.) Still others thought that God created the world *out of God*. On this view, God doesn't choose to create. The world simply radiates out from the Deity as a by-product of God being God, just as your body generates heat as a by-product.

Early Christian theologians quickly rejected these views and asserted instead that God created the world out of nothing. Here is how Irenaeus, in the second century, put it:

> The rule of truth which we hold, is,
> that there is one God Almighty,
> who made all things by His Word,
> and fashioned and formed,
> out of that which has no existence,

---

misleading.

all things that exist.

(*Adv. Haer.* I.xxii.1; trans. ANF I:347).

This teaching was so important to Irenaeus that he describes it as part of "the rule of truth," which is the name for the *core essentials* of the faith. Why did it matter so much to them?

First, they wanted to defend a particular view of God: that God is perfect and unlimited. That meant they had to reject the idea that the world was just there. For in that case, the world doesn't need God to be what it is. Which would make it ultimate and eternal, alongside God. This would limit God. Think of stonemasons or carpenters, whose craft is restricted by the stone and the wood they manipulate. God is not restricted in this way because God creates out of nothing. So Christians quickly rejected the idea that God creates out of preexistent matter.

Second, Christians maintained that God's perfection meant that God is complete in Godself. The Divine lacks nothing and so envies nothing and no one. God does not need to create the world in order to be God. Consequently, the act of creation was a *free choice* of God's, rather than a necessary emanation, like your body heat.

This has important implications. It tells us something about God and something about the world. About God, it says that God is not compelled to create by anything *external to* God, like some cosmic rule or law or power the Deity had to follow, for there are no laws or powers beyond God. More than that, God is not compelled to create by anything *within* God. In other words, it is not that the Divine *has* to make the world in order to meet some inner need or lack. God acquires no extra good by creating the world and God is deprived of no good by choosing not to create it. God's decision to create is thus a *free* decision.

Creation, however, is not an act of unmotivated arbitrary caprice but of purposive love. The Divine is pure goodness, pure love, pure wisdom, pure beauty. What God chooses will always be guided by who God is. What this means is that while God didn't have to create the world, God's choice to create *makes sense*, given who God is. We might say that it's a choice that's not necessary, but it is "fitting." Here is how St. Augustine puts it:

> God made what was made not from any necessity,
> nor for the sake of supplying any lack,
> but solely from His own goodness,
> that is, because it was good.
>
> (Augustine, *City of God* XI.24)

Some people find it disconcerting that the Divine gains nothing by creating the world, but it has important implications. It means that the act of creation is not for *God's* benefit, not an act of divine self-interest. It is an act *entirely* for the good of creation. It is an act of pure goodness and generosity. Consequently, God doesn't create to *gain* something God lacks but to *share* something God has.

Creation out of nothing therefore tells us something about the Divine and something about the world. About the Divine it says that God is perfect, complete, unlimited, gracious. About the world it says that the world is characterized by *utter dependency*. Everything in the world—and the world as a whole—depends for its existence upon God.

2. Divine Transcendence

Reality is thus characterized by the most basic distinction of all—that between Creator and creation. And the Creator is *very* different from creatures. Appreciating the depths of that difference takes time. When we're kids, we often think of God like some giant human being with extra-strong powers and super-knowledge. As we get older, we realize that God doesn't have a body and isn't located in space, unlike an apple or a mountain. We appreciate that God isn't around the corner or in the cupboard or in Japan. However, we're still tempted to think and speak about God as if God were simply another thing in the world. We could count them up: oranges, stones, insects, birds, trees, humans, . . . and God. But God isn't a part of the world. God isn't a particular thing, like my cat Monty. God isn't even a *kind* of thing, like the species of cat. God is utterly unique, unlike anything in the world. God is no-thing.

Theologians speak here of God's *transcendence*. In this context, divine transcendence reminds us that the Deity can't be put into a box with other things. God is *beyond the grasp of our thought and language*.

One challenging implication of this is that thinking and speaking about God becomes very difficult. It's hard enough speaking satisfactorily of things in the world, like the beauty of a sunset. When it comes to speaking of the Divine, our language flails around, trying to get some grip on something it was never crafted for. If you think about it, human languages grew up to help us navigate our way in the world. They pick out things and actions in the world. They weren't shaped to handle the One who transcends our conceptual systems.

Some will still choose to speak about God as if there's no problem here, as if speaking of the Divine is simple. We yap on about God as if our words apply to the Deity in the same way they apply to creatures. For instance, we know what we mean when we say that Sarah is wise. Perhaps we mean *exactly the same thing* when we say that God is wise. But if God is transcendent that will not do. God is not like a supersized, upscaled version of a human.

Others go to the opposite extreme. They say that because God is transcendent we have *absolutely no idea at all* what we mean when we speak about God. We can say that God is wise, but whatever it means it has *no connection at all* with what it means to speak of Sarah as wise. The problem here is that we are reduced to total silence about God, unable to say or think *anything intelligible at all*. But Christians do believe that we can speak truly and understandably about God.

Thomas Aquinas (d. 1274) made a helpful proposal that falls between the naïve simplicity of the first approach and the ultimate agnosticism of the second. He suggested that when we use human languages to speak of the Deity we're not using words in the same way as when we speak of creatures but neither are we using them in a completely different way. Because God is the Creator of the world there's *a real connection* between God and the world—the world images God in various ways. There are thus analogies between Creator and creation. And so words used of creatures can be used meaningfully of the Divine, so long as we are aware that they are being used *analogically*. Consider an example. When we say that God is wise, we shouldn't imagine that God's wisdom is simply an inflated version of human wisdom. Nor should we think that there's no connection at all between human wisdom and divine wisdom. Rather, human wisdom is a dim reflection of divine wisdom, which is its cause. And so there's a real analogy between God's wisdom and creaturely wisdom. God is wise in whatever way it is appropriate for the Divine to be wise. We cannot know a lot about what that is, so a big dose of agnosticism is required, but that doesn't mean that we have *no clue* what we are saying. We can speak of God's wisdom *truly* and confidently, even if we can never fully *understand* what it is for God to be wise.

Why does all this matter? First, it teaches us to recognize that we can't capture God in our thought systems. The Divine will always elude our comprehension. This realization fosters wonder and humility in the presence of Infinite Mystery. It cautions us against simplistic theology. It teaches us to embrace unknowing.

> How great a being, Lord, is thine,
>   which doth all beings keep!
> Thy knowledge is the only line
>   to sound so vast a deep.
> Thou art a sea without a shore,
>   a sun without a sphere;

thy time is now and evermore,
    thy place is everywhere.

"How Shall I Sing That Majesty," by John Mason (c. 1645–94)

    Second, divine transcendence teaches us that God and creation are not to be collapsed into each other; there's a real distinction between God and the world. Beautiful and mesmerizing and awe-inspiring as the world is, it is not God. Consequently, while it should be honored, it is not to be worshipped as divine. This is the dividing line between many forms of paganism and monotheism. Paganisms often, though not always, treat the cosmos (or a part of it) as divine and to be worshipped. Nature is God. The universe is God. But this is to treat a creature as the Creator, to treat that which is not ultimate as though it were ultimate. And this move is considered by monotheists to be a fundamental mistake when seeking the Holy. As Paul puts it in Romans 1, such people "worshiped and served the creature rather than the Creator." God is not a *part* of the world nor the *sum total* of the world.

3. Divine Immanence

Some have worried about this stress on divine transcendence. They fear that it makes the Deity remote, distant, and unreachable. If the world is completely "other" than God, doesn't that make the world empty of God? However, creation out of nothing, rightly understood, does not have this consequence at all. Quite the opposite, in fact.

    To see why we need to grasp something important about God that Christian theologians throughout history have typically affirmed. We can think of God as *the One whose essence is "to be."* A biblical text that was very influential here was God's revelation to Moses in Exodus 3: "I am who I am"—or in the Greek translation, which is what many of the early Christians read, "I am the One who is." God's very essence, the core of who or what God is, is *to be*, to exist.

    Creatures are *not* like that. For any creature there's a clear distinction between its nature and its existence, between *what* it is and *that* it is. For example, I'm a human being. That's the kind of creature I am. In addition, I exist. But my existing is not part of my nature. I didn't *have* to exist. Nothing at all about human nature requires that it exists.

    With God it's different. God's essence and God's existence *are the same*. *Who* God is and *that* God is cannot be distinguished. It is God's nature to exist, for God is the One who *is*. That means God's existence isn't dependent on anyone or anything. God simply *is*.

Created things are fundamentally different. We're dependent at each and every moment of our existence. We receive our being as a gift from God and apart from that ongoing gift we're literally *nothing*. Theologians sometime speak of creation sharing or participating in God. They mean that by granting being to creatures God is enabling them to share in their own distinctive ways in God's own Be-ing and *Is*-ness.

The influence of God on things is *not* like the influence of created things on each other. Imagine a billiard ball that hits another billiard ball and causes it to move. The one ball works as an outside force affecting the other. God's influence on creation is not like that. God doesn't sustain creatures from *without*, but from *within*. God is the cause of our very be-ing, which is innermost in all things. The Divine works in all things intimately.

This is what theologians call divine *immanence*, God's closeness to and presence in all things. The Deity is not at a distance from creation, on the other side of an unbridgeable chasm. God is present to everything, everywhere, everywhen. Nothing exists outside the field of God's influence. As St. Paul said to the Athenians, "God is not far from any one of us. 'For in him we live and move and have our being'" (Acts 19:27b–28b). Think of an artist creating, putting something of him- or herself into that painting. The artwork is in some way "an extension of the artist himself [sic]. He is now in the picture, just as the picture had been in him."[3] So too creation is "in" God and God is "in" creation. This means that the Divine is intimate to everything. There's no "distance" between us and the Creator.

As a consequence, we could speak of the world as sacramental in its very structure—any part of creation has the potential to reveal some aspect of the Divine; we simply need to have our eyes opened to see. The psalmist could see God when he looked up: "The heavens declare the glory of God" (Ps 19:1). Other poets have often reveled in this insight. Elizabeth Barrett Browning (1806–61), for instance, writes,

> Earth's crammed with heaven,
> And every common bush afire with God:
> But only he who sees, takes off his shoes . . . .[4]

And Gerard Manley Hopkins (1844–89):

> The world is charged with the grandeur of God.
>   It will flame out, like shining from shook foil.[5]

---

3. Macquarrie, *Humility of God*, 4.
4. Barrett Browning, from *Aurora Leigh* (1856), Book Seven.
5. Hopkins, "God's Grandeur" (1877).

Macrina Wiederkehr writes,

> You live in a world of theophanies.
> Holiness comes wrapped in the ordinary.
> There are burning bushes all around you.
> Every tree is full of angels.
> Hidden beauty is waiting in every crumb.
> Life wants to lead you from crumbs to angels,
> but this can happen only if you are willing
> to unwrap the ordinary by staying with it
> long enough to harvest its treasure.[6]

It is what the Franciscan Angela of Foligno (c. 1248–1309) meant when, in response to a revelatory encounter with God, she cried out in wonder, "The world is pregnant with God!"[7] Or what Kerry philosopher-poet John Moriarty (1938–2007) is talking about when he describes "the universe as a shimmer of God within God."[8] It is what inspired Lady Julian of Norwich (c.1343–after 1416) to say, "God is everything that is good, and the goodness that is in everything is God" (*ST* 5).

> Lord of beauty, thine the splendour
> shown in earth and sky and sea,
> burning sun and moonlight tender,
> hill and river, flower and tree:
> lest we fail our praise to render
> touch our eyes that they may see.
>
> —C. A. Alington (1872–1955)

Another consequence of the doctrine of creation out of nothing is that we can't talk about any finite creature *adequately* without talking about God. No creature has an identity apart from its relation to God. Our very existence *is* a relation to God. Apart from that relation we are literally nothing.

This in turn means that no creature can ever be fully grasped and understood. Why? Because our being is a participation in God's infinite Being. There is a depth to created things: they all open out into the bottomless depths of Divinity. To understand anything fully, even the humblest microorganism, is impossible because nothing can be understood apart from its relation to God and God's fullness cannot be known. To appropriate William Blake's (1757–1827) famous words, "If the doors of perception were

---

6. Wiederkehr, *Tree Full of Angels*, xiii.
7. Angela of Foligno, *Book of the Blessed Angela of Foligno*, 170.
8. Moriarty, *Serious Sounds*, 9, 63.

cleansed everything would appear to man as it is: infinite."[9] For as Michael Hanby comments, "Reality is bottomless because the heart of each thing is the mystery of being and the heart of being is God."[10]

In sum, the church refuses to affirm divine transcendence apart from divine immanence because that leads to a Creator separated from creation: distant, indifferent, and inaccessible. It also limits God because creation is marked off as a God-free zone. At the same time, and on the other hand, the church refuses to affirm divine immanence apart from divine transcendence because that ends up collapsing Creator and creation into each other. On that view, the world is God; God is the world. That too limits God to the finite sum of finite creatures. Instead, creation from nothing insists that God is both distinct from the world and that the world is saturated with God's presence. The universe exists "within" God. Our world is sacred, but it is not divine.

4. Divine and Creaturely Action

One area in which creation out of nothing is very useful is in helping us to understand what we do *and do not* mean when we speak of God acting in the world. Let me explain. Think about causation. This is a fundamental, everyday aspect of the way we make sense of the world around us. If some event occurs, we wonder what caused it. We don't think that stuff just happens without an explanation. Consider: You hear a sound in the house. You look around to see what made it. Sounds don't just happen—they're caused. Perhaps it was a jug falling off the table. But jugs don't just fall off the table—something will have caused that to happen. Perhaps it was the cat, brushing against it. You get the idea. All day, every day we make sense of the world in terms of causes and effects. And we ourselves are agents who cause things to happen in the world. We act in the world and our actions have effects—they change things. For instance, I make a decision to pour the wine from the bottle into a glass and then I act on that decision. That action has an effect in the world—the wine is transferred from the bottle to the glass.

Christians regularly speak of certain events as divine actions. For example, they thank God for sending rain or see God's hand in the circumstances that led to a positive change in their situation—perhaps a new job or a recovery from an illness. Ordinary, everyday things (like having food to eat or good weather) and major life events and global events (like the end of a war) are often seen as the result of God's work.

9. Blake, *Marriage of Heaven and Hell*.
10. Hanby, *No God, No Science*, 363.

There is, however, a lot of scope for misunderstanding such language. It's very tempting to treat talk of divine action in the same way as we treat talk about creaturely action. We might imagine God to be acting in the world just like we do—except that God is much stronger and more capable. We picture God as a Super Being. But this is to treat God as another thing in the world—a thing in addition to trees, cats, stars, and bubble gum. And it's to treat divine causation as the same basic kind of thing as creaturely causation. And there be the dragons of confusion. For it puts divine action and creaturely action into competition. Consider a believer trying to prove God's reality from an astonishing event for which we have no current scientific explanation. "That must be God," she says, "because science can't explain it." Now think about an atheist arguing that an alleged happening was not God because we have (or soon will have) a scientific explanation for it. Many of the debates between religious believers and nonbelievers fall into this trap.

A classic example is discussions on evolution and intelligent design. In the eighteenth century, William Paley famously argued that the complicated arrangement of parts in organisms is like the complicated arrangement of parts in a watch and just as a watch points us towards a watchmaker so complex organisms point us towards a grand designer. An eye, for instance, has many intricate parts all very precisely interrelated and there is as much likelihood of them all coming together in the right pattern by random chance as there is for all the parts of a pocket watch to simply become the right shape and fall into place. As the watch indicates a watchmaker, so the eyeball indicates an eye-maker. Then in the nineteenth century along came Darwin, who offered a scientific hypothesis to account for the way complex biological organisms could arise from simpler organisms by a process of natural selection. Atheists like Richard Dawkins argue that Paley's divine watchmaker is no longer needed because we have discovered the natural causes of things appearing to be designed.

Both the believer and the atheist have made an assumption about God's action in creation. Both assume that God acts by causing things to happen in the world in much the same way that creatures do. And, as God is outside the system of nature, God is regularly having to intervene in the world—putting together eyes, and such like. On this view, any event caused by God cannot be explained in terms of creational causes and any event that we can explain in terms of creational causes was not caused by God. This way of looking at things considers divine causation to be in competition with creaturely causation.

Exactly the same assumption lies behind many objections to faith. Why are you thanking God for your food? God didn't plant the crop or tend it or harvest it or process it or transport it to your local shop or cook your dinner. Which part did God do? Why are you thanking God that your uncle Bill was saved from near death when the people who really deserve the credit are the ambulance crew and the doctors? Why are you giving God praise for what was obviously the work of people? These questions reflect a very different approach to divine action from the classical Christian approach. Traditionally Christian theologians saw God's relation to creation as *unlike* any relations within creation.

Perhaps the simplest way to get a first grasp of the issue is to imagine the story in a novel. In the story all sorts of things happen, resulting from natural causes and caused by various characters. Let's take an example. In Mary Shelley's novel *Frankenstein*, a young scientist, Dr. Victor Frankenstein, constructs a simulacrum of a human being and uses a lightning bolt to impart life to the creature.[11] The creature's coming to life is the result of the actions of one of the actors in the story and, partly, a natural event—a lightning storm. And we can explain the event satisfactorily (within that fictional world) simply in those terms. Yet we could also speak of it as something Mary Shelley brought about, as the author. But the sense in which Shelley brought about the monster is very different from the way in which Dr. Frankenstein or the lightning did. That is one way to start thinking of divine causation. It's more like the actions of an author than of a character in the story. Authors and characters make things happen in very different ways.

Frankenstein[12]

Now imagine an English teacher saying, "Oh isn't it marvelous how Mary Shelley has her monster brought to life from inanimate matter." Suppose someone responds, "No, that was Dr. Frankenstein. We don't need to appeal to a Mary Shelley to explain the event. It's fully explicable in terms of events in the world of the book." Such a critic is simply confused. Mary Shelley doesn't act in the book at the same level as her characters. And there's no competition between talk of the author doing something in the book and talk of the characters. Bringing the creature to life was fully the work of Mary Shelley and fully the work of Dr. Frankenstein, with the help of some

---

11. I know that the novel doesn't mention a lightning bolt in the account of the animation of the "creature" (though electricity seems to be involved, and lightning certainly served as its inspiration). However, lightning is in the 1931 Universal Studios movie (if I remember right), so let's pretend and just run with it.

12. Universal Pictures, 1931. Reproduced under Creative Commons license.

lightning. It isn't one or the other and it isn't partly one and partly the other. It is fully one and fully the other. Mary Shelley works in her novel *through* her characters and *through* the natural events she puts in it.

Of course, the problem with speaking of God is always that because God's relation to creation is unique, unlike any relations that exist in the world, all illustrations of it necessarily fail to convey the full picture accurately. This illustration is no different. But it makes the basic point. We might say, borrowing the language of Thomas Aquinas, that God is the *primary* cause of what happens in creation and creatures are *secondary* causes.

Creatures, like ourselves, have real powers to cause things to happen in the world. Our actions really do change things. But the Creator is the one who enables us to be and to have the causative powers that we have. In the case of some creatures, such as human beings, those powers are exercised by creatures with a certain degree of free will. Our freedom is not in competition with God's actions—God actually upholds our free will.

If we look at an effect in the world, we don't have to choose between whether it was caused by God or by a created cause. The Creator's actions in creation are realized *through* natural processes and *through* created agents. We see this over and over again in the Bible, where events that are clearly understood to be caused by human beings or by natural events are *also* said to be caused by God. Causation is not a zero-sum game.

Many of the so-called conflicts between science and religion are rooted in confusion about this issue. Scientific explanations of events are simply explanations that work at the level of secondary causation. They are the equivalent to explaining the events in the story in terms internal to the novel—characters and their actions and chance natural events beyond the control of any characters. And it works very well, so long as it doesn't try to overstep its inherent limits. Such scientific explanations are not in and of themselves any threat to theological explanations nor theological to scientific. It is a simple error to imagine a scientific theory could be in competition with the doctrine of creation. The doctrine of creation doesn't tell us the process or mechanism of how the world came to be; it tells us *what the world is*: utterly dependent upon God at every moment of its existence.

This chapter has offered something of a dense detour from the biblical storyline that Christians seek to inhabit. However, I hope that you can see how important the detour was for understanding traditional Christian thinking about creation. So with that in place, it is time to return to the biblical plot.

6

Wisdom Made Text

Israel and the Eco-Spirituality of Torah

IN SCRIPTURE, GOD'S RESPONSE to human sin in creation was not what we might expect. No swift resolutions, but a long, meandering story beginning when YHWH chose one person (called Abram) and made a binding covenant agreement with him. God called Abram to leave his country, Ur in Babylonia, and go to the land that God would show him. Now Abram and his wife Sarai were old and childless and were about to become landless. But YHWH promised to give Abram many descendants, to bless him, and through him to bless the peoples of earth (Gen 12:1–3). Abram and his household obediently left Babylonia on the long trek to Canaan. When they arrived, God promised the land of Canaan to his offspring (12:7). It was many hundreds of years before the people of Israel, the descendants of Abram and Sarai (renamed Abraham and Sarah), inherited the land, but as we shall see, it is impossible to overstate the importance of the land to the covenant relationship between God and Israel, for it was a core feature of God's promises to the patriarchs of the nation.[1] Indeed, the whole Old Testament story is orientated around the land: the books of Exodus to Deuteronomy tell the story of Israel's journey to the land, Joshua tells the story of entering into the land, and the rest of the Old Testament concerns Israel's life in the land, exile from the land, and return to the land.

---

1. Gen 12:7; 13:15; 15:18–20; 17:8; 24:7; 28:4, 13; 35:12.

1. Moses and the Wise Torah

In the biblical narrative Abraham and Sarah's descendants, Jacob and his twelve sons, ended up living not in the land of Canaan but the land of Egypt (Gen 37:1—50:26). And there they remained for hundreds of years, latterly as slave labor under a cruel Pharaoh (Exod 1). God, however, through the leadership of Moses, led the people out of slavery in Egypt and back towards Canaan (Exod 2:1—15:27). On the way God took them via Mount Sinai and there made a covenant with them and gave them his *torah* (meaning "teaching" or "instruction" or "law") (Exod 19:1—Num 10:11). The covenant relationship is two-way: the people of Israel are to obey the divine teaching and God will bless them. He will be their God and they will be his people, his special treasure (Exod 19:5–6). Disobedience, however, would have consequences.

Israel at Mount Sinai[2]

Now the instruction that YHWH gave to Israel on Mount Sinai can be found in our Bibles in sections of the books of Exodus, Leviticus, Numbers,

---

2. Illustration by Jan and Kaspar Luiken, 1723. Reproduced under Creative Commons license.

and Deuteronomy.[3] It became the foundation for the social, political, civic, and religious life of Israel and it remains at the heart of Judaism to this day.

In the context of this book, I want to draw attention to the connection between our discussion of wisdom and the laws. The book of Deuteronomy, which is presented as a speech given by Moses to the Israelites as they camp outside the borders of the promised land, makes a close connection between the torah that God had given at Sinai and God's wisdom.

> See, I [Moses] have taught you decrees and laws as YHWH my God commanded me, so that you may follow them in the land you are entering to take possession of it. Observe them carefully, for this will show your wisdom and understanding to the nations, who will hear about all these decrees and say, "Surely this great nation is a wise and understanding people." What other nation is so great as to have their gods near them the way YHWH our God is near us whenever we pray to him? And what other nation is so great as to have such righteous decrees and laws as this body of laws I am setting before you today? (Deut 4:5–8)

Various psalms too join God's commands with God's wisdom,[4] but the link was brought into special focus in the Second Temple period (586 BC–70 AD). It is most evident when, referring to Wisdom dwelling in Israel, Ben Sirach writes, "All this is *the book of the covenant* of the Most High God, *the law that Moses commanded us* as an inheritance for the congregations of Jacob" (Sir 24:23; cf. Wis 6:8). In an important sense, then, the law of Moses is the concrete manifestation of Wisdom, not the only manifestation, but certainly the *central* one, as far as Jesus Ben Sirach is concerned.

A similar sentiment is found in Baruch 3:9—4:4, a pseudonymous Jewish text written in the name of Jeremiah's secretary Baruch at some point in the second century. There we read how Israel's neighbors (Canaanites, Ishmaelites, Edomites) lacked Wisdom and perished for that lack (Bar 3:20–23). By contrast, God gave Wisdom to Israel (Bar 3:37). And what does this Wisdom look like? *"She is the book of the commandments of God, the law that endures forever.* All who hold her fast will live, and those who

---

3. Speaking very broadly, the law collections in the Torah are (i) the Ten Commandments (Exod 20:1–17; Deut 5:1–21), (ii) the Book of the Covenant (Exod 20:22—23:33), (iiia) the Priestly laws (found throughout later parts of Exodus, and in Leviticus and Numbers), including (iiib) the Holiness Code (Lev 17–26), and (iv) Deuteronomy. The history of their composition is long, complex, and much disputed. We need not concern ourselves with it here as our focus is on the final form of the text.

4. E.g., Pss 33:4–9; 119:89–104; 147:15–20. See Terrien, "Wisdom in the Psalter."

forsake her will die" (Bar 4:1). Indeed, Israel's suffering in exile is a direct result of resisting Wisdom's call in the law of Moses (Bar 3:12).

This is relevant to us for the following reason: the Wisdom of God, through whom God made the world and who is present in the order of creation, is *the same* Wisdom manifest in the torah given to Israel by God through Moses. We could say that *the torah is Wisdom-made-text.* That association is implied by Psalm 19, which falls into two main parts. Part 1 (vv. 1–6) marvels at creation and its revelation of God while Part 2 (vv. 7–14) is a celebration of the law of Moses. They seem completely unconnected, but the simple juxtaposition of the parts along with numerous subtle interconnections between them invites us to grasp that the order of creation and the torah are in fact both expressions of the same divine Wisdom.

> 1 The heavens declare the glory of God;
>   the skies proclaim the work of his hands.
> 2 Day after day they pour forth speech;
>   night after night they reveal knowledge.
> 3 They have no speech, they use no words;
>   no sound is heard from them.
> 4 Yet their voice goes out into all the earth,
>   their words to the ends of the world . . . .
>
> ⁷ The law of the Lord is perfect,
>   refreshing the soul.
> The statutes of the Lord are trustworthy,
>   making wise the simple.
> ⁸ The precepts of the Lord are right,
>   giving joy to the heart.
> The commands of the Lord are radiant,
>   giving light to the eyes.
> ⁹ The fear of the Lord is pure,
>   enduring forever.
> The decrees of the Lord are firm,
>   and all of them are righteous.
> 10 They are more precious than gold,
>   than much pure gold;
> they are sweeter than honey,
>   than honey from the honeycomb. (NIV)

Christians sometimes treat the law of Moses as though it is some intolerable burden from which God needs to liberate people. That mindset is utterly alien to the way that biblical writers saw the torah (including, I would argue, New Testament writers).[5] The law of Moses was received as a wonderful and gracious gift from God, given to guide the people to walk in the ways of YHWH. It was a manifestation of divine Sophia and was to be welcomed with joy. Philosopher Robert C. Roberts helpfully gets to the heart of such a positive approach to the torah:

> The law of God is a rule of order, a prescription, a standard, a blueprint, a map, a sketch, an outline, a perspective, a guide. A standard, blueprint, map, and sketch, *of what*? Of success in living a human life. An order and rule and prescription *for what*? For happiness. A perspective *on what*? On flourishing as human beings. A guide *to what*? To happiness and wellbeing for people, to living a good life. "I will never forget your commandments, because by them you give me life." (Ps 119:93)[6]

Now, the matter of interpreting the torah is complex, especially for modern Christ-believers. This is so for two primary reasons. First, the torah was given to the people of Israel, *not* to the nations. While non-Jews can learn from the law, it was never understood to apply to non-Jews directly. For instance, eating pork was forbidden to Jews but never to gentiles. Similarly, circumcision was obligatory for Israelite men (and remains so for Jewish men today), but it was not expected of gentiles. Most Christ-believers nowadays are not Jewish, so the torah will not apply to them in the *same* way that it applies to Jewish readers (including Jewish readers who follow Jesus). Second, modern people live in *very* different social and cultural contexts from those in which the torah arose. Those ongoing changes of context call for ceaseless interpretation if the text is to speak again in new situations. I am simply flagging this issue and have no intention of wading into the details. It is enough for now to be aware of it.

The point of this discussion is to show that if Christ's people are to be seekers of Wisdom, then they must attend carefully to the torah to see what insights it may have to help them in their quest for ecological discernment.

---

5. This question of Jewish law in the New Testament is a vast issue, much debated by New Testament scholars. But there are many scholars who argue (persuasively to my mind) that Jesus and the writers of the New Testament uphold the ongoing value of the Torah.

6. Roberts, *Virtue Ethics in Christian Perspective*, 58.

2. The Torah and Ecology

a) Israel as an Agricultural Community

The Israel spoken of in Scripture was not some generic "society" that provides a straightforward template for all times and places. Indeed, Israelite society changed considerably over the eras covered by the biblical texts. It existed in a specific place and in particular historical periods and was similar in many ways to the other ancient societies surrounding it. So when Wisdom comes to dwell in Israel, she comes to dwell in and to shape an ancient Near Eastern society in a specific geographical environment.

The topography of the Holy Land[7]

Israel inhabited a small land that was bordered by the Mediterranean Sea on the west and the River Jordan on the east (110 miles north to south, thirty miles east to west). The coastal plain, running parallel to the sea, is composed of shoreline and good agricultural land. Then there are the hills and mountain ranges running from north to south. The southern part of the land, the Negev, was sparsely populated desert. The Jordan valley links

---

7. Topografi Palestina (Bahasa Inggris). This work is licensed and subject to the terms of Creative Commons Attribution 3.0 License.

the Sea of Galilee in the north to the Dead Sea in the south. Within a very small area one finds a range of distinct ecosystems: those of the hill country, the foothills, the broad valley and plain, the coastlands, the high plateau, the steppe land, and the desert.[8]

Deuteronomy presents the "promised land" as "a land of hills and valleys that drinks water from the rain of heaven. It is a land YHWH your God cares for" (Deut 11:11). Rain was a gift, a critical factor on which their food production and hence their lives depended. The rains begin around early October, breaking the drought of the summer. Then December through February see the heavier winter rains, which end by spring as the temperatures are rising.

The Israelites inhabiting the land were primarily agricultural communities whose patterns of life were attuned to the ecosystems and climate of their home.[9] They grew staples like wheat, barley, grapes, figs, pomegranates, olives, and dates. Here is the farming year, as found in a tenth-century-BC Hebrew calendar discovered in Gezer:

Two months for ingathering (olives)	[c. September/October]
Two months of sowing (cereals)	[c. November/December]
Two months of late sowing (legumes and vegetables)	[c. January/February]
A month of hoeing weeds (for hay)	[c. March]
A month of harvesting barley	[c. April]
A month of harvesting (wheat) and measuring (grain)	[c. May]
Two months of grape harvesting	[c. June/July]
A month of ingathering summer fruit	[c. August]

In addition to growing crops, Israelites also reared domestic animals: sheep, goats, large cattle (like oxen), domesticated fowl, donkeys, camels, and horses. And they were very conscious of the wild animals that shared the land with them, not least because some of them, such as snakes, scorpions, wolves, bears, and lions, could be dangerous to both humans and their domestic animals.

Now this is a book on eco-wisdom, and it would be negligent to fail to draw attention to the connection made in Scripture between Wisdom and farming. Consider the important words of Isaiah 28:23–29.

> Listen and hear my voice;
> pay attention and hear what I say.

---

8. If the geography and climate and ecology of ancient Israel are "your thing" then check out Wright, *Understanding the Ecology of the Bible*.

9. For a fruitful insight into the benefits of reading the Bible with agrarian eyes, see Davis, *Scripture, Culture, and Agriculture*.

> When a farmer plows for planting, does he plow continually?
>   Does he keep on breaking up and working the soil?
> When he has leveled the surface,
>   does he not sow caraway and scatter cumin?
> Does he not plant wheat in its place,
>   barley in its plot,
>   and spelt in its field?
> His God instructs him
>   and teaches him the right way.
> Caraway is not threshed with a sledge,
>   nor is the wheel of a cart rolled over cumin;
> caraway is beaten out with a rod,
>   and cumin with a stick.
> Grain must be ground to make bread;
>   so one does not go on threshing it forever.
> The wheels of a threshing cart may be rolled over it,
>   but one does not use horses to grind grain.
> All this also comes from YHWH Almighty,
>   whose plan is wonderful,
>   whose wisdom is magnificent.

The wisdom of the farmer to manage the land well, a wisdom honed through generations of experience, is in fact *the Wisdom of God*. Of course it is!

b) Living Fruitfully in the Land

The laws given by God to Moses are intended to enable the people of Israel to live well in the land that they were to inherit. In effect, Israel's relationship with God in the land was a microcosm or scaled-down model of Adam and Eve's relationship with God in the earth. That insight enables us to make connections between Israel's way of living in the land and wider questions about human life on the earth.

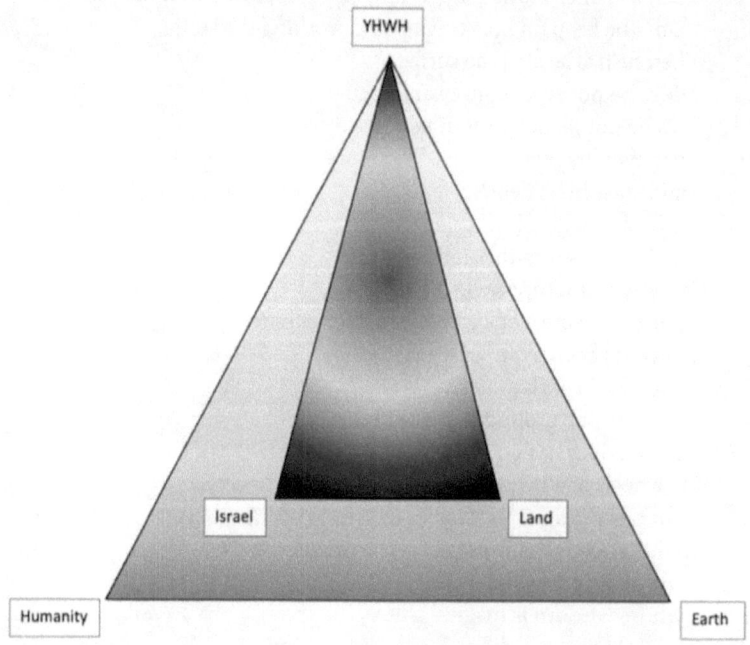

The land was a core element in Israel's relationship with God. Indeed, the land can be seen as a *partner* in the relationship. "And I will remember my covenant with Jacob, and also my covenant with Isaac, and also my covenant with Abraham, I will remember. And the land I will remember" (Lev 26:42). Ellen Davis comments: "The inverted order in which the ancestors are listed—Jacob, Isaac, and Abraham—points to the preeminence of the land, which takes its rightful place in covenantal history, even at the head of the line of ancestors. Before Abraham was, the land is."[10]

i. The land is God's

Israel's understanding of the land has various insights of ecological value. First and foremost, the land was understood to belong to God, not to Israel. "The land must not be sold permanently, *because the land is mine* and you [Israel] reside in my land as foreigners and strangers" (Lev 25:23). In the same way, the earth is God's, not humanity's: "The earth is YHWH's, and everything in it, the world, and all who live in it" (Ps 24:1).[11] Humans/Israel are conceived of as tenants, not landowners. Consequently, land is not ours

---

10. Davis, "Pain of Seeing Clearly," 85.
11. Cf. Exod 19:5; Deut 10:14; Pss 50:12; 89:11.

to do with as we like. We are accountable to God for how we live in it. God freely gives the land and its fruitfulness, but God can take it away, as the exile in Babylon showed.

This insight was reinforced through religious practice. Israel's laws required regular offerings to God in the form of tithes, firstfruits of crops, and firstborn animals (Deut 14:22–23; 15:19–20; 18:3–5). The point here was not that God needed such offerings. Unlike with other ancient Near Eastern deities, which needed feeding, Israel's religious offerings were not to meet a need in YHWH (Ps 50:9–13). The point, rather, was to be a regular reminder to Israel that they were tenants in the land (and, in addition, to help meet the needs of the poor; Deut 14:28–29; 26:12–15).

ii. The land is a gift

Land is important. It provides food, water, shelter, clothing, warmth, and freedom. Land is home. And in Israelite thinking the land was a *gift*. "For YHWH is bringing you into a good land: a land of streams of water, of fountains and depths springing forth in valleys and hills, a land of wheat and barley and vines and fig trees and pomegranates, a land of olive trees and honey, a land wherein you shall eat bread without scarceness; you shall not lack anything in it; a land whose stones are iron and out of whose hills you may dig brass. And you shall eat and be satisfied, and bless YHWH your God for the good land which is being given to you" (Deut 8:7–11). As gift, it was to be received with gratitude and thanksgiving, not assumed as something owed by "right."

This is not a trivial point. An attitude of gratitude for the world is what stops us from taking the earth, whose resources we use, for granted. Practices such as harvest festivals that instill such gratitude, reminding us of our dependence, are important ways of stopping a drift into abusive patterns of domination. (On Israel's festivals, see "N Is for Nature's Rhythms" in chapter 11.)

iii. The land must be respected

Israelites should live in a mutually beneficial relationship with the land. Obviously, humans benefit from the land—its water, its fields and crops, and its resources, such as wood and metals. However, in biblical thought the land should also receive a blessing in return from its human inhabitants.[12]

---

12. Thus, the land "rejoices" at the presence of humans when they live well with

During military conflict, account must be taken of the long-term fruitfulness of the land. One law states: "When you lay siege to a city for a long time, fighting against it to capture it, do not destroy its trees by putting an ax to them, because you can eat their fruit. Do not cut them down. Are the trees people, that you should besiege them? However, you may cut down trees that you know are not fruit trees and use them to build siege works until the city at war with you falls" (Deut 20:19–20). Olive and date trees take years after planting before they start bearing fruit, so uprooting such trees in warfare can have serious implications for a long time to come. Other nations—such as the Assyrians, Hittites, Egyptians, and Babylonians—deliberately targeted such orchards in war as a form of military violence intended to have lasting impact. Israel was forbidden from engaging in such practices.

For Israel, respecting the land meant allowing it sabbath rest. There was to be no work on the land on the sabbath. Then after six years of sowing and harvesting the land shall be allowed to rest fallow for a year in the seventh year (Exod 23:11–12; Lev 25:2–7). There was to be no sowing, reaping, pruning. This was to allow the land to recover, so it could maintain its fertility.[13] It was also intended to benefit the "wild beasts" who could feed on the unreaped crops. Furthermore, according to Leviticus, the Jubilee Year (the fiftieth year) was an additional year of rest for the land (Lev 25:8–12). Israel's expulsion from the land into Babylon in the sixth century BC was to give the land the rest that Israel had not allowed it (Lev 26:34–35, 42–43). So the exile was understood to be, in part, God acting as defender of the land against its mistreatment by Israel. In short, Israel's agricultural practices needed to ensure the long-term sustainability of the land, not short-term gain.

Livestock too had to be given rest on the sabbath (Deut 5:14). This concern for domestic animals is further indicated by the command in Deuteronomy 25:4, "do not muzzle an ox while he is threshing [the grain]." The ox is to be allowed to eat its fill from the grain that the farmers have gathered for their families, even though it meant less for the family to eat. After all, the honorable laborer, which the ox is, has earned the wages.[14]

Concern for the long-term survival of nonhuman species, even wild ones, can be seen in the law in Deuteronomy 22:6–7. "If you come across a

---

it (or when they stop exploiting it, Isa 14:8); indeed, the land celebrates the return of God's people from exile (Isa 49:13). The land will bless humans and other animals with abundant produce (Deut 8:7–9).

13. It is very likely that land lay fallow at other times too.

14. On the issue of the welfare of domesticated animals in Israel and its relevance today, see Grumett, *Bible and Farm Animal Welfare*.

bird's nest beside the road, either in a tree or on the ground, and the mother is sitting on the young or on the eggs, do not take the mother with the young. You may take the young, but be sure to let the mother go, so that it may go well with you and you may have a long life." If humans are to consume animals, it must not be in such a way that the future of the species is placed under threat. Sandra Richter points by way of contrast to a Neo-Assyrian carving of a royal hunt in which the king's dominance is shown in the depiction of a dead lion and *a mother bird with her eggs*, the very thing Israel's torah forbids.[15]

iv. The earth/land is engaged with as a "personal agent"

It will seem very odd to modern Western people, but in Scripture, the land is not merely the inanimate stage on which Israelites lived out their relationship with God; the earth, its soil, trees, rivers, and rocks are often presented *as "persons" that relate to God* alongside and with humans and other animals.[16] The Old Testament does distinguish different kinds of creatures, but *none* of God's creation is "static" and inactive. All creatures participate in the communal life of the world in their own way. In Leviticus land is *an active participant* in God's covenant with Israel. It performs various actions.[17] The ground can choose to give or withhold its produce (Lev 26:4; Deut 11:17) and can even choose to swallow up sinners[18] or vomit them out (Lev 18:28). Indeed, the promised land's responsibility before God *precedes* Israel's arrival (Lev 18:24–28). In Genesis 1, another priestly text, the earth is *an active agent*, working with God in creation (Gen 1:12) and in the ongoing life of the world.

Such ideas are not simply found in the Torah. The Former and Latter Prophets too are saturated with such thinking. For instance, nonanimal nature fights for or against Israel in warfare[19] and is called to mourn after battle (2 Sam 1:21 [mountains and fields]).

Non-animal nature reacts to manifestations of divine presence with terror—just like humans (e.g., Hab 3:10–11 [mountains, water, sun, moon]). The earth also grieves and mourns[20]—a response expressed in stripping off

---

15. Richter, *Stewards of Eden*, 53–57.
16. On this theme see especially Joerstad, *Hebrew Bible and Environmental Ethics*. Her work is a major source of inspiration in this section of my book.
17. Lev 18:25, 28; 19:29; 20:22; 25:2, 4, 5; 26:34, 38, 43.
18. Exod 15:12; Num 16:30–34; Lev 26:38; Ezek 36:13–14.
19. Judg 5:20–21 (stars); Josh 10:12–13 (sun); 2 Sam 18:8 (forest).
20. Isa 24:4; 33:9; Jer 4:28; 12:4, 11; 23:10; Hos 4:3; Joel 1:10.

its lush vegetative covering and sitting in the dust and ashes of drought. On the flipside, nature expresses its joy through rich vegetation and bountiful harvests.[21]

Furthermore, God often directly addresses nonanimal nature (Isa 1:2; Jer 2:12–13; trees in Zech 11:1–3). And prophets speak to it *on God's behalf*. For instance, God calls Ezekiel to address God's message to mountains (7:2; 35:2), soil (21:2), forests (21:7), etc.[22] When God commands nonanimal nature, it obeys.[23] Humans, by contrast, very rarely address nature.[24]

Francis of Assisi adopted a similar pattern of thought and practice in his engagement with Brother Sun, Sister Moon, Brothers Wind and Air, Sister Water, Brother Fire, Sister Earth, our Mother, "who nourishes us and sustains us, bringing forth fruits and vegetables of many kinds and flowers of many colors."[25] Thinking of the land in personalistic terms changes the way one thinks about and relates to it. If the earth is an inanimate thing, a mere resource to be exploited as efficiently as possible, the path is clear for practices that saw off the branch we are sitting on.

c) Animals

The most famous Bible story involving animals, which almost every child knows, is of course the story of Noah's ark. It's a complex story that raises a lot of issues,[26] but I simply wish to make two simple observations regarding it, as it relates to nonhuman animals. The first is that God is determined that all the different species of animal should be preserved from the coming world-destroying environmental collapse. The biblical cosmos is going to be undone, and the ark functioned as a conservation measure to preserve the biodiversity of Genesis 1. The second is that after the flood God reboots creation, although it remains in a flawed condition: humans are still sinful

---

21. Isa 14:7–8; 35:1–2; 49:13; 51:3.
22. As representatives of the humans who inhabit them.
23. Gen 1; Isa 44:24b, 27; Amos 5:8; Hos 2:23–24.
24. Josh 10:12; 2 Sam 1; Hos 10:8.
25. The quotation is from St. Francis's famous *Canticle of the Sun/Canticle of Creation* (1224). Francis did this, according to Bonaventure, "because he knew they shared with him the same beginning [i.e., the Creator God]." Bonaventure, *Works of Bonaventure*, vol. II, 590.
26. At the level of the historical question, I have explored in a series of 2008 blog posts a range of reasons to say that this is not history. But that does not make it "untrue." See "Did Noah's Flood Happen? Theological Reflections" (parts 1–2) on the Theological Scribbles blog. On the ethical concerns raised by the story, see Lynch, *Flood and Fury*, chs. 5–6.

and violent in their hearts and the human relationship with animals has deteriorated (Gen 9:1-4). Nevertheless, God establishes a binding covenant "with you and with your descendants after you *and with every living creature that was with you—the birds, the livestock and all the wild animals, all those that came out of the ark with you—every living creature on earth*. I establish my covenant with you: Never again will all life be destroyed by the waters of a flood; never again will there be a flood to destroy the earth" (Gen 9:9b-11). The sign of this covenant was the bow in the sky, an image of God's military bow held out but *reversed*, a symbol meaning that God will fire no arrows from it at the earth (vv. 12-16). God has disarmed. This covenant relationship is with *all* creatures, not merely human beings, and is "an everlasting covenant" (v. 16).

As mentioned, the world after the flood is not a reversion to Genesis 1. It seems that the Priestly author considered the original humans to be vegetarian—the ideal state for humans—but that after the flood a concession is made that takes account of the ongoing brokenness of the world. Now humans may eat meat (Gen 9:2-3), although with certain restrictions in place—a ban on consuming blood (9:4). What was that about?

We saw earlier that the Old Testament teaches that the promised land itself and the lives of the creatures that inhabited the land, both wild and domestic, belonged to *God*, not to Israel (Ps 50:10-11). This core value was the reason for the strict ban on consuming blood.

> I will set my face against any Israelite or any foreigner residing among them who eats blood, and I will cut them off from the people. For *the life of a creature is in the blood*, and I have given it to you to make atonement for yourselves on the altar; it is the blood that makes atonement for one's life. Therefore I say to the Israelites, "None of you may eat blood, nor may any foreigner residing among you eat blood." (Lev 17:11, cf. Gen 9:3-5)

According to Leviticus, killing animals simply for food was to shed their blood in a way equivalent to shedding human blood (17:3-4). In other words, for an Israelite to kill an animal simply to eat it was considered by this Priestly author to be akin to murder! That is a pretty astonishing perspective! For the meat to be consumable by a human the animal's lifeblood had to be offered to God, ritually transforming the event from a killing to an offering of life, acknowledging God as its source.[27] Counterintuitive as

---

27. Contrary to what many think, sacrifice was not, ritually speaking, about death (theath of the animal is not *ritually* significant in sacrifices), but about life, symbolized by the blood. The death of the animal is simply the means of accessing the blood. The rite seems to be, among other things, a means by which the act of killing the animal can be treated as "not murder," and thus the meat can be consumed.

it may seem at first, the underlying ethic seems to be that animal life was morally valuable and belonged to God.[28] That ritual reminded Israelites that animal life was not to be taken lightly.

A person's treatment of animals was considered an indicator of their moral character. Caring for domestic animals is a sign that one is wise and obedient to God, whereas cruelty indicates the exact opposite.

> The righteous care for the needs of their animals,
> but the kindest acts of the wicked are cruel. (Prov 12:10)

The story of Balaam's ass humorously exemplifies this. Balaam was a Canaanite prophet who was summoned by the king of Moab to prophesy doom on the people of Israel. God was angry that Balaam had gone, and so he sent a sword-wielding angel to block the prophet's path. The joke is that Balaam, the alleged seer, can't see the angel, but the donkey can. It turns off the road into a field, saving Balaam's life. Balaam is angry so he beats the donkey to force it to go where he wants (Num 22:21–23). The angel then stands in a narrow path with walls on both sides so that the oblivious Balaam will find it hard to avoid him, but the donkey presses against the wall so as not to get too close to the danger, again saving Balaam but crushing his foot in the process. That makes Balaam really annoyed. He beats the donkey again (vv. 24–25). Foiled twice by the donkey, the angel repositions himself in a place that even this savvy donkey can't avoid . . . so it stopped still then lay down on the ground. Balaam, utterly frustrated now, beats it with his staff (vv. 26–27). Then begins the most peculiar conversation of Balaam's life!

> YHWH opened the donkey's mouth, and it said to Balaam, "What have I done to you to make you beat me these three times?"
>
> Balaam answered the donkey, "You have made a fool of me! If only I had a sword in my hand, I would kill you right now."
>
> The donkey said to Balaam, "Am I not your own donkey, which you have always ridden, to this day? Have I been in the habit of doing this to you?"
>
> "No," he said.
>
> Then YHWH opened Balaam's eyes, and he saw the angel of YHWH standing in the road with his sword drawn. So he bowed low and fell facedown.
>
> The angel of YHWH asked him, "Why have you beaten your donkey these three times? I have come here to oppose you

---

28. God's love and care for animals is a theme found in both the OT (and Apocrypha) and NT. Pss 36:5–6; 104:10–26; 136:25; 145:8–9; Wis 11:26; Sir 18:13; Matt 10:29.

because your path is a reckless one before me. The donkey saw me and turned away from me these three times. If it had not turned away, I would certainly have killed you by now, but I would have spared it." (vv. 28–33)

Balaam's treatment of his animal is excessive and harsh, exposing his own moral character, but more than that, he is revealed to be a fool, needing to learn wisdom from the donkey, which has more spiritual insight than he does, as the angel confirms. Lessons in humility.

3. Ecological Entanglement in the Prophets

The prophetic texts in Scripture are also full of references to the land and its creatures. Often the oracles and visions of the prophets concern the intimate entangling of the relationship between God, Israel, and the land. The flourishing of the land was seen as a sign of divine blessing and an indication that Israel was walking according to the covenant, whereas disorder in the relationship led to the land resisting the people.

Take this passage from Hosea, in which Israel is pictured as YHWH's wife, who takes the gifts lavished upon her by her husband and showers them on other lovers (in this case Baal, a Canaanite god). As a result, YHWH says he will withdraw those gifts:

> She has not acknowledged that I was the one
>   who gave her the grain, the new wine, and oil,
> who lavished on her the silver and gold—
>   which they used for Baal.
> Therefore, I will take away my grain when it ripens,
>   and my new wine when it is ready.
> I will take back my wool and my linen,
>   intended to cover her naked body. (Hos 2:8–9)

In this way Israel will see that it is YHWH, not Baal, who provides for her through the land, and she will return to YHWH (2:7), who will respond by restoring the land's fecundity (14:6–7).

Environmental devastation following national sin is a recurring prophetic motif. Let me give some examples. Here is Isaiah 24:1, 4–6.

> Now YHWH is about to lay waste the earth and make it desolate,
>   and he will twist its surface and scatter its inhabitants . . . .
> The earth dries up and withers;
>   the world languishes and withers;
>   the heavens languish together with the earth.

> The earth lies polluted
>   under its inhabitants,
> for they have transgressed laws,
>   violated the statutes,
>   broken the everlasting covenant.
> Therefore, a curse devours the earth,
>   and its inhabitants suffer for their guilt;
> therefore, the inhabitants of the earth dwindled,
>   and few people are left.

The people broke the everlasting covenant . . . *therefore* a curse devours the earth. And here's Hosea:

> There is only cursing, lying, and murder,
>   stealing and adultery;
> they break all bounds,
>   and bloodshed follows bloodshed.
> Because of this the land mourns,
>   and all who live in it waste away;
> the beasts of the field, the birds in the sky
>   and the fish in the sea are swept away. (Hos 4:2–3)

Human sin and violence disturb the three-way relationship between God, people, and land, causing the land to suffer and lament, and the creatures that live in it perish as a result. The suffering of the earth is directly connected to human behavior.

The prophets could not imagine any future in which humans thrived and the land did not. If the land falls, humans perish with it. Here, as our third example of environmental devastation, is Jeremiah:

> I looked on the earth, and it was complete chaos [*tōhû wābōhû*],
>   and to the heavens, and they had no light.
> I looked on the mountains, and they were quaking,
>   and all the hills moved to and fro.
> I looked, and there was no one at all,
>   and all the birds of the air had fled.
> I looked, and the fruitful land was a desert,
>   and all its cities were laid in ruins
>   before YHWH, before his fierce anger. (Jer 4:23–26)

Did you notice the *tōhû wābōhû*? That is the Hebrew expression used in Genesis 1:2 to describe the disordered and lifeless pre-world. Jeremiah imagines the devastation to the land of Judah caused by military invaders as a kind of undoing of creation. The image is horrifying, but it can shape the moral imagination by providing word pictures of what environmental collapse can look like. Something similar is seen in Zephaniah's opening oracle:

> "I will sweep away everything
>   from the face of the earth,"
> declares YHWH.
> "I will sweep away both man and beast;
>   I will sweep away the birds in the sky
>   and the fish in the sea—
>   and the idols that cause the wicked to stumble.
> When I destroy all mankind
>   on the face of the earth,"
> declares YHWH. (Zeph 1:2–3)

Don't mistake this for an attempt at a scientifically precise description. Beth Stovel points out that this image too is a kind of *uncreation*, because God removes creatures in the opposite order to which he created them in Genesis 1: first humans then animals then birds then fish. "This is not merely judgment, but an unwinding of the foundational acts of creation."[29] There is a good measure of symbolism and rhetoric at work in prophetic threats[30] and the threat was never literally carried out, but such word pictures do focus the imagination on just how dependent humans and animals are on their environments and what a collapse of those structures might be like. And that is something humans very much need to be conscious of, in our own day more than ever.

The same entanglement is seen in reverse. Thus, the restoration of the people is regularly spoken of in terms of the restoration of the land and its nonhuman inhabitants. For instance,

> I am sending you grain, new wine, and olive oil,
>   enough to satisfy you fully;
> never again will I make you
>   an object of scorn to the nations....
> Do not be afraid, land of Judah;
>   be glad and rejoice.
> Surely YHWH has done great things!
> Do not be afraid, you wild animals,
>   for the pastures in the wilderness are becoming green.
> The trees are bearing their fruit;
>   the fig tree and the vine yield their riches.

---

29. Stovell and Fuller, *Book of the Twelve*, 96.

30. I do not mean to suggest that the threats were not very serious. They pointed to real and present dangers. My point is that prophets will employ devices such as hyperbole in the work of persuasion.

> Be glad, people of Zion,
>> Rejoice in YHWH your God,
> for he has given you the autumn rains
>> because he is faithful.
> He sends you abundant showers,
>> both autumn and spring rains, as before.
> The threshing floors will be filled with grain;
>> the vats will overflow with new wine and oil. (Joel 2:19, 21–24)

Here Judah rejoices in rain (v. 23) and agricultural abundance (vv. 21, 24), but notice that the wild animals and trees are also reassured too (v. 22). The fates of humans and the rest of creation, for good and for ill, were understood to be entangled.

Thankfully the prophets almost always anticipate a restoration. While taking judgment very seriously, they expect an ultimate triumph of mercy. Their message is one of "grace in the end."[31]

---

31. To borrow a phrase from Professor Gordon McConville.

7

Sophia's Shalom
Social Justice and Ecology

1. The Just God

AT THE VERY CORE of the biblical vision of God is divine justice (*mišpāt*) and righteousness (*ṣedāqâ*). "YHWH loves righteousness and justice; the earth is full of his unfailing love" (Ps 33:5). Indeed "right and justice are *the foundation of [YHWH's] throne*" (Ps 89:14), meaning that God's governance of the world is built upon them. It would not be an exaggeration to say that "right and justice" were a part of a biblical understanding of what it meant to *be* divine. Righteousness is thus *essential* to God. A deity that behaved unjustly was no deity at all (Ps 82).

In the Bible, "righteousness" concerns conformity to a standard. Following Jeffrey Niehaus, we could say that at its most *fundamental* level that standard is *God's own being*.[1] God is supremely true to who God is and is thus perfectly righteous. In relation to creation God's righteous acts are God's acting in the world in ways that are consistent with divine Goodness. "Justice," according to Niehaus, is a closely related word but with an

---

1. See Niehaus, *Righteousness*, vols. 1–3. The nuances of the terminology "righteousness" and "justice" in the Bible are complex and much debated, so while I find this proposal attractive, I am not wedded to it.

importantly different meaning in this context. It concerns what is needed to restore a situation to a righteous state. In other words, justice is what righteousness looks like when applied to situations that are out of kilter.

As we shall see, God calls humans to display righteousness (i.e., to behave in ways that mirror divine goodness) and to act with justice to set situations right when states of affairs are unrighteous.

Affirming God as the ground of righteousness means that the justice we're called to implement is not understood to be mere social convention, something that could just as easily have been otherwise, but to be derived from a righteousness that *transcends* the world. It is something we discern, not something we invent.

2. The Shalomic Vision

What is a biblical vision of a social justice? Underlying it is a picture of what a righteous human society would look like. This is an ideal that is not realized in the world but is the standard against which appeals for justice gain their leverage. Genesis 1–2 presents one such idealized picture of relationships within creation. The Hebrew word that best captures this vision is *šālôm (shalom)*, which is not merely "peace" but a holistic sense of "well-being" and rightly ordered relationships at every level. We tend to think of shalom in terms of its implications for intra-human relationships, and this is indeed critical. Shalom *is* about nations ceasing their conflicts and beating their swords into ploughshares (Isa 2:1–4), and it is also social justice within healthy societies. That is why the statue outside the United Nations building in New York depicts this very text.[2] But a biblical vision of shalom is much broader, enveloping not only relationships between humans, but also between humans and God, humans and other animals, and also between humans and the land itself and all that grows on it (Isa 11:1–9). Virtue, for society and for individuals, is those dispositions that tilt towards the order of shalom, or what is elsewhere called "the kingdom of God."

Our world is not like this, nor can we wrestle it into such a shape—not without falling into the common vices that befall all utopianisms. We

---

2. Created by the Soviet sculptor Evgeniy Vuchetich, the bronze statue was installed in 1959. Reproduced under Wiki Commons license.

humans cannot bring about God's kingdom "on earth as it is in heaven." We are never asked to. Only God can bring that about. We pray, we hope, and we engage in prophetic acts of anticipating the future. But we must never imagine that we can or should *enforce* shalom, for the very acts of enforcement would negate it. That is a road to hell, albeit one paved with good intentions.

Nonetheless, we are called to acts of justice that are inspired by this vision, acts that seek to limit and, when possible and as far as possible, to rectify injustice in the world around us. Such justice will always be partial and incomplete, always "on the way," but it is no less important for that.

This shalomic picture of thriving, healthy relationships within and between communities and between humans and the rest of creation helps us to understand why the stress on righteousness and justice took the form that it did in the Bible: namely, defending the rights of those who are most vulnerable when relationships are not righteously ordered.

3. The Just Nation

Ancient Israel had a clear concept of what God's justice meant in relation to human society. It was a narrative-shaped concept, profoundly influenced by their own national story of living as slaves in Egypt. They had been on the sharp end of unjust government policy. They knew what it felt like to be victims of politico-economic exploitation and to be powerless to do anything about it. And they believed that the God of the exodus heard the cries of the oppressed and acted on their behalf (Exod 3:7–10; 6:5–8). This story did not lead Israel to reject political power and authority, but it did temper the vision of how such power should operate. It should be exercised for the common good and in such a way that care for and protection of the most vulnerable was never to be forgotten.

The laws given by God through Moses are presented in the Torah as the foundation of the nation's political and social life. And those laws are to be interpreted within the narrative context in which they are embedded. They are given while the people are en route from Egypt to the promised land and the commands are prefaced with the words "I am YHWH your God, who brought you out of the land of Egypt, out of the house of slavery" (Exod 20:2). They should not be taken out of that relational, redemptive context. That exodus-shaped sense of national identity infused the commands themselves. Israel knew what it was to be slaves, they knew what it was to live as despised foreigners, they knew what it was to be landless and to lack the food they needed, so they should treat slaves, foreigners, the poor, and the landless with compassion and justice. The "at-risk" groups specifically identified in the law included:

- the poor and the landless (remember that land was the source of food, shelter, and clothing)[3]
- the widow and orphan (both groups—being without a male, a husband or father—were very vulnerable in a patriarchal society that lacked any social security)[4]
- the alien/foreigner, whether permanent or temporary residents in the land[5]
- slaves (who faced numerous risks and injustices)[6]

Justice in the legislative texts of the Torah was culturally and socially contextual rather than abstract and timeless. Discernment is needed in interpreting them today because, as Norman Gottwald astutely observes, "the Bible is both grossly irrelevant in direct application to current economic problems and [at the same time] incredibly relevant in vision and principle for grasping opportunities and obligations to make the whole earth and its bounty serve the welfare of the whole human family."[7] (And, we should add, non-humankind.) Additionally, justice as explored in biblical laws was certainly not utopian. It was often a matter of setting up a social safety net, a floor that people should not be allowed to fall below rather than a ceiling that they should be raised to. Thus, much of the focus in the laws is not on setting up ethical ideals so much as with mitigating the dangers faced by certain categories of person in a very non-ideal world and ensuring that such persons were protected and treated with dignity. The laws were focused on matters of fair wages, rest periods, remittance of debts, food and wealth redistribution, working conditions, means-tested payments, equality before

---

3. Exod 20:8–11; 21:1–11; 22:2; 23:10–11; Lev 14:21–22; 19:9–10; 23:22; 25:1–7, 21–22; Deut 15:1–11; 23:24–25; 24:14–15, 19–20, 22–29; 26:12–15.

4. Exod 22:21–25; Deut 10:18; 14:29; 24:1, 19–21; 27:17, 19.

5. Exod 22:21; 23:9; Lev 19:33–34; Num 15:15; Deut 10:19; 23:7; 24:14, 17–22; 27:19.

6. Exod 12:44; 20:10; 21:2, 20–21, 26–27; 23:12; Lev 25; Deut 5:14–15; 15:12–17; 21:10–14. Slavery was a part of social life everywhere in the ancient world, so Israel did not banish it but, having known a harsh form of slavery themselves, put in place a range of protections and routes out of slavery. This is perhaps best understood not as a moral ideal (no person steeped in the story of the exodus could consider slavery an ideal) so much as an attempt to mitigate the worst aspects of a nonideal reality. And the redemptive trajectory of Scripture provides grounds for taking that undercutting of slavery further, to its natural conclusion—abolition.

7. Gottwald, *Hebrew Bible in Its Social World and Ours*, 364.

the law, access to land, and such like. Learning from the wisdom of the Torah today is not a matter of trying to simplistically replicate its specific ways of dealing with the concrete issues faced by its audiences—we are separated by a very large temporal, spatial, and cultural gap—but of grasping the principles and values at its heart: God's righteousness and God's care for justice.[8]

This concern for legal, economic, and social justice for the vulnerable continues right through the Bible, in its historical books, wisdom books, prophetic books, the Gospels, and the NT Epistles. My goal here is not to delve into the details, but simply to register the importance of this theme for any kind of spirituality that claims to be rooted in the Bible.

Israel's political leaders were tasked with defending the poor and needy. Thus, human government, represented by the king, was commanded to implement divine justice, which meant caring for the most vulnerable.

> Endow the king with your justice, O God,
>   the royal son with your righteousness.
> May he judge your people in righteousness,
>   your afflicted ones with justice. . . .
> May he defend the afflicted among the people
>   and save the children of the needy; . . .
> For he will deliver the needy who cry out,
>   and the afflicted who have no one to help.
> He will take pity on the weak and the needy
>   and save the needy from death.
> He will rescue them from oppression and violence,
>   for precious is their blood in his sight. (Ps 72:1–2, 4, 12–14)

The reality, regretfully, was that Israel often fell short of God's righteousness and the leaders often failed to defend the rights of the poor. The rich and powerful often used their position to enhance their own position *rather than* that of the vulnerable—worse, often *at the expense of* the vulnerable.

YHWH did not allow the reality of injustice in society to pass under the radar. Absolutely not! God sent Israel ambassadors, the prophets, to rebuke the leaders and to call the nation back to fidelity to the covenant, because social injustice was not merely a crime against the weak but simultaneously an act of infidelity to God. Why? In part, because to abuse an image of God is to abuse the God whose image it is.

The critique of social injustice is ubiquitous in the writings of the prophets. Amos, in the eighth century BC, for instance, is scathing. Israel

---

8. A helpful study of what this might look like in the modern world is Hartropp, *What Is Economic Justice?*

"trample[s] the heads of the poor into the dust of the earth and turn[s] aside the way of the afflicted" (2:7); they "oppress the poor" and "crush the needy" (4:1). How do the wealthy tread down the poor? Through exploitative taxation in order enrich themselves (5:11), by taking bribes to avoid rendering the justice the law demands (5:12), by defrauding them when selling grain (8:5–6). So those with power have turned the tax system, the legal system, and the economic system to their own advantage at the expense of the vulnerable. God is seriously pissed at this! Do they think that acting all prim and pious is going to make God turn a blind eye to such exploitation? If so, they can think again! YHWH says,

> I hate, I despise your feasts,
> > and I take no delight in your solemn assemblies.
> Even though you offer me your burnt offerings and grain offerings,
> > I will not accept them. . . .
> Take away from me the noise of your songs;
> > to the melody of the harp I will not listen.
> But let justice roll down like waters,
> > and righteousness like an ever-flowing stream. (Amos 5:21–24)

A similar sentiment is expressed by Micah. Do you want to know what kind of religion pleases God? Simple:

> He has shown you, O mortal, what is good.
> > And what does YHWH require of you?
> To act justly and to love mercy
> > and to walk humbly with your God. (Mic 6:8)

The final section of Isaiah applies the same logic to the religious practice of fasting. The prophet's audience considered themselves devout, yet they did not understand the *kind* of devotion God sought. "Yet on the day of your fasting, you do as you please and exploit all your workers" (Isa 58:3). Their lives did not match their worship. YHWH says,

> Is that what you call a fast,
> > a day acceptable to YHWH?
> Is not this the kind of fasting I have chosen:
> > to loose the chains of injustice
> > and untie the cords of the yoke,
> > to set the oppressed free
> > and break every yoke?
> Is it not to share your food with the hungry
> > and to provide the poor wanderer with shelter—
> when you see the naked, to clothe them,
> > and not to turn away from your own flesh and blood?

Then your light will break forth like the dawn,
> and your healing will quickly appear;
then your righteousness will go before you,
> and the glory of YHWH will be your rear guard.
Then you will call, and YHWH will answer;
> you will cry for help, and he will say: Here am I.
If you do away with the yoke of oppression,
> with the pointing finger and malicious talk,
and if you spend yourselves on behalf of the hungry
> and satisfy the needs of the oppressed,
then your light will rise in the darkness,
> and your night will become like the noonday. (Isa 58:5c–10)

4. Wisdom and Justice

What does any of this justice talk have to do with wisdom? The answer will not surprise you at all. God is essentially righteous and just so *of course* God's Wisdom is righteous and just. We read in Proverbs that Woman Wisdom speaks what is "righteous" (Prov 8:6–9). Not only her words but also her actions: she says, "I walk in the way of righteousness, along the paths of justice" (8:20).

And what does that mean for humans? It means that to listen carefully to Wisdom is a great good because "then you will understand righteousness and justice and equity, every good path" (2:9). This is so for ordinary citizens but also for those in political power: she hates the way of evil and enables rulers to "decree what is just" and to "govern rightly" (8:15–16). Those who govern unjustly are, by definition, fools.[9]

This link of Wisdom and justice is exactly as we should expect. That means, however, that one cannot divide the spirituality of wisdom from the path of social and economic justice.

---

9. Proverbs applies Wisdom's guidance to poverty. The poor can become destitute through a wide variety of causes, among which are acts of social injustice (Prov 13:23). Wisdom requires the wise to hear the cries of the poor (21:13), to give to the poor (22:9; 28:27), to be kind to the poor (14:21), and to not "rob" or "oppress" them (22:22–23) or to take land from them (23:10–11). Those in a social position that enables them to render justice for the poor should do so. To insult the poor and destitute, on the other hand, is to mock God (14:31).

5. Justice and the Environment

"Hold on! This is all well and good, but I thought I was reading a book on eco-spirituality, so what does all this social justice stuff have to do with the environment?" That's a good question. It wasn't a connection that was really explored in depth prior to the past fifty years, but it has become a major focus in recent decades. On the surface the answer is very simple, though in the details it is incredibly complex. We'll stick here with the surface.

Human beings are profoundly and inextricably bound up with their natural environments. We cannot talk about relations within human society as if such matters were quite separate from issues of human relationships with the nonhuman creation. And we cannot address environmental degradation without at the same time addressing the way human social interactions contribute to it and are affected by it. As Pope Francis says, "we are faced not with two separate crises, one environmental and the other social, but rather one complex crisis which is both social and environmental. Strategies for a solution demand an integrated approach to combating poverty, restoring dignity to the excluded, and at the same time protecting nature" (*Laudato si'* 139). In God's creation, *everything is interconnected*.

The core insight within the many studies on eco-justice since the 1980s is that the blessings and curses of human use of the environment are not equally distributed. It turns out that the communities that face the worst consequences from modern misuse of the earth's resources are the communities in our world that are the poorest and most marginalized. This is the case *within* nations as well as *between* nations.

Within nations, certain disadvantaged people groups find that, for instance, the places where toxic waste and pollution will be "dealt with" are the areas where they live, far from the homes of the richer communities largely responsible for generating it. The environmental benefits are predominantly enjoyed by the privileged communities while the burden of the corresponding environmental hazards is largely borne by the less powerful, marginal communities. Those risks often come in the form of significant health hazards resulting from exposure to toxic pollution and the lack of financial resources and political influence to respond appropriately. Such communities have statistically significant higher rates of cancer, asthma, and similar health conditions, along with shorter average lifespans. In the United States Indigenous and Black communities have experienced this kind of thing time and time again. It is understandably often spoken of as "environmental racism."

On an international level, consider the way that Western companies buy up vast tracts of land in the Global South for their own businesses, depriving Indigenous people of the land needed for farming. Or the way that the massive resource extraction of timber or minerals or petroleum from the Global South, on which the endless growth of Western economies depends, can create large environmental costs for those who live near the extraction sites or can lead to local communities being displaced to allow for the extraction. Think too of the way poorer nations are often paid to become the dumping ground for excess waste from wealthy countries, often creating environmental problems for them. Or keep in mind the many negative impacts of climate change, which are (and will continue to be) experienced most severely by the poorest countries: including drought, flooding, and devastating weather patterns. In part this is because of where they are located and in part it is because they cannot afford to insulate themselves against the worst impacts in the ways wealthier nations can. It is we in the rich West who have created the problem through our carbon-spewing lifestyles but those who bear the biggest burden are the nations that did least to contribute to the problem.

Poor communities are on the receiving end of what some are now calling "slow violence,"[10] the hidden, gradual, escalating harm brought about by environmental damage. These are very complex issues involving a wide range of multilayered social, economic, cultural, and ecological factors, and the solutions must also be multilayered and contextual, but whatever else we say about them, they are inescapably issues of justice. Furthermore, there is no way to disentangle the ecological problems from the justice issues. To address the one, we must simultaneously deal with the other.

While the Bible does not offer any neat solutions to such complex problems it is very clear that God requires of humanity both (a) *responsible* use of creation's resources and (b) *social justice* for the vulnerable. While Scripture may not offer simple solutions on a plate, it makes it *a spiritual imperative* that we pursue such solutions in our own contexts, using all the resources at our disposal. If we think we can do eco-spirituality without attending in constructive ways to matters of eco-justice, our spirituality amounts to little more than a form of self-therapy and, worse, is at risk of being a pious mask for our silent complicity in injustice.

---

10. A term coined by Rob Nixon in *Slow Violence and the Environmentalism of the Poor* (2011).

8

Wisdom Made Flesh

Jesus-Sophia among Us

THIS IS A BOOK about *Christ-ian* eco-spirituality, so it is time to consider Christ. However, my hope is that by the time we've finished doing so it should become clearer that, in fact, Christ has been present in our field of vision all along. How so? Because *Jesus is Woman Wisdom made flesh and blood*. That point is so central to my understanding of eco-spirituality and is sufficiently unfamiliar to most Christians that I will spend a bit more time than I otherwise would in seeking to show its biblical credentials.

1. More Than a Sage (Matthew's Gospel)

Jesus of Nazareth was a lightning rod, a focus of both fascination and fear, of devotion and denunciation. One thing that everyone agreed on, however, was the Jesus was *a teacher* and that he taught the people in the name of the God of Israel, opening their Scriptures in new and surprising ways. His preaching drew crowds of the intrigued and the committed as well as those suspicious and hostile towards him. And even those who were unsure what to make of him were struck by his wisdom: "When the Sabbath came, he began to teach in the synagogue, and many who heard him were amazed. 'Where did this man get these things?' they asked. 'What's this *wisdom* that has been given him?'" (Mark 6:2). According to the author of Luke's Gospel, wisdom had marked Jesus since his childhood (Luke 2:40, 52) and he presents Jesus as a child of Woman Wisdom herself (Luke 7:31–35). Jesus is one who is greater even than wise Solomon, the image par excellence of the sage (Luke 11:31).

Yet Matthew's Gospel goes a step further. Jesus is not only a wise man; he himself *is* God's own Wisdom. Matthew sidles up to this claim using subtle clues for those with eyes to see. For instance, when the imprisoned John the Baptist had sent messengers to Jesus asking about the "deeds" of the Messiah (Matt 11:2, cf. vv. 5–6), he replied: "For John came neither eating nor drinking, and they say, 'He has a demon.' The Son of Man came eating and drinking, and they say, 'Here is a glutton and a drunkard, a friend of tax collectors and sinners.' But *Wisdom is proved right by her deeds*" (Matt 11:18–19). In context, Wisdom's deeds are either the deeds of Jesus, referred to earlier in the chapter, or Jesus himself—the one announced by the Baptist. In other words, *Woman Wisdom acts in Jesus' acts*.

Or consider the text from Luke in which Jesus says to the Pharisees, "Because of this, *the Wisdom of God said*, 'I will send them prophets and apostles, some of whom they will kill and others they will persecute'" (Luke 11:49). Matthew presents this slightly differently. He has Jesus say, "Therefore, *I am sending you* prophets and sages and teachers. Some of them you will kill and crucify; others you will flog in your synagogues and pursue from town to town" (Matt 23:34). Luke has Woman Wisdom say that she will send messengers to Israel, yet Matthew has Jesus assuming Wisdom's role as the sender. Jesus is Sophia.

The most striking identification of Jesus and Wisdom in Matthew comes in a much-beloved passage. "Come to me, all you who are weary and burdened, and I will give you rest. Take my yoke upon you and learn from me, for I am gentle and humble in heart, and you will find rest for your souls. For my yoke is easy and my burden is light" (Matt 11:28–30). Jesus here speaks as Wisdom. "Come to me" is a common refrain of Wisdom. For instance, "*Come to me*, you who desire me, and eat your fill of my fruits" (Sir 24:19). There is little doubt that in this saying Matthew's Jesus is drawing on certain wisdom texts and themes. Consider:

> Listen, my child, and accept my judgment;
> do not reject my counsel.
> *Put your feet into her fetters,*
> *and your neck into her collar.*
> Bend your shoulders and carry her,
> and do not fret under her bonds.
> *Come to her* with all your soul,
> and keep her ways with all your might. (Sir 6:23–25)

At the end of his book, Ben Sirach considers his lifelong journey with wisdom. At times almost speaking as wisdom, he says,

> *Draw near to me, you who are uneducated,*
>   *and lodge in the house of instruction.*
> Why do you say you are lacking in these things,
>   and why do you endure such great thirst?
> I opened my mouth and said,
>   Acquire wisdom for yourselves without money.
> *Put your neck under her yoke,*
>   *and let your souls receive instruction;*
> it is to be found close by.
> See with your own eyes that *I have labored but little*
>   *and found for myself much serenity.* (Sir 51:23–27)

The last line is echoed by the "rest" that Jesus offers. That too alludes to a theme associated with Wisdom.

> When I enter my house, I shall *find rest with her* [Wisdom];
> for companionship with her has no bitterness,
> and life with her has no pain, but gladness and joy. (Wis 8:16)

> Search out and seek, and she will become known to you;
>   and when you get hold of her, do not let her go.
> For at last you will find *the rest she gives,*
>   and she will be changed into joy for you. (Sir 6:27–28)

When Jesus invites his disciples to come to him, take his yoke, and find rest, he is issuing the invitation *as* the Wisdom of God. He is more than a mere sage; he is Sophia herself.

2. Jesus as Creator (Saint Paul)

The association of Jesus with God's Wisdom predates the Gospel of Matthew. We find it in the very earliest strand of literature in the New Testament, the letters of Paul. Twice in the first chapter of 1 Corinthians (written 53–54 AD) Paul refers to Jesus as Sophia. He speaks of "Christ the power of God and the wisdom of God" (v. 24) and "Christ Jesus, who became for us wisdom from God" (v. 30). That association explains a surprising theme in Pauline thought: that God created the world *through* Christ. Ponder the following passages:

> [F]or us there is one God, the Father, from whom are all things and for whom we exist, and one Lord, Jesus Christ, *through whom are all things and through whom we exist.* (1 Cor 8:6)
>
> [The Son] is the image of the invisible God, the firstborn over all creation. For *in him all things were created:* things in heaven and on earth, visible and invisible, whether thrones or powers or rulers or authorities; all things have been *created through him* and for him. He is before all things, and in him all things hold together. (Col 1:15–17)

Now, as we have already seen, God created the cosmos through Wisdom, but for the early Jesus-followers the identification of Christ with God's Wisdom allows them to see *him* as the one through whom the world was made. The book of Hebrews (not by Paul) makes a similar link:

> Long ago God spoke to our ancestors in many and various ways by the prophets, but in these last days he has spoken to us by a Son, whom he appointed heir of all things, *through whom he also created the worlds.* He is the reflection of God's glory and the exact imprint of God's very being, and he *sustains all things by his powerful word.* (Heb 1:1–3a)

All this places the Lord Jesus into the position of Woman Wisdom, the one *through whom* God created the cosmos. That is an astonishing claim to make about a flesh-and-blood human being who lived and taught in first-century Galilee and Judea.

3. Wisdom Made Flesh and Blood (John's Gospel)

John's Gospel, likely written towards the end of the first century, draws very heavily on the Jewish tradition of Woman Wisdom in its presentation of Jesus. This is evident in the famous prologue. The word *Sophia* (Wisdom) is not found there, but her presence is hidden in plain sight for anyone familiar with Jewish wisdom texts.

Let's quickly look at it, section by section.

> In the beginning was the Word (Greek: *Logos*), and the Word was with God, and the Word was God. 2 He was in the beginning with God. 3 All things came into being through him, and without him not one thing came into being. What has come into being 4 in him was life, and the life was the light of all people. 5 The light shines in the darkness, and the darkness did not overtake it.

Notice the following Wisdom allusions:

- The Word *existed in the beginning*, just as Wisdom was there in the beginning (Prov 8:22–26; Sir 1:4; Wis 9:9).

- The Word was *"with God"* in the beginning. Being alongside God is a motif associated with Wisdom (Prov 8:30; Wis 9:4; Sir 1:1). Not only was Wisdom with God but she was loved by God (Wis 8:3–4), just as the Father and the Son love each other in John's Gospel.

- The Word *"was God."* In a single mind-expanding sentence John *distinguishes* between God and the Word (the Word was *with* God) and *identifies* them (the Word *was* God). John's paradoxical statement of distinction and identity between the Word and God has clear parallels in traditions about Wisdom and God (see chapter 1).

- God created all things *"through"* the Word. Wisdom is the divine figure through whom God created all things (Prov 3:19; 8:30), who is accordingly called "the architect of all things" (Wis 7:21, cf. 9:1–2).

- In the Word is *"life."* Wisdom too is closely linked to life (Prov 8:35; Sir 4:12; Wis 8:13).

- The Word is associated with *"light"* and indeed is "the true light . . . coming into the world" (cf. 1:6–9). The light metaphor indicates the spiritual enlightenment brought by the Logos to people. We find a similar association between Wisdom and light (Wis 7:26)—perhaps unsurprising given her role in revealing God's ways to people.

> 10 He [the Logos] was in the world, and the world came into being through him, yet the world did not know him. 11 He came to what was his own, and his own people did not accept him. 12 But to all who received him, who believed in his name, he gave power to become children of God, 13 who were born, not of blood or of the will of the flesh or of the will of man, but of God.

As the incarnation of Christ is not mentioned until v. 14, these verses most likely refer to the work of the divine Word in the world and in Israel *prior to* the incarnation (while at the same time anticipating the same pattern played out in the ministry of Jesus). This helps us to see various Wisdom connections:

- Sophia is presented in wisdom texts as being active in mediating God's blessing and salvation and judgment throughout the history of Israel and beyond the borders of Israel (cf. Job, who was not an Israelite character). Wisdom is at work everywhere and everywhen.

- The Word *comes into the world, seeking people*. This is true of the ministry of the Word prior to the incarnation but supremely in the incarnation, as the rest of this Gospel makes clear. And this is how we first encounter Woman Wisdom, walking on the streets, in public, calling out to people to listen to her (Prov 1:20–33). The idea of Wisdom seeking a place to dwell among people is a recurring one (Prov 1:20–33; Sir 15:7; 24:28–29; Bar 3:12, 23; 1 En 42).

- The Word is inexplicably *rejected by some*, even his own. That theme is true of Israel's history and is clearly displayed in Jesus' ministry as the gospel story is unpacked by John. So too Wisdom is rejected by some, a rejection pictured in Proverbs in the image of embracing Wisdom's nemesis, Dame Folly (Prov 7; 9:13–18).

- Yet *some welcome the Word* and are affirmed as *children of God*. Similar things can be said of Wisdom. Those in whom Wisdom dwells can call God "Father" and are "children" of God (Wis 2:13, 16d; 14:3; Sir 23:4; 51:10).

> 14 And the Word became flesh and lived [lit. "tabernacled"] among us, and we have seen his glory, the glory as of a father's only son, full of grace and truth.

This passage continues the theme of the Word looking for a home amongst people. Here we reach a pivotal moment: the *enfleshing* of the Logos. And this too resonates with Wisdom:

- The idea of Wisdom seeking a place to dwell and coming to live in Israel is present in certain wisdom texts. The presence of Wisdom in Israel is focused especially in the law of Moses (Sir 24:23; Bar 3:37—4:2) and in the figure of the high priest (Sir 50). John, however, takes this trajectory to new and unprecedented levels: the Word (=Wisdom) *became flesh*.

- The glory (*doxa*), grace (*charis*), and truth (*alētheia*) of the Word are *God's* glory, truth, and grace. Wisdom too is associated with divine glory (Wis 9:11; 7:25–26); grace (Sir 24:16, cf. 37:21); and truth (Prov 8:6–7; 14:22; 23:23; Wis 6:22; Sir 4:24–25).

- Here the language of Father and Son is introduced for the first time in the Gospel, terms that are core to John's sense of Jesus' relationship with God. Wisdom is obviously never referred to as God's Son, but she is arguably presented as God's daughter in Proverbs 8—God, at least, begets her (as her father) and gives birth to her (as her mother) (cf. Wisdom as "God's daughter" in Philo, *Fug.* 50–52).

> 15 (John testified to him and cried out, "This was he of whom I said, 'He who comes after me ranks ahead of me because he was before me.'") 16 From his fullness we have all received, grace upon grace. 17 The law indeed was given through Moses; grace and truth came through Jesus Christ. 18 No one has ever seen God. It is the only Son (*monogenēs*), himself God, who is close to the Father's heart, who has made him known.

- The Logos is utterly unique. The word John uses in v. 18 is *monogenēs*, "one and only." This same word is used of Wisdom: "There is in her a spirit that is intelligent, holy, unique (*monogenēs*) . . ." (Wis 7:22).
- The Son reveals God (who is otherwise inaccessible to humans). In John's Gospel as a whole, Jesus is the revealer of God, revealing what he has seen and heard (3:11, 32; 8:26, 38, 40; 15:15), his own glory (2:11), the works of God (9:3), and God's name (17:6, 26). What he reveals is not information about God but *God's own self*. What qualifies Jesus for this role is that he was with God before the world began, sharing glory with him, and has come down from heaven to make him known. This is in synch with a theme in wisdom literature, that Sophia is qualified to speak of God's ways because of who she is, where she's from, and what she's seen (Wis 9:9). She is a reflection (*apaugasma*) of God (Wis 7:25–27, incidentally, the same word used to describe Christ as "the radiance/reflection [*apaugasma*] of God's glory" in Hebrews 1:3) and she understands the created world. She too descends from above to reveal God and God's ways (implicit in Proverbs, as Wisdom is with God and then down at street level, with the people, calling out to them; Sir 24:3–17; Wis 9).

All of this in just the first eighteen verses of John! The rest of his Gospel continues unpacking many of the themes introduced here, also offering other possible Wisdom allusions.

I have spent a long time spelling out the case for Jesus understood as Sophia-made-flesh. The reason for this indulgence is that the idea will be dismissed out of hand by some people as just some "crazy ass, politically correct, bleeding-heart liberal (and woke)" attempt to subvert traditional Christian theology. It is not. It is, I believe, the teaching of the New

Testament.[1] And that it was such was recognized by the early church fathers, who for the most part understood Woman Wisdom to be the second person of the Holy Trinity.[2] So, if you want biblical and traditional Christianity, behold: Jesus-Sophia!

4. The Eco-Spirituality of Incarnation

In terms of the story of the world that Christians tell, this is of foundational importance. It makes Jesus-Sophia central to the way we understand the cosmos. God creates all things through the divine Wisdom/Word. So Christ-believers relate to the world around them as the holy craftwork of Christ.

Precisely because of that, the *Sophia* or *Logos* of God present in all things is none other than the one who walked among us as Jesus. St. Athanasius writes, God "has placed in each and every creature and in the totality of creation a certain imprint and reflection of the Image of Wisdom. ... [And God] has made the true Wisdom herself take flesh and become a mortal human being and endure the death of the cross, so that henceforth all those who put their faith in him may be saved" (*Against the Arians* 2.78, 81). When we discern the patterns and presence of divinity in the world, it is *Christ* we are seeing, even if we do not realize that. When you are struck by wonder at the patterns of the wind or the complex eye of the mantis shrimp or the moving harmonies in a piece of music, your awe is a response to the work and presence of Sophia, whether or not you are aware of it.[3]

But perhaps the real shock of John's prologue is that God's Logos "became flesh" (1:14). The *enfleshing* of Holy Sophia as Jesus of Nazareth is hugely important for shaping the spirituality of Christian engagement with the world. As we have seen, in Israel's wisdom tradition Sophia has never shirked the materiality of created life, seeking a place to "live" and be "embodied" in the world. But becoming a human being in the person of Jesus takes her inhabiting of creation to a new and unprecedented level! As one New Testament author puts it, "For in Christ all the fullness of the Deity lives in bodily form" (Col 2:9). Think about that: the *fullness* of God ... *in*

---

1. The literature on Wisdom Christology is large, but for starters I recommend Dunn, *Christology in the Making*, 163–268; Douglas, *Early Church Understandings of Jesus as the Female Divine* (and for a more accessible version, Douglas, *Jesus Sophia*). On Matthew's Gospel, see Lodahl, "Wisdom's Invitation." On John's Gospel, see Scott, *Sophia and the Johannine Jesus*.

2. See esp. Dowling, "Proverbs 8:22–31 in the Christology of the Early Church."

3. This idea is captured beautifully in Kathleen Raine's poem "Word Made Flesh." It is easily found online.

bodily form. There can be no body-hating for those who find a home in this story. Instead, we find as profound an affirmation of the goodness and value of the physical world as one could ask for. God's Wisdom identifies with the materiality of the cosmos to the point of taking on that materiality as a fitting habitation.

Neil Darragh put it like this: "To say that God become flesh is not only to say that God became human, but to say also that God became an Earth creature, that God became a sentient being, that God became a living being (in common with all other living beings), that God became a complex Earth unit of minerals and fluids, that God became an item in the carbon and nitrogen cycles."[4] Denis Edwards develops this further:

> Like us, Jesus is part of evolutionary history, dependent on the hydrogen that formed in the beginning of the universe, on the carbon and other elements synthesized in the stars, and of the long history of evolutionary emergence on Earth. . . . In Jesus of Nazareth, God becomes a vital part of all the interconnected systems and physical processes of our planet, part of the evolutionary history of life on Earth, part of the story of the expanding and evolving universe. God embraces all this in order to bring it to completion.[5]

Some recent theologians thus speak of "deep incarnation" in this regard: "The flesh assumed in Jesus Christ connects with all humanity, all biological life, all soil, the whole matrix of the material universe down to its very roots."[6] Thus it is that Jesus can represent *all creation* before God and God before all creation. And that insight is the pulsating heart of Christian eco-spirituality.

---

4. Darragh, *At Home in the Earth*, 124, quoted in Edwards, *How God Acts*, 123.
5. Edwards, *How God Acts*, 74, 123.
6. Johnson, *Ask the Beasts*, 196; the phrase was coined by Niels Gregersen.

9

Saving Wisdom

The Cosmic Implications of Christ's Death and Resurrection

And [Jesus] said to them, "Go into all the world and preach the gospel to *every creature*."[1] (Mark 16:15)

THE CHRISTIAN YEAR HAS two key focal seasons, Christmas and Easter, which serve as the gravitational centers that everything else orbits. The former celebrates the coming of God in the coming of Christ, the latter celebrates the salvation of the world in the death, resurrection, and ascension of Christ.[2]

Now the stories of Jesus' birth, death, resurrection, and ascension are often spoken about in relation to human beings, and rightly so, but what is often missed is the cosmic dimension of this story.

The foundation for appreciating this cosmic dimension is the understanding of the incarnation sketched in the last chapter. It is critical to

---

1. Or "preach the gospel to all creation" or "to the whole creation."

2. In reality these two are like the colors refracted through a prism that while seeming to be quite distinct really belong inseparably together in the pure, primal, unified light. Easter is anticipated in Christmas and Christmas reaches its climax at Easter. Neither makes sense apart from the another. Indeed, all Christian festivals are aspects of a single gemstone, which is Christ.

appreciate that in Christian thought Christ is not simply an individual human being, *but a representative figure.*

- As the Jewish messianic king, he represents the covenant nation of Israel.
- As the second Adam (Rom 5:12–19; 1 Cor 15:22, 47–49), the origin of a renewed humanity, he represents the whole human race.

Those two are the focus in New Testament texts, but the early church understood Christ to be the archetypal Human Being,[3] and in that capacity he also symbolically represents:

- animals (as he is a sentient and rational animal)
- living organisms (as he is a living organism)
- non-living creation (as he is made from the inanimate "dust of the ground")

It is precisely because of this understanding of Christ's significance that the story of the death, resurrection, and ascension was never thought of by his followers as merely a story about Jesus but always also as a story about Israel, about the nations, and about the whole cosmic order.

1. The Cosmic Death of Jesus

> 15 The Son is the image of the invisible God, the firstborn over all creation. 16 For in him all things were created: things in heaven and on earth, visible and invisible, whether thrones or powers or rulers or authorities; all things have been created through him and for him. 17 He is before all things, and in him all things hold together. 18 And he is the head of the body, the church; he is the beginning and the firstborn from among the dead, so that in everything he might have the supremacy. 19 For God was pleased to have all his fullness dwell in him, 20 and *through him to reconcile to himself all things, whether things on earth or things in heaven, by making peace through his blood, shed on the cross.* (Col 1:15–20 NIV)

---

3. In early Christian thought, building on the letters of St. Paul, Christ is the "second Adam" in order of appearance, for he came after Adam. However, he is in truth the archetypal Human, the true Image of God upon whom Adam was modelled. Thus, Christ is the Image of God and we are in the image of the Image. Christ is the true Human and we are en route to becoming human (in the full-blown image-and-likeness-of-God sense). So in the order of being, Christ precedes Adam.

This passage in Colossians is crucial because it highlights how the stories of creation and redemption in Christian thought are not two distinct and unrelated stories but *one story*—and it is a *Jesus-centered* story. The passage moves from the creation of all things through and for Christ to the salvation of all things through Christ. This is the story of *everything*, "in heaven and on earth, visible and invisible." Nothing is left out of its gravitational pull. Thus, when redemption is addressed, its scope is as broad as creation: "God was pleased to have all his fullness dwell in [Christ], and through him to reconcile to himself all things . . . by making peace through his blood, shed on the cross." Here the cross of Jesus reconciles *the whole cosmic order*, not merely human beings, to God.

Most of the New Testament teaching about the cross is focused on its role in the redemption of humanity, but in biblical thinking even that focus appears to be relevant to its cosmic dimensions. Human sin afflicts the whole order of life on earth and liberation for the earth and its nonhuman inhabitants is tied up with the transformation of human beings. With the redemption of humanity, the blockage to the redemption of the rest of terrestrial life is removed. This is perhaps why "the creation waits in eager expectation for the children of God to be revealed" (Rom 8:22). This unveiling of the children of God refers to the resurrection of the dead, and when the children are manifest in divine glory the whole cosmic order will in turn be set free.

However, beyond this, it seems not unreasonable to speculate that as Christ can be seen to represent both humans and nonhumans, his death is a sharing not only in the death that human beings face but also in the death and decay experienced by the whole creation. In Christ, God stands in solidarity with the universe. In Christ's death, God faces the ultimate annihilation of every creature, going beyond the point of no return into oblivion . . . and then returning. In this way, the cross of Christ becomes the means by which God astonishingly changes death, the termination of the journey, into a transition to its next stage. Christ "suffers the self-destruction of creation in order through his sufferings to heal it."[4] Switching metaphors, death is now a comma, not a full stop. Or, switching imagery again, Christ enters into the heart of the prison cell of death, from which no one and nothing can escape, and leads a jailbreak. The dungeon has become the doorway. And this is possible because Christ died for all creation.[5]

---

4. Moltmann, *God in Creation*, 16.

5. Not all *claimed* "wisdom" is God's wisdom, so discernment is needed to sift competing claims to spiritual insight. See Brookins, *Rediscovering the Wisdom of the Corinthians*, on 1 Corinthians 1–4.

2. The Cosmic Resurrection of Jesus

Just as Jesus' death is on behalf of creation, so too is his resurrection. When God raised Jesus from the dead, he was raising him as the representative of:

- Israel, the covenant people
- The nations of the earth
- Creation as a whole (animate and inanimate)

In Christ's resurrection, Israel, humanity, and all creation are liberated, restored, reanimated. In his resurrection a new age of a wholly different order has begun. Jesus did not simply *die* for us; *he was raised for us too.* As he shared in creation's death so creation will share in his new life.

This is why Christians make such a big deal about Easter. The resurrection of Jesus is the ground zero of Christian eschatology. It is where the eternal life "detonated" in the midst of the world, bringing not devastation and destruction but new horizons of hope.

You see, the concept of resurrection in first-century Judaism was indissolubly linked with the idea of a coming new creation, the new heaven and earth spoken of by the prophet Isaiah (Isa 65:17–25). This coming new age would be a time of shalom. War between nations would end (2:1–4). Conflict between different kinds of creatures would cease (11:1–9). Even death would be banished (26:19). The resurrection body was the body transformed and transfigured into a form fitting for such a life. St. Paul discusses the nature of the transformations he expected in resurrected human bodies in a fascinating and important passage.

> 35 But someone will ask, "How are the dead raised? With what kind of body will they come?" 36 How foolish! What you sow does not come to life unless it dies. 37 When you sow, you do not plant the body that will be, but just a seed, perhaps of wheat or of something else. 38 But God gives it a body as he has determined, and to each kind of seed he gives its own body. 39 Not all flesh is the same: People have one kind of flesh, animals have another, birds another and fish another. 40 There are also heavenly bodies and there are earthly bodies; but the splendor of the heavenly bodies is one kind, and the splendor of the earthly bodies is another. 41 The sun has one kind of splendor, the moon another and the stars another; and star differs from star in splendor.
>
> 42 So will it be with the resurrection of the dead. The body that is sown is perishable, it is raised imperishable; 43 it is sown in dishonor, it is raised in glory; it is sown in weakness, it is

raised in power; ⁴⁴ it is sown a natural body, it is raised a spiritual body.

If there is a natural body, there is also a spiritual body. 45 So it is written: "The first man Adam became a living being" [Gen 2:7]; the last Adam [Christ], a life-giving spirit. 46 The spiritual did not come first, but the natural, and after that the spiritual. 47 The first man [Adam] was of the dust of the earth; the second man [Christ] is of heaven. 48 As was the earthly man, so are those who are of the earth; and as is the heavenly man, so also are those who are of heaven. 49 And just as we have borne the image of the earthly man, so shall we bear the image of the heavenly man. (1 Cor 15:35–49)

It is important to pay very careful attention to both the *continuity* and the *discontinuity* between our current body and our resurrection body in Paul's thought. His agricultural metaphor brings out both aspects: a seed is sown and a plant grows from it. The plant is the *same* organism as the seed, but it is significantly *changed*. In the same way, when we die our body is like a seed planted in the ground. The resurrection body is the plant that emerges. It is the same body, but it is *very* different. Paul highlights some contrasts

THE CURRENT BODY Sown...	THE RESURRECTION BODY Harvested...
...perishable	...imperishable
...in dishonor	...in glory
...in weakness	...in power
...a natural body	...a spiritual body

Our body is currently like Adam's—of the dust of the earth. And, importantly, it is mortal, like his body. It gets sick, it ages, and it dies. Now this dusty body is not a bad thing; it is a good thing. But according to Paul it is *not the final stage* of the body. It is the caterpillar stage. God always intended humanity to reach a new phase in its life: the butterfly. Human sin blocks this transition from happening, but Christ has dealt with that obstacle. And Christ has become the one in whom our humanity is transformed from caterpillar to butterfly.

Jesus' risen body was the *same body* as before, not a substitute. That's why the tomb was empty and why Jesus still had the wounds from the crucifixion. Yet, he is not a mere resuscitated corpse or a zombie or a ghost. Jesus had been radically *changed*. While his glorified body could be touched (Luke 24:39; John 20:27) and could eat (Luke 24:41–43), it could also appear and disappear (24:31). It could get into locked rooms (John 20:19). And it is a body that is eternal, having an "indestructible life" (Heb 7:16). Our resurrection body, says Paul, will be like Christ's resurrection body—a real body, but a "spiritual" one, for the Holy Spirit, the very life of God, is animating it.

Now beyond this rather general claim we ought to have a large dose of agnosticism. The First Epistle of John says it well: "Dear friends, now we are children of God, and *what we will be has not yet been made known*. But we know that when Christ appears, *we shall be like him*, for we shall see him as he is" (1 John 3:2). We know *very little indeed* about the new age of the resurrection. The Bible provides hints and glimpses and a lot of symbolic imagery, but we need to own our ignorance. We have a lot of questions, and we simply don't know the answers. And that's fine. Because what we do know is enough: "we shall be like him."

3. The Death and Resurrection of Creation in Christ

Resurrection is not restricted to human beings. We can see this logic coming to the surface in St Paul's thought in Romans 8. Paul assures his audience that Christ's resurrection has future implications for them: "And if the Spirit of him [i.e., God, the Father] who raised Jesus from the dead is living in you, he who raised Christ from the dead will also give life to your mortal bodies because of his Spirit who lives in you" (Rom 8:11). Indeed, the resurrection has present implications too, for the Spirit of God, which resurrected Jesus, is already living in the believing community, so they should live lives *even now* empowered and guided by the Spirit of Life (8:12).

For New Testament writers, the resurrection remains a future hope, even if it can be "tasted" to some degree in the present age such that we can be said to have "eternal life" already. But what a hope! And how it enabled struggling and suffering believers to cope with situations that seemed hopeless: "I consider that our present sufferings are not worth comparing with the glory that will be revealed in us" (Rom 8:18). At this point, Paul expands his focus from his Christ-believing audience to the whole cosmos!

> 19 For the creation waits in eager expectation for the children of God to be revealed. 20 For the creation was subjected to frustration, not by its own choice, but by the will of the one who subjected it, in hope 21 that the creation itself will be liberated from its bondage to decay and brought into the freedom and glory of the children of God. 22 We know that the whole creation has been groaning as in the pains of childbirth right up to the present time. 23 Not only so, but we ourselves, who have

the firstfruits of the Spirit, groan inwardly as we wait eagerly for our adoption to sonship, the redemption of our bodies. 24 For in this hope we were saved. But hope that is seen is no hope at all. Who hopes for what they already have? 25 But if we hope for what we do not yet have, we wait for it patiently. 26 In the same way, the Spirit helps us in our weakness. We do not know what we ought to pray for, but the Spirit himself intercedes for us through wordless groans. 27 And he who searches our hearts knows the mind of the Spirit, because the Spirit intercedes for God's people in accordance with the will of God. (Rom 8:19–27)

Several important points are worth noticing here.

Creation—by which Paul means primarily *nonhuman* creation—is currently "subjected to frustration" and in "bondage to decay." For that reason, it has been "groaning as in the pains of childbirth." It has not chosen of its own will to be in this condition, but was subjected by the will of another, probably a reference to human mistreatment of the earth.[6]

Nonhuman creation is moaning in lament at its wounded and enslaved condition. This parallels the earlier discussion in the chapter in which Paul talks about sharing in Christ's sufferings (8:17). Suffering believers share in Christ's sufferings, but the nonhuman creation also shares in Jesus' passion. Precisely for that reason, while creation's lament is a howl of grief, it is not a cry of despair, for to share in Christ's passion opens up the hope of sharing in his resurrection glory. Thus, the inarticulate moans are also a cry of hope, for they are a prayer to the God who raises the dead. They are a plea for re-creation, making the groaning akin to the pained cry of a woman in childbirth, a precursor to new life. Along with the afflicted creation, the suffering Christ-community also groans and so too does the Spirit of God, which joins with creation in intercession, praying *in* and *through* the moans of nonhumans and humans. We might refer to this as "lament in the Spirit." God's Pneuma is at work even in the travails and sorrows of the earth, leading the world towards new creation. And that will be its exodus, its liberation from slavery, its glorification.

Here Paul is stretching the logic of Christ's resurrection beyond its implications for human beings to the entire cosmos.[7] *All of heaven and earth will share in Christ's risen life.* This is the "new heaven and earth" that Scripture anticipates (Isa 65:17; Rev 21–22). And just as we need to speak of both

---

6. For a defense of that claim, see Burroughs, *Creation's Slavery and Liberation*, 160–66. On the creation in Romans 8, see Moo and Moo, *Creation Care*, ch. 6.

7 For an excellent discussion of how this relates to the possibility of extraterrestrial life, especially intelligent extraterrestrial life, see Davison, *Astrobiology and Christian Doctrine*.

continuity and discontinuity between the old and the new when speaking of the resurrection of humans, so too with the rest of creation: new creation is not a displacement of or replacement for creation. Rather, it is *creation transfigured and elevated to the glory for which it was always intended*.[8] It is creation reaching its telos.

And just as we need to acknowledge our vast ignorance concerning our own human future with God, so too we must confess that we have nothing more than hints at the nature of the future glory of creation. In the end, our confidence and hope are grounded not in our great insight into the future, for we have little, but in the God who raised Jesus from the dead.

And here we see that in the Christian story, Jesus is the ultimate key to the grand mystery and meaning of the cosmos: where it is from, what it is for, where it is going, and how it gets there. The cosmos is *from* God and *to* God in its origin and destiny, but its relation to God is always actualized *through* Christ, the Wisdom of God—in its creation, in its salvation, and in its ultimate glorification. Knowing this changes the way we see the world and live in the world.

---

8. For a defense of this understanding of the fate of creation in NT eschatology, see Middleton, *New Heaven and a New Earth*, and Juza, *New Testament and the Future of the Cosmos*. For an excellent guide to understanding the cosmic dimensions of the new creation, see Moo and Moo, *Creation Care*, chs. 8–9.

10

The Spirit of Wisdom
Pentecost and Eco-Spirituality

1. The Spirit of Wisdom and the Trinity

WHAT OF THE HOLY Spirit? The very name "Spirit" is itself a metaphor. The Hebrew word *rûaḥ* and the Greek *pneuma* both can mean "breath" or "wind" or "spirit." The connection is not hard to understand. Breath and wind are both invisible to the human eye yet have a noticeable effect on the world around us. So, to speak of the spirit of a creature (whether human or nonhuman) or of God's Spirit is to use a metaphor drawn from our mundane experiences of the movement of the air and of our own breath. It's a way that our language and thought can get some feeble grasp on that which is fundamentally mysterious.

Now, God's Holy Breath is also connected with divine Wisdom. The Spirit imparts to human beings the wisdom needed for practical activities, from craftsmanship (Exod 32:2–5) to service (Acts 6:3) to governance (Isa 11:2). As such the Spirit of God is:

> the Spirit of *wisdom* and *understanding*,
> the Spirit of *counsel* and might,

the Spirit of *knowledge* and the fear of YHWH. (Isa 11:2, cf. Deut 34:9)

There is thus an especially strong connection between the Spirit and the *revelation* of God's wisdom. The Spirit inspires the prophets with oracles and visions (2 Pet 1:21). This prophetic and apocalyptic strand in Israel's Scriptures was prominent in the thought of St. Paul, who speaks of the wisdom of God's purposes in human history, hidden from sight for generations but now revealed in the Christ-event. And the meaning of the Christ-event—that, contrary to appearances, God's power and wisdom are ultimately manifest in this man and his humiliating death—is made known to the community of believers *through the work of God's Spirit* (1 Cor 2:1–16). This is why Ephesians speaks of "the Spirit of wisdom and revelation" (Eph 1:17).

It would seem then that the Spirit is very closely associated with God's Wisdom. Not in the sense that the Spirit is *identified* with her. Rather, the Spirit *mediates* or *imparts* or *reveals* God's Wisdom to people. The Spirit is "the Spirit of wisdom" because it is the Spirit *of Jesus*. The Wisdom that the Spirit reveals is, at its most fundamental level, *Christ* (John 16:12–15), and Christ crucified (1 Cor 1:18—2:16).

In terms of a wisdom vision of God, then, we might speak of:

1. the wise God
2. the Wisdom of God (Christ)
3. the Spirit of Wisdom

As Christians reflected on and clarified this vision over the early centuries of the church, these three were understood to be the three "persons" of the one God—usually referred to as the Father, the Son, and the Spirit, though that is not the only biblical pattern of naming the three.[1]

The Spirit is ever present and active in the world as the means through which Christ-Sophia is present and working in creation. The Spirit *connects* us with Christ-Sophia, conducting the presence and activity of Jesus like water conducts electricity.

Consequently, *any* human wisdom that reflects true Wisdom from above is ultimately rooted in God and is an encounter with Christ-Sophia mediated by the Spirit of Sophia, even if we do not realize that it is such, indeed, even if we do not believe in the reality of God.

---

1. On diverse patterns of naming the three "persons," see Soulen, *Divine Name(s) and the Holy Trinity*.

EXCURSUS: Relationality in Creation and the Trinity

The doctrine of the Trinity—that God is one being (Greek: *ousia*) in three "persons" (Greek: *hypostases*)—is mind-blowing, marvelous, and mysterious, and I have no intention of getting into it here, save to make a single point. It reveals God—the most fundamental level of reality, the "Ground of all being"—to be *essentially relational*. To use traditional language: the eternal identity of the Father is constituted by his relationship to the Son, and vice versa. The Spirit is the bond of love between them and is co-beloved and co-lover.[2] Each of the three "persons" is only who they are by virtue of their relation to the other "persons."

As creation reflects something of the Creator, similar to the way that art reflects something of the artist, this leads us to expect a world that is not merely a collection of self-contained parts, parts complete in themselves, which are then simply put together into relationship. Rather, no part has an identity apart from its relationship to the other parts. The world is relationships all the way down to its foundations. And that is precisely what the sciences, including biology and ecology, are making clearer and clearer to us. Ecosystems are complex *systems*, defined by the interrelationships within them and between them. No part can be understood apart from its relations.

And it is not only biology and ecology, modern physics is also pointing in this direction. Zachary Hayes comments:

> By and large, it has been assumed that the subatomic particles are isolated and independent particles. Yet in the quark research being done at Fermilab near Chicago it seems that quarks are discerned only in groups. If quarks are really the end of the line in the search for the ultimate building blocks, this may mean that the so-called building blocks are not isolated monadic blocks but are relational complexes. This points to the possibility that the cosmos is really systems within systems all the way down, and all the way out. If this is the case, then it seems that created reality is through and through relational. With that in mind, we can recall the core insight of the traditional Trinitarian concept of God: namely, that the divine reality is intrinsically relational in character. It may well be, then, that Christian believers today can see the cosmos as grounded in and as reflecting the relational character of the Trinity.[3]

---

2. This is an essentially Augustinian theology with a twist from Richard of St. Victor.
3. Hayes, *Gift of Being*, 69.

A creation in which we find that everything is interrelated, interconnected, and interpenetrating is a core insight of recent ecological thinking and is very "fitting," given the identity of the God revealed in the gospel.

2. The Spirit in Creation

All God's acts in relation to creation are the activity of the three "persons" of the Trinity working as one. God always engages the world *through* the Son and *by* or *in* the Spirit. This is so whether we are speaking of the activity of creation, providence, redemption, or the final re-creation of the world. And the reverse is true too: creation's approach to God is *through* the Son, *by* the Spirit (Eph 2:18), even if we are oblivious to it.

With that in mind, let's return our gaze to the "third person" of the Trinity, the Breath of God, but move the focus to matters concerning creation. The Spirit is deeply connected to the cosmos. And this shouldn't surprise us.

In the opening creation story of the Bible, the curtain lifts on a disorderly, swirling chaos, incapable of supporting life: "Now the earth was formless and empty, darkness was over the surface of the deep . . ." (Gen 1:2a). Yet even then, in this primeval state, we see that the *Rûaḥ* (Wind/Spirit) of God is moving over the surface of the deep (Gen 1:2b). No explanation is given of the presence of the divine Wind here, but it hints at a sense of pregnant expectation—of God's *Rûaḥ* moving, perhaps in anticipation of what is to come.

Other biblical texts understand the Spirit of God to be ubiquitous in the world; most famously in Psalm 139's rhetorical question: "Where can I go from your Spirit? Where can I flee from your presence?" (v. 7). The answer is: *nowhere*. The enigmatic divine Breath is everywhere we go, before we get there and after we leave.

In the Bible, there's a particularly strong association of the Spirit with life. It's not hard to see why. The connection between breath and life is intuitive: when we're breathing, we're alive; when we stop breathing, we die. So the Bible associates God's Breath with the impartation of life in creation. "Then YHWH God formed a human from the dust of the ground and breathed into his nostrils the breath of life, and the human became a living being (Hebrew: *nepheš*)" (Gen 2:7); "This is what YHWH God says—the Creator of the heavens, . . . who gives breath to its people, and spirit/breath (*rûaḥ*) to those who walk on it" (Isa 42:5).

And it's not only humans: *everything* that has breath has its life-breath from God and is "a living being" because of God (e.g., Gen 7:22). That is most clearly put in a section of Psalm 104. God provides food to sustain creatures, and in due course God takes away the life-breath from them (vv. 27–30). Then God sends out his own Breath so that life is renewed on the earth, as the circle continues.

> When you send your Breath [Spirit] (*rûaḥ*),
> they [all creatures] are created,
> and you renew the face of the ground. (v. 30)

This isn't describing miraculous divine interventions in a world that otherwise functions perfectly well without God. It's about the mundane, everyday emergence and sustaining of life in the world, through processes immanent within the world—and the Spirit of God is seen to be at work *in* and *through* this. In the twelfth century the Benedictine nun Hildegard of Bingen captured something of the Spirit's dynamic life-giving role in a beautiful hymn:

> O comforting fire of Spirit,
> Life, within the very life of all creation.
> Holy you are in giving life to all. . . .
>
> O mightiest path which penetrates all,
> from the height to every earthly abyss,
> you compose all, you unite all.
>
> Through you clouds stream, ether flies,
> stones gain moisture,
> waters become streams,
> and the earth exudes life. . . .

This connection of the Spirit and life not only concerns ordinary biological life. The New Testament places a special emphasis on the spiritual, eternal, resurrection life of the age to come. This new life or new creation is also bestowed by God's Pneuma. It was through the Spirit that God raised Jesus from the dead and this is the very same Spirit who now lives in Christ's followers. The Spirit's presence in them is both a gift of eternal life in the present (for the Spirit *is* the eternal Life-Breath of God in them) and a promise of a fuller, resurrection life yet to come in the new age (Rom 8:11).

And it's not only human beings who can anticipate resurrection life: as we've seen, Paul speaks of *the whole nonhuman creation* longing to share in this same liberation, this new creation achieved through the work of Jesus. And share it will (Rom 8:22–25).

The Spirit is at work in creation guiding it towards the life to come, a life that the Spirit imparts; indeed, a life that the Spirit herself *is*. This is what Gregory of Nyssa meant when he said "every activity that pervades from

God to creation . . . *starts off* from the Father, *proceeds* through the Son, and *is completed* by the Holy Spirit."[4] Or as Jürgen Moltmann puts it, "It is always the Spirit who first brings the activity of the Father and the Son to its goal."[5] The Spirit works within the world to draw it towards the destiny for which it was created, a destiny of eternal union with God, of Life in all its fullness.

Physicist and priest John Polkinghorne developed the implications of recent physics in ways that resonate with a theology in which Wisdom/Word is manifest in the order of the world and Spirit in its life, freedom, and movement towards the future:

> The scientific picture implies that creation is a world of true becoming and not a world of static being. . . . Here order and openness so interlace that the state of affairs is neither so rigid that nothing really new can ever come about, nor so haphazard that nothing new can ever persist. . . . A Trinitarian theology of nature has some resonance with this insight. The Father is the fundamental ground of creation's being, while the Word [Wisdom] is the source of creation's deep order, and the Spirit is ceaselessly at work within the contingencies of open history. The fertile interplay of order and openness, operating at the edge of chaos, can be seen to reflect the activities of Word and Spirit, the two divine Persons that Irenaeus called "the hands of God."[6]

3. Pentecost and the Christ-Community

What of the church? Fifty days after the resurrection, during the Jewish Feast of Weeks/Pentecost, God poured out the Spirit upon the Christ-community in a new way, as Jesus had promised (Acts 1:8; 2:1–4). Many Jewish people were expecting the new age of God's kingdom to be marked by the giving of the Spirit to change Israel from the inside out and empower them to walk in God's ways (Ezek 36:24–28). This would be the mark of a new covenant (Jer 31:31–34). The earliest followers of Jesus understood themselves to be experiencing the dawning of this new-covenant era of the Spirit—the time of new creation, the coming of the kingdom—even in the middle of the present era.

For the writers of the New Testament, the life of Christ-followers is currently one of tension, living caught in the messy crossover of the current

---

4. Gregory of Nyssa, "On Not Three Gods, to Ablabius."
5. Moltmann, *God in Creation*, 9.
6. Polkinghorne, *Science and the Trinity*, 80–81.

age and the future age. The resurrection life given by the Spirit still lay ahead of them and was experienced in the present as a *hope*. Their current experience is marked by the cross, the suffering and darkness of this age. But *even now*, in anticipation of the resurrection, the Spirit had been given to them, as a down payment (Eph 1:13–14) and to grant them a foretaste of the coming age (Heb 6:4–5). It is the Spirit of the new creation that gives boldness and empowers witness (Acts 4:31), that gives gifts for ministry (1 Cor 12–14), and that works to transform the believing community into the pattern of Jesus (Gal 5:13–26). It is the Spirit that defines the Christ-following life. In truth, *Christian spirituality is nothing more nor less than a life lived in Christ (i.e., living out our baptism) through the Spirit.*

However, Christians tend to think of the Spirit's work simply in terms of building up the church community and empowering its mission. And those are indeed components of the Spirit's work. Yet, when we appreciate the Spirit's activity in creation, both its day-to-day rhythms of life and in drawing the creation towards its resurrection future, we need to consider what it might look like to co-inhabit our environments in "pentecostal" ways.

a) Acts of Faithful Eco-Witness

The church's first calling is not to save the world but *to be the church*. Saving the world is not our responsibility. Rather, the church is called *to bear witness to God's redemption of the world in Christ*, and it does this by seeking to live its communal life in Christ, with the help of the Spirit.

You might think that sounds very otherworldly. And that would be understandable. It would also be a mistake. The church sees itself as a community gathered by Jesus and constituted by the Spirit as Christ's body (1 Cor 12:13). As the body of the risen Lord, it is called to anticipate the restoration of humanity in its way of being in the world, to embody something of the new creation in the present. That future is one without sin, and so believers are called to walk in the Spirit and not to satisfy the desires of the flesh (Gal 5:16). This is a journey of sanctification, never complete in this age but always pursued. Similarly, the new creation is a time of shalom, so peaceable and loving relations are to govern the Messiah-community and its engagement with others.[7] The vices that early Christ-followers were to reject were mostly community-destroying vices (like gossip or greed or anger or marital infidelity), while the virtues encouraged were community-building traits (like love, gentleness, and generosity). The coming kingdom

---

7. John 13:34; Gal 6:10; Rom 12:9–21; 13:8–10.

is pictured as an age in which every nation on earth will set aside animosity and conflict and join peaceably with Israel in worshipping the one true God. So the church was to be a multiethnic rainbow community of equals drawn from every nation and language worshipping as one (Gal 3:26–29). In these and other ways, the church is supposed to exist as *a prophetic foretaste of the age to come*, to model a more human way of being in the world. Depressingly, the reality is often *far* from the calling. *Nonetheless, the calling remains.*

So the church's first responsibility is *to be the church*—to inhabit the world in a Spirit-filled, gospel-shaped, new-creation way, and in doing so to bear witness to the gospel of Christ—to proclaim his good news in word and action.

And what does any of that have to do with ecology? A lot. To live in creation as Spirit-filled human beings representing Jesus is to seek to live in creation as it currently is, facing the reality of its travails, but also with a vision of its origin and destiny in God and all that such entails. It is to seek to live truly wise human lives—as individuals and as a Christian community at local, national, and international levels—in relation to other humans and to the rest of the world. And that *cannot but* include how we treat our natural environments.

An analogy with sin in general may help to explain this. For Paul, Jesus broke the power of sin over humanity in his death and resurrection. Those who are baptized have been baptized into his death and resurrection (Rom 6). They have been baptized in the Spirit into Christ (1 Cor 12:13). As such, they have entered, albeit in an anticipatory way, into the resurrection age. Thus, Paul urges them to *live out their baptism:* to put to death sin and to walk in newness of life. Sin has no place in the life in Christ. So the journey of sanctification—of becoming more like Jesus, more human—is a journey into a future already achieved in Christ and made possible by Christ in the Spirit. For Paul and all the other early Christ-believers, and for the church ever since, the suggestion that we can carry on sinning with impunity and must simply await the future in which God will fix us is anathema (Rom 6:1–2). *Exactly the same dynamic* is at work in the way Christians interact with the wider creation. The liberation from oppression and destruction Christ has achieved for the cosmos is something those "in Christ" *must seek to anticipate in the present*. As creation will rejoice in redeemed humanity, which will no longer oppress it, so the church must seek to model such non-oppressive ways of relating to the rest of the world *right now*. That is what God's kingdom and walking in the Spirit look like in relation to our environments. A church living in the world in creation-abusing ways is rejecting an important dimension of the gospel. It is "giving the finger" to the new creation. Indeed, it is quite literally *anti-Christ*. Such behavior still bears witness, but a *false* witness. It proclaims a "gospel," but not the gospel of Jesus.

The mission of the church is really nothing other than its participation in the *missio Dei*, *God's own* mission in creation. God eternally "sends out" (Latin: *missio*, to send) his Wisdom and his Spirit. They were described by Irenaeus in the second century as "the two hands of the Father." What he meant was that every engagement of God with creation is by means of God's Wisdom and God's Spirit. Through them YHWH creates the world and works in the world to guide it and redeem it and bring it to its destiny. The *missio Dei* has always been creation-wide in its scope. And the mission of the church, as a participation in God's mission, is likewise broad in its scope. The church is called to play its part, joining in with the liberating mission of Jesus through the enabling of the Spirit.

Perhaps a helpful analogy for Christian environmental action is the healing stories we find in the New Testament. Jesus and the apostles were known as healers. When they encountered sickness, they sought to bring healing. And such healings were understood to be a sign that the coming kingdom of God was erupting into the present. Nevertheless, those healings were only temporary. All those who were healed eventually died. And even those brought back from the dead eventually died again. The healings were not the fullness of life, which only the final resurrection of the dead can bring. Rather, they were *prophetic anticipations* of it. Signs.

Does that mean that they were a waste of time, being only temporary fixes? If we thought that, nobody would ever be a doctor and nobody would bother going to a hospital. Healing, even partial improvement, brings real transformative blessing. It is to be pursued and welcomed with thanksgiving. And it can be a sign of a deeper healing to come.

In the same way, the church is called to a healing ministry that extends beyond humans to the wider creation. Healing and blessing creation are goals to be pursued and welcomed with thanksgiving, for they are, among other things, signs of the new creation. That they are temporary does not make them pointless. Acts of environmental blessing and healing are acts of gospel witness. This is why, in 1984, the Anglican Communion defined five marks of the church's mission, the fifth of which is "to strive to safeguard the integrity of creation, and sustain and renew the life of the earth." There may well be more to mission than this, but there is certainly not less.

b) Eco-Prophets in the Spirit

The church is not called to save the world, but it is called to embody in its communal life the values of the future. It is called to engage in acts of kingdom witness in the world. One specific aspect of that is to speak truth to those with power and influence.

The Spirit inspires prophets who speak YHWH's challenging (and often unwelcome) word for their times. There is a prophetic aspect to the mission of the church today: speaking the word of the Lord to the wider world, empowered by the Spirit. And a part of that prophetic ministry will be ecological. Indeed, we should note that Israel's prophets spoke messages into their own specific situations, words for their time and season. So in our own time of unprecedented ecological emergency, it should not be surprising that the prophetic ministry of the Christ-community is taking on an increasingly ecological edge. *Of course* God has something to say about our treatment of the planet! *Of course* God is calling for a change of mind and behavior.

And sadly, though unsurprisingly, some in the community of the church are triggered by the prophets and mock them and seek to silence them, even imagining that by doing so they are serving God. Witness the climate change denial amongst some Christians. Their response is dressed in a few conveniently selected scraps of clothing from theology and science, feebly covering up its nakedness and trying to pass as both devout and reasonable, but at its root it is motivated by neither science nor faith but by very different commitments and fears. The Spirit of Sophia, however, will not be silenced. The prophets will keep on speaking. And we will either listen, and live, or reject their word and perish.

The Spirit is not restricted to the church. Just as God's Wisdom was believed to be found beyond the community of Israel, so too the Spirit was believed to be able to speak through prophets outside of Israel (like Balaam in Numbers). There are many voices speaking into ecological matters that could be seen as influenced by God's prophetic Spirit of Wisdom. Both Sophia and the Spirit are at work across the world, so we look and listen for their presence wherever it manifests.

c) Saints

The word "saint" translates the Greek *hagios*, meaning holy one, someone who has been set aside for God. In the New Testament it refers to *all* followers of Jesus. However, certain Christ-followers model what it means to live a life set aside for God in a more exemplary way, and they are the folk usually referred to in churches as "the saints"—we might say that "the saints" are saints whom the church feels were especially good at being saints. They exemplify aspects of the Spirit-filled life in ways that can inspire the rest of us.

One recurring feature of the lives of many saints is their relationship with the rest of the natural world. The saints very often love nature. For, as St. Athonite notes, "Anyone who loves God loves not only his fellow man, but the entire creation as well: trees, grass, flowers. He loves everything with the same love."[8] And the natural world often responded to saints with mutual "love." I think, for instance, of the story of the lion from whose paw St. Jerome extracted a painful thorn. In the story, the lion showed its gratitude by becoming the saint's companion.[9]

The stories of the saints abound with tales of nature becoming more harmonious in the vicinity of holy people. The idea of peaceful Edenic relations between humans and animals seems to lie behind such stories. One example is the tale of a fifteenth-century Russian hermit, Paul of Obnura. A visiting monk was said to have been astonished to find the saint with

---

8. Quoted in Theokritoff, *Living in God's Creation*, 119.

9. "Saint Jérôme dans son cabinet" de Colantino (Musée du Louvre, Paris). Reproduced under Wiki Commons license.

birds perched all over him, eating out of his hand, while a bear sat nearby waiting its turn. Around them ran foxes and rabbits getting along peaceably and showing no fear of the bear. In a way, it does not matter whether this is a historically accurate account, for its value is in offering a vision of ideal relations between humans and nonhuman animals.

Saints also seem able to persuade animals to stop terrorizing human communities. For instance, a desert father who through his gentle approach managed to persuade a giant hippo and a crocodile to leave a harassed farmer's land alone.[10] Or the famous wolf that struck fear into the citizens of the city of Gubbio yet was tamed with a word by St. Francis.

St. Francis is, for good reason, seen as a saint of special interest for those with an ecological focus. He regarded all creatures as his brothers and sisters, addressing them as such, and stories abound about his interactions with birds, insects, worms, mammals, fish, plants, and inanimate creatures such as rocks and water. His last great contribution before his death was the beautiful "Canticle of Creation," a hymn of praise to God for the manifold blessings of creation.[11]

St Melangell and the hare[12]

I have to mention just one more example: St. Melangell, a seventh-century Irish woman who lived as a hermit in Wales. One day the prince of Powys was taking part in a hunt in the valley in which she lived. The hunt was pursuing a hare, and the terrified creature fled for cover beneath Melangell's cloak. She stood her ground and refused to allow the hunting party near the creature. A holy hunt saboteur. So impressed was the prince that he gave her the valley as a place of sanctuary for animals and paid for a place of worship to be built for her. She subsequently became the abbess of a community there and remains the patron saint of hares.

Saints, while not perfect, and very much people of their own times and places, can be seen as Spirit-inspired examples of godliness who gesture towards more respectful relationships with nonhuman creation. As such, they can be a resource for Christian eco-spirituality.

---

10. Russell, trans., *Lives of the Desert Fathers*, 66.

11. On St. Francis and the Canticle, see Cocksedge, Double, and Worssam, *Seeing Differently*.

12. Handcrafted model by Hannah Parry.

4. The Spirit and Eco-Spirituality

Eco-spirituality, as I understand it, is a holistic matter of a life increasingly integrated, in which belief, worship, prayer, character, and everyday living form a seamless garment of love for God and love for neighbor (whether that neighbor be human or not). However, what makes this integrated life a "spirituality" is not merely that it concerns the human "spirit" or the "spirit" of nature or such like. For Christians, it is a first and foremost a spirituality because it is enabled by *God's Spirit*. Let me very briefly sketch this idea to close the first section of this book.

Think about religious belief. In the New Testament, the Spirit of Wisdom is the Spirit of truth and of revelation,[13] the one who reveals Christ-Sophia and enables our hearts to open up to Wisdom in faith.[14] There is no true knowledge of God that is not the result of the work of the Spirit. God reveals God through God.

Worship and prayer are also a fruit of the Spirit's work. Believers approach the Father through Christ *in the Spirit* (Eph 2:18) and are urged to "pray in the Spirit" (Eph 6:18). When we don't have the words, the Spirit prays for and in us in groanings that cannot be put into words (Rom 8:26–27). Worship too is to be "in Spirit and in truth" (John 4:23–24). As Paul comments, we "worship by the Spirit of God" (Phil 3:3).

Likewise, ethical living: "the fruit of the Spirit is love, joy, peace, forbearance, kindness, goodness, faithfulness, gentleness, and self-control" (Gal 5:22–23). These are the character traits, the virtues, that God seeks to cultivate in the community of Jesus, and they are the Spirit's work.

Similarly, we could see the Spirit as integral to the *relationality* of creation. A cosmos is not a collection of discrete things-complete-in-themselves, thrown together and bouncing off each other, but a web of things-in-relation, things that are only what they are by virtue of their interconnections. As Paul's metaphor of the church as the body of Christ makes clear, the Spirit connects and unifies without obliterating diversity and distinctiveness—allowing individual creatures to thrive as the creatures they are in relation to others (Rom 12; 1 Cor 12). Jürgen Moltmann suggests that:

> God the Spirit is also the Spirit of the universe, its total cohesion, its structure, its information, its energy. . . . The evolutions and catastrophes of the universe are also the movements and experiences of the Spirit in creation. That is why Paul tells us that the divine Spirit "sighs" in all created things under the power

---

13. Isa 11:2; John 15:26; 16:13; 1 Cor 2:10–16; Eph 1:17.
14. John 15:26; 16:12–15; 1 Cor 2:10–16; 12:3.

of futility. That is why the divine Spirit transcends himself in all created beings. This is manifested in the self-organization and the self-transcendence of all living things.[15]

A Christian eco-spirituality will seek to discern and cooperate with the Spirit's work in facilitating and healing relationships within creation, including those essential for the health of the earth.

There is no Christian spirituality, no integrated life of faith, love, and hope, without the Spirit. Which means that any Christian eco-spirituality—its belief, praxis, affections, liturgy—must understand itself to be a *Spirituality*. It is of course *our* response to God's initiative, but even that response is a *"gifted* response,"[16] one utterly dependent upon God.

---

15. Moltmann, *God in Creation*, 16.

16. Credit to Matt Redman for this phrase, which he coined under the inspiration of J. B. Torrance.

Conclusion to Part I

WISDOM THEOLOGY AFFIRMS THE divine goodness, beauty, and wisdom in the cosmic order, from the micro-level to the macro-level. There is a way that the world *is*, which is simply a given. We discover it, we do not invent it. We either work with it, going with the grain of the universe, or we foolishly ignore it and pay the price. Christians will see that the wisdom perceived in the world is not only the *same* divine Wisdom that was revealed in the law of Moses but also the same Wisdom who walked among us as a human being. Walking the path of wisdom is walking the path of Christ.

The *enfleshing* of Holy Sophia as Jesus of Nazareth is hugely important for shaping the spirituality of Christian engagement with the world. "The flesh assumed in Jesus Christ connects with all humanity, all biological life, all soil, the whole matrix of the material universe down to its very roots."[1]

And the resurrection of Christ-Sophia is God's affirmation of the goodness of embodiment and a promise of hope for its future.

It is the Spirit who works to guide the creation towards its eschatological destiny and who empowers the Christ-community to participate in prophetic anticipations of the age to come.

---

1. Johnson, *Ask the Beasts*, 196.

PART II

Inhabiting The Story

A Wise Worship

11

The A to Z of Wild Worship

OK. I LIED. This chapter title is misleading. For a start, there is no entry for A or for Z, perhaps because my musings here are neither the first nor the last word on the subject. Secondly, the points are not arranged alphabetically. Maybe that's to make the point that there is no single, logical, and tidy way through this subject. Or perhaps the whole chapter was an alphabetic experiment that went horribly wrong. You, the reader, must decide.

We turn our gaze to worship. Now, I am not going to tell you how creation-attuned worship should look—at least not in any detail. It can look like all sorts of things, depending on your local environment, your church tradition, the people who gather with you, your cultural context, and a whole host of other variables. Instead, what I aim to share is some of the principles that have helped me to think through what creation-attuned worship might look like. I hope that you find at least some of them to be useful provocations.

1. Y is for YHWH-Centric

Christian eco-spirituality is not creation-centered, it is *God*-centered. That may sound like semantics, but it's an important principle to keep in mind if our worship is to be an expression of Christian faith. We can gather as Christians and do all sorts of worthwhile things out in nature, "spiritual" things included, like mindfulness. And we should. I am not criticizing any of that for a moment. But when it comes to worship, we need to remember that worship is offered *to God*.

Why does God require our exclusive worship? Is worship merely a way to boost a flagging divine self-esteem? Or is God some kind of supreme egomaniac in constant need of flattery, craving for everyone to lick his boots?

As we saw in chapter 5, according to the Christian doctrine of creation out of nothing, God does not *need* the universe at all. God has no inner "hole" that needs filling. Consequently, whatever worship is for, it isn't for *God's* benefit (Ps 50:10–12; Acts 17:25). So how should we think of it?

Let's approach that question by entering through the doorway of an olde word. The English word "worship" derives from the Anglo-Saxon *weorthscipe* (worth-ship). It's an acknowledgment through our ritual actions of the value of someone. It could be a recognition of the worth of a noble person, whom we honor, or of God. Now, with that in mind, recall the Sophia worldview sketched throughout Part I of this book. God, out of gratuitous goodness and love, created the cosmos. The world derives its being from the Creator at every moment of its existence. Its patterns and rationality are the work of the second person of the Trinity (Sophia/Logos) and its life and development that of the third (the Spirit). For human creatures to worship God is for us to discern and acknowledge something of the most fundamental contours of the world we indwell and to seek to orientate ourselves accordingly, to work with the grain of the universe, to sing in tune with the world. Worship is about such orientation.

This offers an angle on what makes idolatry problematic. Idolatry is to treat something that is not of supreme value as though it is of supreme value. Whether that "something" is a part of the universe or the whole universe[1] itself, it is to invest ultimate value in the *creation* rather than the transcendent *Creator* (Rom 1:25). It is to have immanence without transcendence. This is to misread the contours of the world and to orientate our lives in ways that run, in some respects at least, contrary to them. And that's not what is best *for us*. It grates against the very deepest structures of our identity as creatures, for, in the words of St. Augustine, "You have made us for Yourself, and our hearts are restless until they find rest in You" (*Confessions* 1.1).

From a Christian perspective, not only can idolatry be harmful to humans, but it's also dishonoring to the objects of our worship. Ironically, if we worship, say, the universe as "God," we are disrespecting it, because the universe finds its meaning and destiny *beyond itself*. It cannot bear the weight of ultimate value we place upon it and, as a creature, if it "sought" such worship, it would be harming itself. That's why the angel in the book of

---

1. Or "multiverse" if that is your tipple.

Revelation tells John not to worship him (22:9). Angels, as all other creatures (including the cosmos as a whole), are simply fellow worshippers. Hence, the vision of worship in the book of Revelation: a throne at the heart of reality on which is seated God and Christ (Rev 4–5). Around that throne in concentric circles expanding outward like ripples on a pond, we see "every creature in heaven and on earth and under the earth and on the sea, and all that is in them" (Rev 5:13). This is the unified community of creation with their compass needles directed to true north.

However, all that said, the theology of creation outlined in this book does advocate both for the recognition of the true goodness, truth, and beauty of God's creatures and for the need to honor them. Creation may not be the Divine, but *it is sacred*. Ironically, some Christians who are hyper-eager to avoid idolatry can, in their zeal, sometimes end up *dishonoring* God's good earth, evacuating it of divinity, and in so doing they dishonor *God*. This is the danger of divine transcendence without divine immanence, a theological mistake that makes God "distant." There's a tightrope to walk here, for there *is* an appropriate kind of "worship" that can be offered to creatures. Perhaps we might say that Worship (capital W) is due to God alone, but worship (lower case w) is due to creatures.[2] After all, aspects of the Divine can be seen in creation, from the humblest amoeba to Mother Earth herself. The world is saturated with divine presence and glory, a fitting palace for God. As Calvin writes, the Lord "irradiates the whole world in his splendour," the world being "the garment in which he, hidden in himself, appears in a manner visible to us."[3] And honoring nature around us, treating it with deep respect and learning to love it, perceiving and acknowledging the refracted presence of God in it, is precisely the kind of thing Christians *ought* to be doing. We do not worship creation, but we must reverence it.

This helps us to see that some of what Christians consider misdirected worship is misdirected in a very particular and understandable way—a way in which we can discern real goodness. From a Christian perspective, those who (capital W) Worship Mother Earth or the sun, for instance, can be thought of as genuinely perceiving and acknowledging the immanent presence of the Divine in the world. And they seek to honor it and love it, as Christians do. How can that not be a *good* thing? The error, from a Christian perspective, is to lose sight of transcendence, thus not track the beauty and life we perceive back to its True Source. It is like looking at light streaming through a window and becoming fixated on the window as the source of light rather than peering *through* it. Or perhaps it is a little bit like getting

---

2. For the rest of this Y section, I shall retain this capping practice.
3. Calvin, *Psalms 93–150*, 145.

on a train from Glasgow to London and getting off at Carlisle. It's the right train, heading in the right direction, but we mistook the end of the line.

What I am saying is that Christians should welcome and seek to learn from the insights and instincts behind any sincere responses to genuine glimpses of the Divine Light in the world.[4] After all, some biblical authors regarded stars and the sun and moon as gods. Yes, you heard that right.[5] The celestial lights were the astral bodies of deities, and as such they were glorious and honorable. They "rule" the night and day on behalf of God (Gen 1:16). In biblical thought, the sun in its glory could even serve to symbolize YHWH himself.[6] Remember, its light is a participation in, and dim reflection of, the Divine Light. It is a symbol pointing beyond itself. The instinct behind that biblical association is running along similar tracks, at least for a while, to the instincts of those among ancient pagans who saw the sun as God. Nevertheless, biblical authors were clear that the celestial deities were not to be the objects of Worship. They are esteemed created gods, not the Creator God; they are divine, not the Divine; they even deserve worship (in the sense of a respectful recognition of their worth), but never Worship.

One final thing to flag up: Christian eco-worship will not be blandly theocentric, for the God at its center is the *triune* God of Israel revealed in Christ. Thus, it will be *Christ-centered* and *Trinitarian* (with due acknowledgement of and openness to the Spirit). The Sophia theology outlined in Part I provides the basis for thinking through such worship.

2. F is for Formation

So the God-focus of worship is for *our* benefit. It should orientate us and equip us in an ongoing way in our journeys towards Christlikeness. It is, in other words, *formative*. Worship shapes us and forms us in our faith and actions: *lex orandi, lex credendi, lex vivendi* ("the rule of what is prayed is the rule of what is believed is the rule of what is lived"). It should be a school that contributes to our learning in our bones how to be human in God's world. It teaches worshippers habits of thought and imagination and practice.

---

4. C. S. Lewis suggests that God might even count Worship offered to "idols," even if not ideal, *as* worship offered to God if (a) it was a response to a genuine revelation of divine presence in creation and (b) was a sincere attempt to respond aright to that divine revelation (cf. the conversation between the idolater Emeth and Aslan in Lewis's *Last Battle*, 164–65).

5. For a defense of this seemingly outrageous claim, see Parry, *Biblical Cosmos*, ch. 5, "Eyes in Their Stars."

6. See Brown, *Seeing the Psalms*, ch. 4, "Sun of Righteousness."

What difference would it make to us if our worship was more alive to the breadth of creation? If we made it integral to its warp and weft to worship God, yes, *for* nonhuman creatures, but also *with* nonhuman creatures and *on behalf of* nonhuman creatures?

Worship *for* creation is not so alien to us. We give thanks to God "for the beauty of the earth, for the glory of the skies." We express gratitude for the harvests and rains, and awe when we "see the stars and hear the distant thunder, thy power throughout the universe displayed." And this is important. It fosters our sense of *wonder* at, our *gratitude* for, and our *esteem* of the gift of creation. All that is very formative. But what about worship *with* and *on behalf of* other creatures?

What if we spoke, with Saint Francis, of "Mother Earth"; of "brothers" sun, wind, bee, and wolf; of "sisters" moon, water, sparrow, and cow? What if our worship encouraged such ways of relating? How might it affect our patterns of thinking and feeling and acting?

Practicing worship *with* other creatures reminds us that the cosmos is not all about us-and-God. Locating our relationship with God in relation to God's engagement with other creatures knocks us down a peg or two, as Job discovered. It helps us to appreciate that God and nonhuman creatures relate to each other, and in some mode "address" each other. *What* they say to one another is mostly none of our business, and that too is important for us to grasp. Such worship could help us to *feel* the truth that other creatures are, like us, *creatures*. And each has its own valuable niche and place within the whole. Such worship can decenter humans, without demeaning us. It places our worship within a wider context—singing our part in a cosmic hymn of praise that needs *all* the voices.

The words we use in worship can help in this shift in consciousness, but it's never only the words. What if we made *outdoor* communal worship a feature of our practice and incorporated hands-on, fully embodied, multisensory engagement with and blessing of the natural world around us as part of the worship? How might that help form our affections and motivate healthier, integrally Christian ways of living in the world?

Here there is much to learn from animism (worldviews in which all things are alive and in some sense "persons"). Tim Ingold states, "animism is . . . not a way of thinking *about* the world but of being alive *to* it."[7] Thomas Hughson adds that "Being alive to it is being alive with it and in it. The characteristic of animism lies in 'heightened sensitivity and responsiveness, in perception and action, to an environment that is in perpetual flux, never the

---

7. Ingold, *Being Alive*, 214.

same from one moment to the next."[8] Perhaps we need to relearn something of that *being alive to nature*, and perhaps worship can be one way of doing so.

My intuition is that such liturgy has the potential to foster a more reverential way to understand our fellow creatures. Considering a forest or an animal as a co-worshipper suggests certain ethical ways of relating to them and treating them. It also frames other ways that we might relate to them as sacrilegious. "Mountaintop removal, clear cutting, aggressive use of fertilizers and pesticides, and careless oil drilling looks very different when these acts are not only extractive resource management, but also dysfunctional relationships with persons created and valued by God."[9] Jesus said not to come and offer our sacrifice of worship if our neighbor has anything against us. What if we expand our understanding of who our "neighbor" is? What would that do?

Finally, taking up our priestly role as humans and worshipping *on behalf of* nonhuman creatures is to "elevate" creation's praises in our own, thereby *focusing on* and *making manifest* something of the divine glory in creation. This is worship as a mode of art, of craft, of imagination, of poetry. And it too has the potential to shape the way we "see" and value nonhuman creation.

Becoming aware of the formative power of worship, it can be tempting to think that the key reason it should be more creation-attuned is so that Christians can be better equipped to deal with the ecological crises of our time. I think that this, while understandable, would be a mistake. I hope that it is clear from Part I of this book that creation-attuned worship makes good sense from a Christian perspective *even if we faced no ecological emergencies*. Such worship is simply a liturgical approach that resonates with a Christian understanding of *who* we are, *what* we are, *where* we are, and *whose* we are. It's inherently valuable, irrespective of *when* we are. Yet, it can, of course, better equip people to respond in more image-of-God-like ways to such problems. Indeed, I suspect that if it had been more embedded in Christian practice, Christians would have been among the "first off the blocks" in pioneering responses to environmental emergencies instead of lagging behind. And so, in these days of environmental threat the need to cultivate wild worship is even more pressing.

---

8. Hughson, *Neanderthal Religion?*, 164, quoting Ingold, *Being Alive*, 214.

9. Joerstad, *Hebrew Bible and Environmental Ethics*, 6.

3. R is for Revelation

The church believes that we can only know the Divine because God has made Godself known. We depend upon revelation. There's an ancient tradition in Christianity that the Creator has written two books, the book of God's *word*, the Scriptures, and the book of God's *works*, creation.[10] Both of these bear witness to Christ-Sophia—the perfect self-revelation of God—and so wise Christian reflection attends to both, seeking Christ's word in them. Hans Urs von Balthasar makes this point well:

> Christ gathers up in himself all the words of God lying scattered in the world, . . . not only the "words spoken in many ways" of the Old Testament [i.e., Scripture], but equally those scattered throughout creation, stammered or muttered in it—words uttered in the great and small things of nature, in the words of the flowers and the beasts, words of overpowering beauty and paralysing horror, words manifold and confused, this word full of promise and disillusionment of human existence—that all these belong to the one, eternal, living Word become man for us; they are wholly his property, and on that account are governed by him, to be interpreted by his light and no other.[11]

i. The book of God's word

It is no great insight to see that the Bible has always been fundamental to any faith that claims to be Christian. Being faithful to Scripture is a requirement for the followers of Jesus, even if questions and disagreements will always remain over what constitutes fidelity to Scripture. The Bible matters for the church. Everyone knows that. But it's worth stressing two ways in which it should be central to Christian eco-spirituality.

First, the philosophy that underpins and shapes any version of Christian eco-spirituality must be deeply rooted in the teachings of Scripture. I was drawn towards eco-spirituality through reading the Bible. I subsequently sought (and continue to seek) to draw on other sources of wisdom to enrich that spirituality, but the origin and basic shape of my eco-spirituality was, and remains, Scripture-inspired. That's not to say that you can't be eco-spiritual without the formative influence of the Bible. Of course you can!

---

10. For this idea in the early church, see Mann, "Church Fathers and Two Books Theology."

11. Balthasar, *Prayer*, 16.

Many are. It's to say, rather, that *Christian* eco-spirituality will actively seek to be biblical through and through.

This may seem blooming obvious, but I mention it because it is not always prioritized. There's a deep yearning among many Christians for building a creation-attuned spirituality, yet as the scriptural and theological foundations for such are often not taught in churches, Christians sometimes mistakenly feel that their own tradition is somewhat impoverished in this area. Now, I am not for one moment suggesting that Christians shouldn't seek to learn from Sophia's work beyond the church. On the contrary, there is much to learn. My point is that Christian eco-spirituality must be *true to itself* and that means that it gets its foundations and supporting structures from the Bible, guided by the Christian tradition. Then, out of a confidence in its own core identity, it seeks to listen to and learn from other spiritual traditions, pursuing mutual enrichment. Dialogue is always more fruitful when both partners have a sense of their distinctive identities, even if such identities are rightly always porous.

With this in mind, I would encourage anyone involved in shaping outdoor worship and preaching to seek out recent biblical and theological works on creation-related issues. In the past twenty years we have witnessed a blossoming of eye-opening new work in biblical studies. And theology too continues to see exciting and innovative studies emerging. If you thought everything that can be said about the Bible, theology, and creation has been said, you are very wrong. Keeping alert to some of this new work will enrich the possibilities for worship and action.

Second, the biblical pillars supporting such spirituality should be regularly and clearly articulated in public and private acts of worship. In our own outdoor worship, we read the Bible aloud at every service. And we always include a short talk explaining the relevance of the passage(s).[12] We want our worship not only to be biblical but also for it to wear its biblical heart on its sleeve.

ii. The book of God's works

Underpinning the notion of "the book of God's works" is the biblical idea that God created the cosmos through the Logos or Sophia. As Irenaeus put it in the second century, "[Christ] is Himself the Word of God Almighty, who in His invisible form pervades us universally in the whole world, and encompasses its length and breadth and height and depth" (*Demonstrations of the Apostolic Preaching* 1.34). As such, the world manifests God's

---

12. With occasional exceptions when we replace the talk with a lectio divina.

Reason or Word or Wisdom. We can learn to perceive the complex patterns in creation and to marvel at them, but for ancient Christians, when we do this, we are detecting the fingerprints of the Divine. We might say that the Word speaks itself in the world. Reading this "book" is not at all easy—and is always provisional—and so in the tradition it is read alongside the book of God's word in a mutually interpreting way. That is an always open, never finished task.

> The works of God, above, below,
> Within us and around,
> Are pages in that book to show
> How God Himself is found.
>
> —Hymn by John Keble, 1827

It seems obvious to us that if we want to live well in the world, we need to pay careful attention to how it works. There are various ways in which we do this, not least of which is science, but when it comes to worship, any act of public worship "in the green" (or "in the blue" for those of you beside the sea) must take nature seriously by directing and cultivating *attention* to what is around us: the variety of plants and animals, the annual cycles of the vegetation, the wind in the trees, the play of the light, the movement of the sun and moon, the behavior of the insects, the changing temperature. Here is Peter of Damaskos, an eleventh-century monastic:

> By . . . contemplating dispassionately the beauty and use of each thing, he who is illumined is filled with love for the Creator. He surveys all visible things in the upper and lower worlds: the sky, the sun, the moon, stars and clouds, water-spouts and rain, snow and hail, how in great heat liquids coagulate, thunder, lightning, the winds and breezes and the way they change, the seasons, the years, the days, the nights, the hours, the minutes, the earth, the sea, the countless flocks, the four-legged animals, the wild beasts and reptiles, all kinds of bird, the springs and rivers, the many varieties of plant and herb, both wild and cultivated. He sees in all things the order, the equilibrium, the proportion, the beauty, the rhythm, the union, the harmony, the usefulness, the concordance, the variety. . . . [C]ontemplating thus all created realities, he is filled with wonder.[13]

13. From *Philokalia*, vol. 3, quoted in Christie, *Blue Sapphire of the Mind*, 159. To explain: to see "dispassionately" means learning to see things without those "anomalous thoughts and feelings that often clouded the mind and prevented it from apprehending reality freely and openly, . . . to see things clearly—unencumbered by the clinging, egoistic mind. It is to be free and open enough in oneself to see things for what they are, to appreciate their peculiar qualities, and to see them as part of a whole." Christie, *Blue Sapphire*, 159.

This attention is perhaps the most obviously distinctive feature of "wild worship." And "learning to pay attention . . . may well be one of the most important contributions we can make to the work of ecological renewal."[14] We'll say more about it in what follows. And it feeds back into the praise and confession and intercession.

4. T is for Tradition

The Christian tradition, as any ancient tradition, is a vast and complicated thing, and, as every other tradition, it contains both helpful and unhelpful elements. A healthy tradition, like a healthy person, is not static. That would be a corpse. A healthy tradition is a dynamic system of both sedimentation and innovation, an ongoing story that is constantly drawing on its past and refreshing itself to face the present. "Tradition," writes G. K. Chesterton, "means giving a vote to the most obscure of all classes, our ancestors. It is the democracy of the dead."[15] We listen carefully, respectfully, reflectively, and discerningly to the Christians of yesteryear, for they help us to "remember our future."[16] And it is precisely when we do this that we discover that our tradition is surprisingly rich with potential sources for eco-spirituality. Such resources include things like:

- Liturgical practices, some of which we'll discuss later.
- Classic prayers, such as The Song of the Three or St Francis' "Canticle of Creation."
- Numerous creation-attuned "events," such as harvest festivals, rogation festivals, clipping services, beating the bounds, and the blessing of trees, fields, seeds, crops, rivers, wells, seas and oceans, and of course animals.[17]
- Pilgrimages, where the journey is the point as much as the destination.
- Sacred sites, which are often natural features—like wells, rocks, trees—that have special associations with saints or salvation history.
- Local folk legends or symbols or images, such as the so-called "Green Man."[18]

14. Christie, *Blue Sapphire of the Mind*, 143.
15. Chesterton, *Collected Works, Volume 1*, 251.
16. A phrase I owe to Professor Andrew G. Walker.
17. For some helpful resources on these, see Mayhew-Smith with Brush, *Landscape Liturgies*.
18. We do not know the meaning or origins of the figure now referred to as "the

- The teachings of theologians of the past, often rich in creation theology.
- Traditional religious imagery, such the picture of Christ crucified "on a tree"—a rich symbol, explored in art and literature, linking the cross to the tree of life in Genesis. (E.g., the Anglo-Saxon "Dream of the Rood" in which the rood, i.e., the tree of the cross, offers its own perspective.)
- Saints, who often (though alas not always) model respectful relationships with nonhuman creatures.
- Traditional practices, like religious restrictions on meat-eating (e.g., the traditional Lenten fast was a fast of meat).
- Monastic traditions of simplicity of life—which if embraced by churches today would be a strikingly prophetic act against the world-eating consumer cultures we now swim in (and drown in).

5. D is for Divine Presence

> I have felt
> A presence that disturbs me with the joy
> Of elevated thoughts; a sense sublime
> Of something far more deeply interfused,
> Whose dwelling is the lights of setting suns,
> And the round ocean, and the living air,
> And the blue sky, and in the mind of man,
> A motion and a spirit, that impels
> All thinking things, all objects of all thought,
> And rolls through all things.
>
> — William Wordsworth

What evocative words! If our faith embraces the ubiquity of divine presence in creation, then we need to have *confidence* in that presence. Such confidence allows us to step back from the temptation to manipulate people's engagement with God. Leave space for God to meet with people in whatever way they need in this moment. Don't be in a rush. Don't fear silence.

Green Man," and all sorts of proposals abound (some very different, e.g., it is a Christ figure, it is an Adam figure, it is a demonic figure, it is a pagan god, it is a symbol of nature). I am not qualified to adjudicate between them. However, in light of the fact that in the popular imagination he is now widely considered to be a pagan symbol, it is worth pointing out that before the modern period he is only found in Christian contexts, most especially churches and cathedrals. At the very least, he was considered a fitting symbol for churches and is possibly a Christian innovation (even if drawing some inspiration from pagan precursors).

If you are leading such worship your task is simply to help people to posture themselves in ways that enable them to be receptive to such presence.

> The soul should always stand ajar,
> That if the heaven inquire,
> He will not be obliged to wait,
> Or shy of troubling her.
>
> —Emily Dickenson

Keep your soul ajar. Don't bolt the door. What a thought-provoking image. In worship we can learn to be *open* to the Light, but then we relinquish control. You cannot manipulate God. Do not even try.

6. P is for Place

Obviously, while creation-sensitive worship can take place inside a building (see later), it makes most sense when it takes place outside. That is where one comes face to face with a plethora of nonhuman creatures and where consciousness of their reality most forcibly impinges upon us.

The beauty of place is that every place is a particular place, and every particular place is distinct and different. And this teaches us to deal not merely in generalities (e.g., the beauty of trees) but in particulars (e.g., the beauty of *this* tree at *this* moment). Wild worship needs to pay close attention to what is happening all around. It needs to work *with* a place and not to be rigidly superimposed upon it.

Let me give an example. I was asked to lead an outdoor act of worship for clergy on a parkland site. The very first thing I did was to scout out the site, to see what was there, and how all the parts stood in relation to the whole. Only then did I start thinking how to craft an act of worship that would make sense in *that* place at the time of year we'd be there. Failure to do this seems to me to be a betrayal of the ethos of eco-spirituality. How are we learning to worship alongside other creatures if we don't pay careful attention to them and accommodate what we do to their presence?

We live in increasingly mobile societies, where we may not live in any one place for a long time. And we often travel through (or fly over) places quickly and inattentively as we rush to and from work and holiday and distant relatives. All of this makes it harder to learn to attend to particular places or to become attached to them. Many of us feel less and less at "home." There is much to be said, therefore, for worshipping in the same place, week after week, over a long period of time, for this allows people to become more intimately familiar with a particular landscape and to observe how it changes over the seasons. One temptation to be avoided is the restless pursuit of the exotic, the thrill of the new. I have nothing against seeking out the new and exotic from time to time, nor with being wowed by it, but if we never take sustained and repeated time to attend to the particular in the natural world, we will not learn to love nature. It will become merely a source of stimulation for us rather than an object of care.

The place you meet may not be spectacular. You may not have a lovely river or lake or woods or mountains or grand vistas. You may simply have a modest plot of land with some grass and a few trees. Don't see this as a loss. See it as an opportunity. What we need in the first instance is not new, inspirational vistas but new eyes with which to see the wonders that lie before us. A small space allows us to take time focusing on the details—there's a landscape in a leaf if we just make the effort to look, and there's a whole universe in the soil. I love Francis Thompson's (1859–1907) poem "To a Snowflake" about the wonder of one single tiny and fleeting creature:

> What heart could have thought you? —
> Past our devisal
> (O filigree petal!)
> Fashioned so purely,
> Fragilely, surely,
> From what Paradisal
> Imagineless metal,
> Too costly for cost?
> Who hammered you, wrought you,
> From argentine vapor? —
> "God was my shaper.
> Passing surmisal,
> He hammered, He wrought me,
> From curled silver vapor,
> To lust of His mind —
> Thou could'st not have thought me!
> So purely, so palely,
> Tinily, surely,
> Mightily, frailly,
> Insculped and embossed,
> With His hammer of wind,
> And His graver of frost."

Small invites attention. And a small place also gives you the chance to learn. You may be like me and have a somewhat meager knowledge of the natural world. Well, don't try to learn it all—focus on knowing your little space, the trees and plants and insects and birds that populate it. Come to know *them*. That is more far important than being able to recite the Latin names of every species of shrub.

Finally, being in the same space week on week, even if it's a modest area, and learning about the plants and animals you share it with, enables a group to invest in *blessing* that place—to give to it and to enrich it, as it enriches us.

These matters of location lie close to the heart of eco-spirituality. This is because we humans learn to love, in part, by paying attention. We spend time in the presence of the object of our affection—a parent, a friend, a lover. We watch them carefully, catching their distinctive mannerisms, the way they smile, the way their eyes crinkle when they laugh, their peculiar hand gestures when they are animated, the way they like to spend their time. We listen, learning to catch the nuances in their voice, even the different ways they breathe. We touch them and embrace them. And we do all this over and over again. When we learn to love, we do not love universals and generalities, we love particulars—we don't love humanity, we love *this* person. Our love can expand, through empathy, but it starts with particulars.

It is precisely the same with learning to love the natural world. Such love is fostered and nurtured in the first instance through learning to attend to the particular: this tree, this fox family, this pond, this field, this hill.

A poem by the great Jesuit poet Gerard Manley Hopkins movingly illustrates this connection between attention to the particular and the affections. It concerns the cutting down of a row of poplar trees he was familiar with near the village of Binsey, beside the River Thames outside Oxford. Take some time to ponder his words.

> "Binsey Poplars"
>
> *Felled 1879*
>
> My aspens dear, whose airy cages quelled,
>   Quelled or quenched in leaves the leaping sun,
>   All felled, felled, are all felled;
>   Of a fresh and following folded rank
>   Not spared, not one
>   That dandled a sandalled
>   Shadow that swam or sank
> On meadow & river & wind-wandering weed-winding bank.
>
>   O if we but knew what we do
>   When we delve or hew—
>   Hack and rack the growing green!
>   Since country is so tender

> To touch, her being só slender,
> That, like this sleek and seeing ball
> But a prick will make no eye at all,
> Where we, even where we mean
>   To mend her we end her,
>   When we hew or delve:
> After-comers cannot guess the beauty been.
> Ten or twelve, only ten or twelve
>   Strokes of havoc unselve
>   The sweet especial scene,
> Rural scene, a rural scene,
> Sweet especial rural scene.

Worship is never about merely forming how we *think*. It is holistic, sculpting our patterns of affection too. And as Wendell Berry observes, "The primary motive for good care and good use is always going to be affection."[19] To develop such affections we need to have a regular place that we return to again and again and again.

7. N is for Nature's Rhythms

When I look at the sky, I am like a toddler looking at a novel. I just don't know how to read it. Indeed, it usually doesn't even occur to me that it is something to be read. The ancients saw the sky very differently. For them it was how they measured the time of day, by the location of the sun; the time of month, by the phases of the moon; the seasons of the year, by the movements of the constellations. They knew the sky intimately. And they calibrated the patterns of their lives to the natural rhythms of the world. They "felt" time in a very different way to the way that we do.

The modern world changed everything. Mechanical clocks were invented in the thirteenth century, and that sowed the seeds for a schism between our awareness of time and what was happening in the world. The shift was gradual, with a major change in England in 1840 when the needs of the new national railways required the synchronization of times across the country to a single, standard time. Now we all measure time using extremely accurate mechanical devices we carry about with us. And our lives are synched together by this standard time, requiring little or no attention to the world around us.

Modern urban life is less and less tied to natural rhythms. In older times human sleep patterns varied across the year, with people sleeping

---

19. Berry, *It All Turns on Affection*, 32–33.

longer when the days were shorter and then rising earlier on brighter, longer days. Work too for most people in agricultural societies waxed and waned and varied with the seasons. And because their lives were so interconnected with the patterns of daylight, weather, and the cycles of plant and animal life, people knew intimately the little signs of change from season to season. My life is not like this. Not one bit. I awake at the same time every day (though in the dark months an alarm helps to override what my body naturally wants to do). My work in an office does not vary across the year: same hours, same tasks, same sights and sounds, day in day out, month in month out, year after year. And I wouldn't know a gerbera if it kicked me in the shins.[20] Artificial lighting now serves to diminish the differences between night and day. It is literally never dark where I live. Never. Which makes it harder to see the stars at night, let alone make sense of them. And globalization means that I don't even know which fruits are in season when I go shopping. When I was a kid, you could only obtain certain fruit at certain times, but now you can buy everything everywhen. Nature plays less and less of a role in regulating our embodied lives, but these bodies of ours are made from the "dust" and still want to move in time with the earth. And there is a potential health cost when we try to overwrite such bodily instincts.

An eco-spiritual orientation would push us towards reconnecting our life rhythms with natural rhythms, even if we keep our watches. Worship is one place to do that. And here the tradition again has much to teach us, for since ancient times the church has observed a lovely annual array of special seasons and days, built around the story of Jesus, which make each year a variegated journey with great potential for spiritual formation.[21]

I am aware that there are some modern Christian traditions, most particularly some evangelical traditions, that eschew almost all of these seasons. I spent decades in such churches. However, while valuing those churches deeply, I think they're missing a trick. The danger with abandoning the traditional Christian year is that gatherings for worship become more and more like modern work in the office: you could pick any individual day and swap it for any other and no one would know the difference. They're all

---

20. OK, that is a tad hyperbolic, I do know what a gerbera looks like, but my basic point stands.

21. In liturgy "[o]ur sense of time is more kairological than chronological, meaning that we feel some times to have different significances than other times. We experience time as folded in on itself, crumpled together rather messily, not as neatly strung up as clothes on a washing line to be read as one reads the words in a book." Reyburn, *Roots of the World*, 83.

interchangeable and much the same. There's little sense of moving with the year: it's just "one darn thing after another."

The Bible models a different pattern. Ancient Israel, as we have already seen, was an agricultural society and was very attuned to earth cycles, using the sun, moon, and stars to chart time. Families spread the risks of subsistence by diversifying, working with grains, olives, fruits, and livestock. The year was composed of two meteorological seasons, a dry season and a rainy season, with the spring and autumn equinoxes roughly marking the breaks. Crops were harvested in the dry season and planted in the rainy.

But not only did their pattern of life and work track the seasons, so too did their religious life. Weekly rhythms were punctuated by the Sabbath (Saturday), a day of rest from work to free up space for worship of God. This was tied into a creation story in which God made the world in six days and rested on the seventh. Thus, the natural rhythm was inseparable from the religious rhythm. Sabbath, for them, was cosmic.

Additionally, annual seasons were marked by various harvest festivals. Six of Israel's seven annual festivals fell next to either the spring or the autumn equinox (the exception being the Feast of Weeks).

Season	Season	Agriculture	Dates	Festival
Spring Equinox	Spring	Barley harvest	14th day of 1st month (full moon)	PASSOVER (in Jerusalem)
		Start of lambing season	15th day of 1st month	Firstfruits
			15th–21st days of 1st month	Unleavened Bread
Dry season		Wheat harvest	c. 8th day of 3rd month	FEAST OF WEEKS (in Jerusalem)
	Summer	Tending of fruit (dates, pomegranates, figs, olives, grapes) and vegetables (onions, leeks, garlic, cucumber, melons, chickpeas, lentils, beans); tending cattle and flocks		
Autumn Equinox	Autumn		1st day of 7th month (new moon)	Feast of Trumpets
			10th day of 7th month	Day of Atonement
		Fruit harvests	15th–22nd of 7th month	FEAST OF TABERNACLES (in Jerusalem)
Rainy season	Winter	Planting and plowing and pruning		

The first three festivals take place over the same week and celebrate the first harvest of the year (barley), taking place just before the main work of gathering the barley began. After that intense week there is a long break, allowing the main barley harvest to be collected. Then in late spring a second pilgrimage festival is held in Jerusalem, the Feast of Weeks. This marks the start of the wheat harvest, with wheat bread being offered to God. The summer was free of festivals. It was a busy time, spent tending fruit, veg, and animals. Autumn kicks off with Trumpets, marking the countdown to the Day of Atonement (a time for fasting, not feasting), which in turn prepares for the climax of the year, the Feast of Tabernacles, a time of great rejoicing when firstfruits of the summer fruit and vegetables were brought in worship.

What's fascinating is that Israel's annual religious festivals integrated the natural rhythms of creation—its new moons and varying harvests—with Israel's own salvation story of deliverance from slavery in Egypt and rest in the promised land. Each harvest festival was linked to a part of Israel's founding story of deliverance from slavery in Egypt and journeying to "rest" in the promised land. Passover and Unleavened Bread commemorate the first Passover meal on the eve of Israel's departure from Egypt, Firstfruits anticipates the harvests to come when Israel would have its own land; Weeks (Pentecost) links to Israel's arrival at Mount Sinai and the covenant God made with them there, in which the law of Moses was given. The Feast of Tabernacles recalls Israel's time wandering in the wilderness, living in booths, prior to entering the promised land.[22]

It is sometimes said that ancient paganism was tied to the earth and saw time as endless cycles whereas Israel, in light of its salvation history, saw time as linear, forward-moving, not cyclical. And this, we are told, lies beneath modern Western thought about the arrow of time. Well, yes, but . . . no. Israel saw time as *both* cyclical *and* linear. Perhaps a spiral is a more accurate image, cycling round and round but moving forward as it does so. And the church through the ages has sought to do the same, respecting both the cycles of the year and the forward movement of creation towards its *telos*.

In fact, Israel's integration of harvest celebrations with salvation-history celebrations might serve as an invitation for the church to likewise bring natural and liturgical seasons into more overt and close alignment. Easter is a prime candidate.

> When . . . we celebrate Easter, we do not merely do so as an "anniversary" of the paschal mystery but as a participation in the divinely given order of creation. Easter, in the western tradition, at least, is on *the first Sunday after the first full moon after the Spring Equinox*, when days becomes longer and brighter, and when new life springs forth. This way, creation reminds us of how life and light become victorious over darkness and death.

---

22. For a detailed and fascinating study of Israel's religious calendars, see LeFebvre, *Liturgy of Creation*. The book makes a very convincing case that every dated event in the Pentateuch (Genesis to Deuteronomy) is offering the dates not for the purposes of chronological precision (thus, they should not be read as attempts at historical accuracy) but for liturgical purposes. Imagine telling the Christmas story in which Mary gives birth to Jesus on December 25. The point is not that Jesus was actually born on that date. He wasn't. Rather, such a telling helps us to link the story to the festival. That, according to LeFebvre, is what the Pentateuch offers. The whole pentateuchal story was shaped to guide the liturgical life of the community.

The dating of Easter, then, is cosmic because the cosmos itself is liturgical.[23]

Now the associations of Easter and spring are noticed by many, as is the association of Easter sunrise with the resurrection. Such connections should not be avoided but embraced.

Given that liturgical seasons like Christmas occur in different natural seasons in different parts of the world, the kind of connections made will be contextual. In the northern hemisphere Advent and Christmas fall in the winter, with short days and long nights. It's a time of dark, awaiting the light; a time with little growing, waiting for the new life of spring. Christmas always comes immediately after the winter solstice, the turning point in the year marking a shift from darkness to light. There are suggestive links to be explored here. The church in the Southern Hemisphere will need to take a somewhat different path. And that is all for the good.

To sum up, Christian eco-spirituality will be inclined towards marking time using both natural and liturgical seasons (and will seek to find resonances between the two). It will also see equinoxes and solstices and phases of the moon as events that can fittingly be marked with a religious response. Some Christians fret about suggestions like that. "Pagans celebrate those things," they cry. True enough, they do, but so flipping what! If ancient Israelites in Bible times sought to avoid anything that pagans did then they would not have had a temple or sacrifices or prayers or sacred texts or prophets or religious festivals or proverbs or laws or holy sites. And neither Judaism nor Christianity would exist. So, stop being daft! Go, kiss a tree.

8. W is for Weather

You will have some of this. You will have no control over it. And whatever weather you get, it will affect what may and may not work. Challenge? Yes. Problem? No. Don't bemoan the fact we can't control weather. Embrace it as a *positive* thing. It puts us in our place and reminds us that we can't manipulate everything. Enjoy that powerlessness.

Our rule in our own outdoor worship is that we gather together whatever the weather (except dangerous weather, like lightning or hurricanes). As the old aphorism says, there's no such thing as the wrong weather, there's only the wrong clothes. So just make sure you tell people to dress for the weather. (Sure, I know that most people do, but there's always one!)

---

23. Kringlebotten, *Liturgy, Theurgy, and Active Participation*, 61–62.

The unpredictability of the weather can make some services tricky to plan. For instance, I have wanted to do services about clouds and about the moon and stars, but you simply cannot know in advance that such things will be visible. (I did take a gamble on stars once, and it paid off—but it was touch and go until very close to "the moment.") The sun is a little easier because even if it is obscured by clouds, its light is visible. And you can even do a sun service indoors—at least, if you have windows. Plus, you can move with the circumstances. For example, in an outdoor service we did on the sun, the sky was overcast and the rain felt like the days of Noah. It wasn't what I was hoping for, but you work with it. My point shifted to be about the blessings of the sun, which (to fit the moment) include the evaporation of water, the formation of clouds, and the fall of rain. The very rain we were experiencing was the sun's work, yet one more way that it is essential for life on earth. Thank you, sun!

Finally, and as mentioned previously, weather in the Bible is seen as manifesting, while at the same time as hiding, the Divine. The sun's light is a created symbol through which we can see God's Light, the storm clouds and lightning and wind can represent the awesomeness of God, the thunders can sound God's voice.[24] All this makes weather another aspect of creation to enfold within the event of worship.

9. B is for Bodies

In biblical faith, as we have seen, human beings and animals are not immaterial souls trapped in bodies. We are essentially embodied, material creatures, even if we are certainly more than matter. This high biblical valuation of bodies leads us to seek out ways of expressing worship that takes seriously our embodied creaturehood. This should not need saying, but unfortunately there is sometimes a tendency in Christianity to pursue an almost disembodied kind of spirituality focused on ideas and the mind and what is going on "inside" us.

Well, it's a big thumbs up from me for ideas and minds and what is going on inside, but if we imagine we can do that well without attending to our bodies then we are forgetting ourselves, quite literally. So what might a more holistic approach look like? Thankfully, the Christian tradition provides a lot of helpful resources here. (Plus, some that are unhelpful—I did say tradition was complicated.)

---

24. On weather, see Wiggins, *Weathering the Psalms*.

i. Engaging the Senses

Outdoor nature-located worship offers the perfect opportunity to engage all the senses. We're surrounded by sights and sounds and smells and things to touch and (if safe) taste. Make the most of that. Actively encourage consciously embodied interaction with the surroundings. So, for instance, near the start of our regular outdoor service we always have five minutes of silence in which people are encouraged to wander and to "be" in the garden spaces: looking, listening, touching, and smelling. Remember: "Creation is not a vast lump of valueless matter. It is God's love made visible, fragrant, tactile, audible, and detectable."[25]

ii. Movement

Worship in church can often be relatively static, a matter of standing up and sitting down at the right times. Moving makes us more aware of space, and ritual movement makes us more aware of the significance of space. Here traditional patterns of worship have a lot to teach us.

Let me illustrate what I mean with a couple of examples from our regular worship. Close to the start we turn to face the four points of the compass, one by one, accompanied by prayers that focus on the presence of Divine Wisdom in this sacred place at this holy time. The integrated prayers and actions seek to heighten our awareness of God in the space we inhabit.

The service moves, step by step, from the far west of our area to the far east, the place the rising sun, the direction of Jerusalem, the place where Christ was raised. This makes use of the traditional symbolism of the east in churches, but we develop it into something of a symbolic pilgrimage eastward. Our crude altar, made from sections of tree trunks, is located at the far east end and is the focus for the climactic part of the worship.

iii. Symbolic Liturgical Action

Traditional symbolic actions, eschewed by some Christians as "empty superstition," are actually wonderful ways of training the body in spiritual perception. In the early church it was understood that our bodily senses can be elevated by the Holy Spirit to be spiritual senses.[26] The physical symbols of the divine—the Scriptures read and preached, the baptismal water, the

---

25. Wirzba, *From Nature to Creation*, 21.
26. See Lucas, *Sensing the Sacred,* for a superb discussion of the spirituality of the physical senses in fourth-century catechesis.

eucharistic bread and wine, the anointing oil, incense, candles, laying on of hands, and so on—became the means by which we "see" and "hear" and "touch" the Lord, by which we "smell" the aroma of Christ and "taste and see that the Lord is good." Additionally, engaging in *traditional* liturgical actions is a way of participating in something that far transcends our own modern context, helping us to share more deeply in the life of the ancient, global Christian community. It's about being a part of something that's bigger, that precedes you and will continue long after you.

So in our outdoor worship we actively encourage people to swallow their pride and give it a go: use your body. At appropriate points, bow, raise your hands in the traditional posture of prayer,[27] kneel (if physically able), make the sign of the cross, share the peace. The reason we do this is precisely because humans are psychosomatic unities. Making fuller use of our bodies in worship is a part of embracing our identity as creatures.

I will never forget a prayer meeting that I attended when I was a teenager. I considered myself to be a cool Christian, much more "in the flow of the Spirit" than the rather conservative and stuffy Christians I was praying with. So, there I was, slouching in my chair, praying to my "mate" Jesus, when the leader of the meeting stopped the proceedings and rebuked me. "Who do you think you're talking to? Your buddy down at the youth club? You are in the presence of a holy God. Now sit up and show some respect!" Somewhat embarrassed, I did. And the simple act of moving my body-posture transformed my prayer. When I sat up straight, held my hands out, palm-upwards, and raised my face heavenward, my whole attitude changed. I owe that man more than he will ever know. What we do with our bodies really matters because our "outside" and the "inside" form a single person, and what God has joined together . . . you get the idea.

And you can add some nontraditional symbolic actions into the mix too, so long as they are "fitting." For example, as part of our intercessions we will use pebbles or twigs or some such object to represent our individual prayers. The leader will pray a short general intercession focused on a particular area, such as the work of local environmental groups, and then leave an extended silence for those present to make that prayer more specific in their own way. Then we use the call and response, "Creator in your mercy,

---

27. This is known as the orans position, and it is the traditional prayer posture adopted by priests. For this reason, some feel that *only* priests should adopt it. I disagree. First off, in Scripture *all* believers are encouraged to pray that way (1 Tim 2:8). Second, the priest adopts that position in his or her role as a *representative* of the praying community. He or she prays not instead of the community but *on its behalf*, summing up the community's prayer. And the community prays with the priest. Raising hands when one does so is perfectly appropriate. However, if you feel uncomfortable then keep your hands down.

hear our prayer." At that point we each drop one of our pebbles into a bucket of water (or pile it into a cairn, or lay it in front of the altar, or drop our twig into a fire). This very tactile action represents our offering of our prayers to God.

So my advice is this: don't avoid traditional and liturgical actions in the desire to be culturally relevant—embrace the weird.

iv. Eating

Eating is a reminder of our embodied existence, both in the variety of bodily senses that are engaged when we eat—basically all of them—and in the sheer reminder of our physical need. More than that, eating together is profoundly culturally meaning-full and community-building. It is no accident that Jesus made meals such a central part of his ministry nor that the church embraced the Eucharist as the central rite of its worship. So make eating together a part of what you do, at least from time to time. You can cook together outside, perhaps even using ingredients you have grown yourselves.

10. L is for Liturgy

"Forest church isn't just normal church happening outside."[28] This sentiment is often a major point flagged up by those promoting forest church. Forest church isn't just a matter of relocating your normal Sunday service into a field and then carrying on as usual. And that is true, importantly so. But it is only true *to a point*.

Over the centuries Christian worship has been sifted and configured in particular ways and certain core elements have come to stand out as key ingredients. These include things such as:

- A liturgical welcome
- Bible readings
- A sermon
- Thanksgiving, praise, and adoration
- Prayers of confession
- Prayers of intercessions
- The Lord's Prayer

---

28. Stanley, *Forest Church*, 12.

- The Eucharist (including sharing "the Peace")
- A blessing and sending out

And those elements are not randomly thrown in but are arranged in certain intelligible orders, so that the worship experience is a journey across a liturgical landscape. Such liturgical patterns are the fruit of much reflection and experience over two thousand years—more, in fact, as they reach back into ancient Jewish worship.

Now, outdoor Christian events of spirituality do not need to include all (or even most) of those elements. At our cathedral we run a monthly event called Sacred Garden, which always begins with a short Scripture text and prayer and always ends with a short prayer. In between, however, the bulk of our time is spent engaging God in less direct ways—through gardening, through art, through contemplative prayer, through wild crafts (like whittling, wood chopping, *hapa zome*, etc.). We seek to glimpse God in the corner of our eye, as it were. And it is very worthwhile. Nonetheless, I am always careful to explain that "This is not a service of worship." For it to be a service of Christian worship it really needs to contain all the kinds of elements listed above. And that means it *is* going to look in many ways like the kind of things that happen inside a church building. If it does not, then while we may be enriched by some of the new things we take up, we will simultaneously be impoverished by the things we have put down. So one key principle for outdoor worship is not to fear including those staples of "ordinary" worship. Don't try to avoid them just for the sake of being different or hyper-naturey. Embrace the sifted wisdom of the past and allow the traditional aspects of Christian worship to interact creatively with the surroundings.

Now, let's be honest, liturgy can be too wordy. So we have made a deliberate choice to thin out the number of words in our outdoor liturgies. The reason was threefold: first, for acoustic reasons—to reduce the amount of listening to unamplified talking;[29] second, because of the need to create more space for silence and extra activities, such as gardening; third, to get away from overfocusing on the intellectual aspects of worship. I am a great believer in not drowning a liturgy with words. Less is often more, and in this case that is most certainly true. Give it space to breathe.

---

29. This is especially so for the sermon, which in our case is four or five minutes long. (The short sermon is also partly for temperature reasons, for sitting still outside while listening to a sermon in the middle of winter is not anyone's idea of fun. People need to move.) It's amazing what can be said in that brief time *if you prepare carefully*. Sure, it's not enough time for more substantive teaching, but there are other contexts in which such teaching can be given.

11. E is for Eucharist[30]

Holy Communion is usually considered by Christians to be the most significant ritual in our common worship. And here there are eco-spiritual veins running through its body.

Eucharist means "thanksgiving" and the sacrament celebrates an upward spiral of mutual and transformative giving and receiving. Think of this prayer which some Christians pray at the preparation of the table. "Blessed are you, God of all creation. Through your goodness we have this bread to set before you, which earth has given and human hands have made. May it be for us the bread of life." So first we have the fruit of the earth—a plant: the wheat. This is received with thanksgiving as God's gift. But then we transform the gift through the work of our hands into bread. What we offer is not just wheat; it is bread, a product of human culture. And the same applies to the wine: fruit of the vine received with thanksgiving and turned into wine, which we then offer back to God.

God receives the bread and wine from us and, by the Holy Spirit, transforms them for us into the bread of life and the cup of salvation. God then offers them back to us as a gift, now elevated as a means by which the transforming presence of Jesus comes to us: the bread of life, the cup of salvation. Christ *is here*. We receive these holy gifts with thanksgiving, and we ingest them.

As with all food, they are metabolized and become a part of us, but as Spirit-elevated elements they are a means by which Christ himself is present to us and works within us. Indeed, instead of *our* bodies absorbing Christ and conforming him to the pattern of *our* lives, *Christ* assimilates *us* and makes us a part of *his* body—"though we are many, we are one body because we all share the one bread."

Then, having received heaven's transformative gift within us, we ourselves become the gift. Thus, the worship concludes with us offering ourselves back to God. We pray something along the lines of: "Through [Christ] we offer you our souls and bodies [notice the bodies] to be a living sacrifice. Send us out in the power of your Spirit to live and work to your praise and glory."

So this spiral of giving and receiving begins with plants growing in the soil and ends with people living lives of service in the world. And on the journey, there are multiple transformations: grain and grapes to bread and wine; bread and wine to the body and blood of Christ; body and blood of

---

30. Baptism too is a ritual well fitted to wild worship if your site has access to safe, clean water. I will leave it to others to comment on outdoor baptisms—which, after all, is how baptism started in the River Jordan.

Christ to a community filled with Christ and serving the world in Christ's name. Notice too that the spiral comes back to where it started: the community comes to the sacrament from the world of daily living and then returns at the end back to that same world. However, God's intention is that community is sent back *changed*—albeit incrementally—and that through them the world receives something of the healing touch of Christ. We are called to be the hands and feet of Jesus in creation.

OK, what does any of this have to do with ecology? For now, let me just mention two things, which can serve as seeds for your own reflection.

First, it is noteworthy that the bread and wine are not incidental to the worship, but *central*. And bread and wine, as grain and grapes, are deeply *material, physical* things. This act of worship is overtly "earthed," "grounded" we might say. Some Christians think that spirituality is all about non-physical things, but the Eucharist affirms the *importance* and *goodness* of the physical world—of the natural world of plants and animals, and of human culture. What else would you expect in a religion that teaches that the Word became flesh! In a religion of incarnation, matter matters. The Eucharist underlines for us the *spirituality* of the material world—that God is found *in* and *through* it. The world around us has the capacity to become, by the Spirit, a site of encounter with God. And in the Eucharist, by God's grace, it does. Imagining, as many do, that the physical and the spiritual are separate realms and that we must abandon the material to discover the spiritual is a mistake. In Holy Communion, God comes to us in a multi-sensory ritual, involving sight, sound, touch, smell, and taste, in the very bodily act of eating and drinking. This physicality is not a distraction from the spiritual side of things, it is *integral* to it. Think about that. Don't try to ignore the sensual experience of the ritual. Attend to it.

Second, notice that the spiral does not take us *away* from the world of creation, elevating us higher and higher into otherworldliness. On the contrary, it keeps us very much grounded in the world, but it illuminates that world with the light of heaven, so we can see it with new eyes; it cracks the world open like a perfume jar, thereby allowing the aroma of Christ to infuse our lives. Then it sends us right back into the world of plants and animals and ecosystems and human culture, of work and rest, of family and friends, of struggles and joys, and successes and failures, of holiness and sin. But it sends us back with resources to live in creation in more Christlike ways. This spirituality is not about *abandoning* creation but *transforming* creation. And that has all sorts of ecological implications.

So here is my challenge: How does one celebrate the Eucharist out in nature in such a way as to bring out some of those ecological connections?[31]

12. G is for Gratitude

At the heart of the Christian theology of creation is that creation's existence is granted to it by pure grace. This is a vision of creation as *gift*. And the natural response to gift is first wonder then gratitude. Now gratitude can seem so mundane that it hardly warrants comment, but it is a *fundamental* ingredient of Christian life. Indeed, it seems to be very important to us simply as human beings, whatever our spiritual beliefs (or nonbeliefs). Numerous psychological studies have shown the many positive health benefits for mind and body that come from regularly expressing thanks. Such benefits include:

1. it can make you more patient and better able to make sensible decisions
2. feeling grateful towards another person can improve numerous aspects of your relationship with them
3. it can improve your self-care
4. it can help you sleep better
5. it can help ease depression, often more effectively than anti-depressants
6. it can improve happiness. In the words of one researcher at Stanford and Yale, Emma Seppälä, "Gratitude is something that leads to much more *sustainable* forms of happiness, because it's not based in that immediate gratification; it's a *frame of mind*."[32]

None of this should be surprising for Christians. Living with thankfulness is one of the ways that worship helps us to work with the grain of the world, and naturally that is good for us.

A few years ago, I listened with great interest to an atheist who was very excited about the benefits of gratitude. He was speaking positively of religion precisely because it encourages "an attitude of gratitude." He himself had started to practice gratitude each day, when he woke up, and he'd found it transformative. The problem was, he said, that he could not answer

---

31. Specific denominations will have certain restrictions on what they can and cannot do in a Eucharist, and these should be respected. As an Anglican community, for instance, our Eucharists must have certain key elements in the liturgy, must use an approved Eucharistic Prayer, and must be presided over by an ordained and licensed priest. But those restrictions still leave plenty of room for maneuver.

32. Quoted in Ducharmie, "7 Surprising Health Benefits of Gratitude."

this question: *"Whom* am I thanking?" For the very *grammar* of gratitude implies (i) a person who is grateful, (ii) something they are grateful for, and *(iii) someone to whom they are grateful*. Without that final element, one can be pleased or happy about a positive aspect of one's life, but can one be *grateful* for it? Not in any straightforward way. Be that as it may, worship teaches us to be thankful to God by regularly involving us in the practice itself. We learn gratitude by practicing gratitude.

When it comes to the natural world, there are an infinite number of things to be grateful to God for. Those seeking to curate eco-worship must be alert to the need to make gratitude a central aspect of all acts of wild worship, and to find multiple ways to do so.

13. K is for Keeping (i.e., Guarding)

In Genesis 2, humanity was created "to tend and keep (i.e., protect)" the garden. This is a vision of gardening as priestly service. To my mind, it makes a lot of liturgical sense to incorporate some act of engaging and blessing creation as a feature of our public worship. This is not terribly traditional, so let me illustrate what I mean. As part of our regular service, we include a fifteen- to twenty-minute time in which we take part in some activity aimed at looking after or blessing the garden space in which we meet. Maybe picking fruit or planting, maybe filling bird feeders or placing bug hotels, maybe seeking to enhance the biodiversity by looking after the pond or keeping the brambles from swamping out all the other plants. We're still very much figuring out how best to tend the space. The point is that this act of gardening is not a short break from the worship but is offered *as* an act of worship. We deliberately frame it as such within the service.

Our intention in making gardening a formal part of worship is to ritually symbolize that *all* our acts of tending creation, any time and any place, can be offered as worship. For gardening is no frivolous activity: "Gardening ... is the complex activity that leads us into deeper encounter with and understanding of creation, creatureliness, and the Creator's life."[33] Obviously, the small time in the service given to this is more of a symbolic gesture rather than an attempt to have a major impact on the place. But it's enough time to make a positive contribution, even if small, and that is adequate.

---

33. Wirzba, *From Nature to Creation*, 104. On a theology of gardening, see Wirzba, *From Nature to Creation*, 98–107.

14. S is for Silence

In my experience, we're often bad at silence. The modern world is one of hyperstimulation and constant distraction. If we sit down, we have to be *doing* something or *watching* something or *listening* to something. Many find sitting in silence to be excruciating. Our brains won't stop buzzing. Silence is boring, and if we are in the presence of other people, silence is deeply awkward and embarrassing. There is a compulsion to fill it with chat, even if we are just scrabbling around desperately for something, anything, to say—anything to avoid the void. It's not infrequently the same in church. Liturgies often have spaces for silent pauses built in, but it is usually the case that such silences are brief indeed. A silence of even ten seconds has people looking around as though someone has forgotten what they should be doing. And I can't count the number of charismatic services I've been at in which the worship leader says, "Let's be silent before the Lord . . . while the musicians continue playing." At which point we stop singing for a while, and although such moments are very valuable in themselves, we do not have any actual *silence*. Actual silence would freak people out, because we are so unused to it.

Silence, though, has been an integral part of Christian prayer for many centuries. It is so important that I have added an extended appendix on the subject, because discussing it all here would take too much space. For now, it will suffice to say that being silent in worship is a very healthy and worthwhile practice, for a number of reasons, not least of which is that it enables us to connect with God at levels other than the cognitive. It is, however, something that needs to be learned and something that we need to be very intentional about. It will not usually just happen but must be cultivated. Outdoor worship is a great opportunity to make sustained silence a normal way of being together.

In our cathedral in Worcester we have used a couple of different approaches. Sometimes we have more extended periods of group silence for contemplative prayer. These would typically be ten to thirty minutes, depending on the group. And we almost always have a brief sustained silence (five minutes) near the start of each act of worship, and other, shorter silences are used at key points thereafter. We do not direct how people should use the opening silences. Some people choose to engage in meditative prayer while others attend carefully to what they see around them. Both are spiritually valuable activities.

"Leisure"

What is this life if, full of care,
We have no time to stand and stare.
No time to stand beneath the boughs
And stare as long as sheep or cows.
No time to see, when woods we pass,
Where squirrels hide their nuts in grass.
No time to see, in broad daylight,
Streams full of stars, like skies at night.
No time to turn at Beauty's glance,
And watch here feet, how they can dance.
No time to wait till her mouth can
Enrich that smile her eyes began.
A poor life this if, full of care,
We have no time to stand and stare.

—W. H. Davies (1911)

15. C is for Creativity

The God who created the world is an artist. And when we use our imagination and creativity, we are echoing the original divine artisan. Indeed, exercising creativity could be seen as a kind of "sub-creation,"[34] one aspect of our imaging God.

There are two sides to the spirituality of art: the act of *creating* a work and the act of *receiving* a work. Both can have a place in nature-based spirituality, though in a public service of worship time is too restricted for creating artworks (with a few exceptions). Creativity usually needs to be unhurried and unpressured. However, receiving a work of art can easily be an aspect of worship: a song that is sung or listened to, a poem that is read and contemplated, a beautiful painting displayed, a lovely garment that is simply worn.[35] And all such things can have a creation-attuned focus, which enhances the service.

While acts of worship have limited scope for creating art, there are other opportunities for that. Let me tell you a little more about our Sacred

---

34. A term I take from C. S. Lewis.

35. Here I must mention a beautiful stole my eldest daughter made for me in 2018. It's green and has wheat on one side, to represent the eucharistic bread, and grapes on the other, to represent the wine. Around it in gold embroidery are the Hebrew words בְּרֵאשִׁית בָּרָא אֱלֹהִים אֵת הַשָּׁמַיִם וְאֵת הָאָרֶץ (In the beginning, God created the heavens and the earth). Various creatures—a caterpillar, a butterfly, a snail, a ladybird (= ladybug), and a robin bird—adorn it. On the back is a gold symbol of the Trinity.

Garden event. As I mentioned, this is put on as an event of Christian spirituality, but not as an act of formal worship, and our strapline is "Engaging God in creation through creativity." It's an informal time in which people are free to be in silent prayer (we have a silent zone), gardening, a wild-craft activity (like sawing, log splitting, and weaving string from our grasses and then making bowls from it), simply being in the garden (perhaps using ID sheets to identify birds, insects, trees, etc.), or an art activity. Folk can choose to do any or all of those activities in our two hours together. For the art activity we work with a local Christian artist who has explored a range of ideas, all of which encourage attention to the space around us. Some of the art activities are overtly Christian (using Bible verses) and others are not. She is also working on a project making paper and paint pigments and inks from our garden plants to be used in the activities. One project is to make paper that includes wildflower seeds from our gardens, then to write letters on it, which can then be planted.

16. M is for Music

Christians have sung psalms and hymns and spiritual songs since the time of Jesus and his first followers. Music can connect with levels of the soul that other kinds of prayer cannot reach.

And there's no reason that this would not be so outside as well as in. There is no shortage of songs that would fit a creation-attuned service. Singing is not a major component of our own services, but we usually have one or two (occasionally three) songs. We have also wondered about writing musical settings for some of the regular liturgy, so that we can sing that.

There are some practical matters you will need to consider. If you are not indoors you are probably not amplified and the musical instruments you can use are limited. We do not use any. We sing unaccompanied. There is something beautifully empowering about hearing the human voice "naked" as it were. We are not awesome singers—I certainly am not! But it's amazing what a bunch of ordinary, unspectacular singers can do together. What it needs is (a) songs that people are familiar and confident with or are short and simple enough to learn easily and (b) someone who can lead the singing with confidence.

17. J is for Journey

Journey is in the DNA of biblical spirituality. The exodus story is paradigmatic here, leaving its pilgrim footprints all the way through both Old and

New Testaments. And the narrative journey of Christ's life—incarnation, birth, baptism, temptations, ministry, passion and crucifixion, burial, resurrection, ascension, and pouring out of the Spirit—becomes the pattern for the Christian Year. We literally worship our way through that story each year, allowing it to inform our own life journeys.

For such a journeying faith, pilgrimage seems a fitting form of religious expression. Israel's faith included three pilgrim festivals each year, which involved a journey to Mount Zion in Jerusalem, the symbolic focus of God's presence with the people. And both Jesus and his earliest followers, as observant Jews, kept these pilgrim festivals. In due course pilgrimage became a part of Christian spirituality for non-Jewish followers of Jesus too, with pilgrimage sites springing up all around Christendom. It remains to this day a vivifying part of Christian practice for many.

For those who, for one reason or another, could not make a literal pilgrimage, symbolic pilgrimages in the form of labyrinths were developed. These are not to be confused with mazes. The aim of a maze is to avoid the dead ends and find the hidden route through. In a labyrinth there is only one way through. The point of a labyrinth is prayerfully walking the path in and then out. This allowed worshippers to go on a kind of "virtual pilgrimage," in lieu of a literal pilgrimage. There has been something of a revival of interest in labyrinths in recent years.

Journey can feature in eco-worship in various ways. In the first instance, each service can be structured as a journey, involving literal movement, in stages, from a starting point to a climactic end point. A little landscape is traversed, both liturgically and literally. I have already described how we try to do this.

A second mode is to develop some one-off services that (literally) cover more ground, as it were. Let me illustrate from a Forest Church service for younger children and their families we did in this mode. It was based around a journey with four stopping points in different natural locations. On the journey to Stop 1 we looked out for signs of animals, insects, and birds (both the animals themselves or clues of their presence, like webs, footprints, feathers, and poo). We then gathered at Stop 1, shared what we'd seen, and took time to give thanks for the animals. The journey to Stop 2 required us to look out for wildflowers, paying special attention to their shape and color. When we regathered and shared what we'd seen, we blew bubbles, using the bubbles—ascending and then bursting open—to represent our prayers of blessing on the bees and other pollinators. The trek to Stop 3 required the worshippers to collect one blade of each different kind of grass they found. We then gathered at 3 to see how much variety there was in a single field. This was followed by a Bible reading about grass (Gen 1:11–12).

Stop 4 was in woodland. En route we chose a fallen twig from the ground. At the stop we stood in silence for a minute listening to all the different sounds we could hear. We then talked in families about people and issues we know that need prayer. We used the sticks to represent them and then placed them in a pile, gathering our prayers. We closed with the Lord's Prayer, a blessing, and a sending out. One could easily expand that mini-journey model into a grander and a more adult format.

Further, I am sure that there is eco-spiritual potential in labyrinths, though I confess to not having given it much thought. And, of course, one could always go on an actual pilgrimage. Some go on religious pilgrimage to climate events or protests, making the journey to the event an important part of the whole, framing the event itself in a spiritual light. Others go on traditional pilgrimages, traversing both outer and inner landscapes in creation-mindful ways.

18. V is for Veritas

Veritas is the Latin for "truth." One thing we must avoid in outdoor worship is getting so lost in the beauty of creation that we lose sight of the very real and desperate challenges confronting the natural world (mostly as a consequence of human activity). Wild worship is not a matter of having "a chill out" in Wonderland, blind to the harsh and difficult truths we'd rather forget. It is a time in which such truth can be named and brought into the presence of God.

I will have more to say about this in the next chapter, but here I simply note that the most obvious spaces in the service for such truth-telling are:

- the sermon/talk
- self-examination and confession of sin
- prayers of lament
- prayers of intercession

All these parts of worship can deal directly, albeit in different ways, with the fact that we inhabit a fallen world. Additionally, certain seasons of the year, most especially the penitential seasons of Advent and Lent, provide an opportunity for sustained self-examination (on the part of individuals and groups) in relation to some of these issues.

Finally, outside of the space of a formal service of worship, Christians can address a range of such matters in more depth. For instance, our cathedral's eco-group runs a whole series of wide-ranging talks and educational events on numerous troubling matters of ecological concern and how we might actively respond to them.[36] Christians can also organize an array of active responses to these issues, and many Christian ecological organizations and groups exist for this very purpose.

19. I is for Integration

Two of the features that need careful consideration are fittingness and integration. Our services always have a focus, and that will be one fitting for the time of year, alert to the both the natural rhythms of the year and the patterns of Christian liturgical seasons. Once we have a theme, the various elements in the service are built together to serve that focus. Let me illustrate this from the way that we would plan our regular children's forest church service (a service for 0–11s and their families). That service had various fixed elements (determined by the need to count as an Anglican act of worship) in a fixed order.

Zone 1

- A liturgical greeting (The Lord be with you. **And also with you**.)
- A welcome and introduction to the service
- An opening prayer (of one to two sentences)
- An act of praise (which was quite varied and used a range of engaging activities)
- A collect prayer (one sentence)
- A short Bible reading
- A talk about the reading (of about two minutes)

[Process to Zone 2]

Zone 2

- Activities (a selection of nature-based craft activities—and this was a bit of an exception to my earlier comments about not having time for acts of creativity in services: we saw some lovely little acts of creativity from the children).

[Gather in Zone 3]

---

36. Worcester Cathedral's eco-group won the *Church Times* 2024 Green Church award (in the training and education category) for these events.

Zone 3

- Intercessions (interactive, accessible, short)
- The Lord's Prayer (which we also sign)
- A blessing
- A dismissal (Go in peace to love and serve the Lord. **In the name of Christ, amen.**)

That structure provided a skeleton shape with a few simple and basic prayers that the children could feel comfortable with. It sounds like a lot, but it only took forty-five minutes from start to finish (including a significant chunk of time doing activities), with a lot of variety and movement, and all of the children, from toddlers to eleven-year-olds, were engaged throughout.

However, despite the similar skeleton, every service was distinctly different. The theme varied a lot, and *it infused every single aspect of the service*, apart from the brief liturgical greeting and dismissal and the Lord's Prayer.[37] This is what I mean by integration.

20. X is for Mystery

For me, one of the inspirational things about classical Christian theology is that the God at its heart is forever beyond comprehension, utterly mysterious. Without revelation we could know nothing of God, and even with revelation—including the supreme revelation of the incarnation—God remains concealed. This truth is wonderfully captured by Charles Wesley in "Hark, the Herald Angels": *"veiled* in flesh, the Godhead *see."* Six words bearing the weight of infinity. The journey into knowing God is a journey that never ends.

Not only is God a mystery, but *every single created thing*, because its being is grounded in the infinite Being of God, is never fully explicable. There is an ineradicable element of excess and mystery in all things, from a galaxy to a raindrop. The mundane is a marvel. Think of a human being, for instance. Despite all we know about humans, and continue to learn, there is no sense in which we could ever know all there is to know about any single human, ourselves included. Unfathomable depths will ever remain. "The mysterious nature of being is not due to its unintelligibility, but rather its superabundant intelligibility in relation to the scope of human intellect, which it always surpasses. Reality will always exceed our comprehension of

---

37. Our regular adult service is also fully integrated, though it contains fewer flexible elements and so is not as variable as the children's forest church service.

it, yet we can comprehend it truly and deepen into its truths in an endlessly fruitful way."[38] Philosophy, as Socrates taught, begins in *wonder*—a childlike astonishment before reality as it presents itself to us. And the love of wisdom continues in that vein. Cultivating wonder is a key to insight.

Worship is one place to learn to be in awe and wonder in the presence of such mystery, both the mystery of the infinite God and the mystery of finite creatures. That is another reason why symbol and ritual and poetry and silence and art and story and multisensory awareness are important. They do not need to be exhaustively understood in the mind to do their work. Indeed, sometimes they don't need to be understood much at all. So be vigilant to maintain mystery.

21. U is for Unicorn

You did not misread that. Bear with me. Weird as it may seem, unicorns have a place in the history of Christian spirituality, even appearing in the King James translation of the Bible (Num 23:22; Deut 33:17; Pss 29:6; 78:69; Job 39:9).[39] The myth of the unicorn predates Christianity but was incorporated into Christian art and storytelling, often as a symbol of Christ. There are, for instance, many images of the Virgin Mary with a unicorn.

Now unicorns as such have no special eco-spiritual interest to me. They do speak, however, of the value of myth, and myth certainly does have importance for contemporary eco-spirituality. Christian authors such as George MacDonald, C. S. Lewis, and J. R. R. Tolkien appreciated the great truth-communicating power of myth, even in a modern culture obsessed with "empirical facts." And each of these writers made use of imaginative fantasy and myth to address issues of nature-spirituality. Let me take just one example. In C. S. Lewis's novel *The Voyage of the Dawn Treader* the travelers encounter an old man with long silver hair and a long silver beard. He said,

> "I am Ramandu. But I see that you stare at one another and have not heard this name. And no wonder, for the days when I was a star had ceased long before any of you knew this world, and all the constellations have changed."
>
> "Golly," said Edmund under his breath. "He's a *retired* star."
>
> "Aren't you a star any longer?" asked Lucy.
>
> "I am a star at rest, my daughter," answered Ramandu. . . .

---

38. Taylor, *Foundations of Nature*, 9.

39. Hebrew *reēm*, beast with a horn (i.e., wild ox), which the seventeenth-century translators took to be a unicorn (as one does).

"In our world," said Eustace, "a star is a huge ball of flaming gas."

"Even in your world, my son, that is not what a star is but only what it is made of."[40]

Here Lewis is hinting that there is more to stars, *even in our world*, than the sciences can tell us. Michael Ward, in his books *Planet Narnia* and *The Narnia Code*, has argued persuasively that Lewis's long-term fascination with Ptolemaic cosmology underlies all seven of the books in the Narniad. Lewis was well aware that the medieval cosmology he felt so drawn to was, if believed literally, false. But while not factually true (in the way in which people used to think it was), it was deeply beautiful and, at an aesthetic level, was truthful. Lewis wrote, "the characters of the planets, as conceived by medieval astrology, seem to me to have a permanent value as spiritual symbols."[41] Might it be that in this capacity some of the myths in Scripture—such as that stars are gods, members of the divine council—retain a permanent value and even warn us against the kind of scientific reductionism that seeks to disenchant the cosmos?[42]

Eco-spiritual worship is not the place to recount extracts of fantasy novels. However, it can be a place to use some mythic motifs that offer re-enchanted ways of understanding the world. These must not be understood as attempts at speaking science and their poetic nature should be clear, but worship is one of many human spaces in which we learn to appreciate that the language of the empirical sciences is not the only language for engaging reality. Worship is a place for speaking truth in many tongues.

22. H is for Hospitality

Welcoming of guests and strangers has been important to the Christian tradition since its origins, and eco-spiritual worship must find ways to manifest that tradition of hospitality. Everything from welcoming people on arrival, explaining what will be happening, making sure all are included in what is going on, providing food and drink, and doing whatever is needed to accommodate any special requirements individuals have for participation. Never forget, though, that hospitality is at heart about *the heart*; it is first and foremost an attitude towards others, not a list of things to do. And if

---

40. Lewis, *Voyage of the Dawn Treader*, 158–59.

41. Lewis, "Alliterative Metre," 23.

42. Parts of the above paragraph were taken from Parry, *Biblical Cosmos*, 189–90. Reproduced with permission.

you seek to become a community with that heart then you will figure out the practical issues that need attending to as you go along.

Don't forget that we are thinking about eco-spirituality. So this attitude of hospitality should extend beyond your human visitors. Like St. Francis, we should learn to open hospitable hearts towards God's nonhuman creatures. Nurturing such an attitude and discovering what it looks like in practice is a part of the journey of eco-spirituality.

23. O is for Outside-In

While the bulk of this chapter has been about outdoor acts of worship, I do not think for one moment that creation-sensitive worship has to take place outside. It is perfectly possible to use songs and prayers and biblical texts and sermons that embrace creation while inside a building. It happens all the time. And animal-blessing services often take place in churches. After all, church buildings are as much a part of creation as a forest is.

In fact, traditional church buildings present interesting opportunities for creation-spirituality and are underused resources. Let me illustrate what I mean. Perhaps your church has a tapestry or a stained-glass window or a carving that lends itself to creation-spirituality. At Worcester Cathedral we are very blessed to have a huge west window that is a magnificent pictorial presentation of Genesis 1–3. Not only is it beautiful, but it is packed full of good theology. And even if you do not have a window like that, you can always decorate the church with creation art. Again, at Worcester we had on display a stunning sequence of silk tapestries by Jacqui Parkinson on the days of Genesis 1 called "Threads Through Creation." This thought-provoking art was seen by thousands of people. Alternatively, a computer and projector can be a helpful way to lead a guided meditation on a piece of artwork with a nature theme or a guided reflection on a poem.

And there's more. The *very church building itself* may have eco-spiritual potential. Take a cathedral. Now I don't want to reduce the multiple layers of meaning in a cathedral to one—these buildings have more layers than an onion—but for our purposes it's helpful to draw attention to one fascinating aspect of them. The medieval cathedral isn't just a beautiful building—*it's a symbolic representation of the cosmos*. Not some crude attempt at a realistic scale model or map. Medieval people weren't stupid. They knew that the world didn't *literally* look like this. No. A cathedral is a way of bringing out some aspects of the *meaning* of the world and shaping those who worship within its walls so that when they go out "to love and serve the Lord" they perceive the world around them in Christian ways.

Consider: there are three basic levels: Ground level, the space we inhabit. Beneath is the crypt, where the dead bodies were placed. Above is the vault of the heavens, far beyond our reach. In Worcester Cathedral, as you move closer to the high altar, look up and you'll see that the heavens are opened and you can glimpse hosts of angels, saints, and martyrs in glory. And directly above the high altar is Christ, seated on his throne, surrounded by circles of angels. One of the most striking aspects of a Gothic cathedral is the way that your eyes are drawn up to the heavens by all the vertical lines. You can't help but look up. The cathedral is orientated heavenward, but not to encourage escape from the earthly realm. In our worship we don't try to climb up to the ceiling. Rather, in this space, there's an open interaction between the earthly and heavenly; the heavenly infuses the earthly with the divine light, bringing life and blessing.

And these cosmic cathedrals are full of representations of the living world. In Worcester there are plants and animals all over the place, in glass, wood, stone, and metal. A quick scout around would reveal dogs, deer, boars, goats, donkeys, snakes, monkeys, scorpion, crabs, fish (including flying fish), and the ever-popular lions; owls, swans, pelicans (of course), eagles (naturally), and that's not to mention a cat and our infamous pink giraffe; plus a few lovely mythic beasties: a winged horse, a centaur, mermen, and dragons everywhere. There are trees, and herbs, and flowers, and a wide assortment of leaves. As we gather in that space to worship the Creator, the building itself reminds us that *we don't worship alone*. We worship as creatures, alongside other creatures, all of whom have their place in God's house.

The fabric of the cathedral is itself very earthy—and rightly so. Wood, stone, metals, glass, and don't forget the very powerful use of sunlight. And all these elements have their own stories. If you are sitting in a pew, think: that pew you are sitting on was made from a tree—a living creature with a story and an ancestry, almost certainly with descendants still living today. Look at the wall: we have Cotswold limestone, around 195 million years old; and that's a wee bairn compared to the Carboniferous green sandstone next to it, which is about 345 million years old. There's a *spirituality* to stones—ask a stonemason. And in a cathedral these stones are shaped into an edifice in which they serve to bring praise to their Creator. But in an important sense, that's merely to reveal to us something of the meaning of *all* stones—there is a God-ward orientation to the whole creation. *Every* stone declares the praise of God in its own rocky way. The cathedral teaches us that the material stuff of the world directs us to its transcendent Source.

Then there's mathematics. The geometry of the cathedral is full of meaning. In the Middle Ages, geometry was believed to reveal some of the hidden order of creation, its *logos*. The proportions of the cathedral are very carefully worked out to achieve a divinely beautiful balance and proportion that brings out an aspect of the cosmos. It says, *"Although it may not always be immediately obvious in your day-to-day life, you actually inhabit an ordered and unified world that manifests divine Reason."*

The music too—and never forget that for a medieval worshipper in a cathedral, as today, the music was *central* to their experience of worship—the music too presented the same mathematical patterns as the architecture, the same ratios and proportions in the musical scales, harmonies, and the intervals between notes as those that informed the building. So, in subtle multisensory ways, worshippers were imbibing Christian ways to understand and to inhabit the world. The cathedral taught them: the cosmos is divinely ordered and beautiful.

Perhaps you think this is too "tame"—it seems to have no place for all the pain and suffering of creation, the groaning and lamenting that St. Paul spoke of. Is a cathedral too beautiful? Notice, however, that the entire building forms the shape of *a cross*. This cosmic cathedral is not free of the memory of pain, injustice, and death at all. However, it frames that suffering in the context of the story of Jesus. In doing so, it places God's presence right at the center of the pain—in the crucified Christ. In the cathedral's cosmos, God stands *with* creation, *as a creature*, in its most God-forsaken moments—and in Christ God holds out the hope of cosmic resurrection on the other side of death. There *is* death here, but it is enfolded within the hope of life.

In a way, a cathedral is in part an interpretation of Genesis 1 and Romans 8, preaching its own silent sermon. So what does a cathedral say to us about living in God's world? It says, this is God's house, not our house. We are guests, alongside nonhuman guests, and while we're invited to make ourselves at home, we are *not* invited to trash the joint. We inhabit the world as we inhabit the cathedral—with *awe* and *wonder* and *love* and *service* and *worship*. And we learn that just as God's presence fills the cathedral, so it fills the cathedral of the cosmos. Cathedrals have the potential to send us out into the world with refreshed eyes and ears and a heart newly attuned to see and hear and touch and taste and smell the glory of God in the world around us.

24. Q is for Questions of Practicality

Last but not least—Q. Hmmm. That sounds weird. Q is for the boring but important questions of practicality to consider. Matters such as the following:

i. Acoustics

We do not use amplification. So careful consideration needs to be given to audibility and acoustics. What background noises will you be in competition with? How will you deal with noise from wind or rain? Where is the best place to stand to use natural features to aid in the amplification? How do you need to project your voice to be heard? Are there times you need to break into smaller groups so that more quietly spoken people can be heard by others? What can you do for those who are hard of hearing or even deaf?

ii. Toilets

Where are people going to go to the toilet? This is about hospitality and embodiment, so think this through. (And for the intellectual, yes, there is a theology of poo waiting to be written. And what fun you'd have thinking of titles and cover images. I'll leave that as homework.)

iii. Accessibility

Is the space you meet regularly accessible to those with mobility challenges? Wheelchair users? Older people? What can you do to improve accessibility? Is there a way to help those who have impaired sight?

iv. Health and Safety

You will need to risk assess your site and all your activities. And if you're using fire or tools and such like, do you have people properly trained to oversee that? Do you have a first aid kit? Are all the safeguarding concerns for vulnerable adults and children adequately taken care of? Failure in these areas is not a mere failure in admin and red tape, it is a failure to love.

v. Planning

You can't just rock up and improvise your wild worship if you want it to be good. Every service will need careful and clear planning, and you will also need to consider general planning across a longer span of time—if you are going to take changing seasons seriously.

We took a very deliberate decision to develop a basic service for a non-Eucharist and for a Eucharist, which we would alternate between. This keeps a shape that people can become familiar with, learning the essential calls and responses, liturgical actions, and so on. Having a core of people who know what to do means that the leader does not need to explain what is about to happen at every stage, which is distracting. And the more familiar people become with the basic shape of it, the more they can relax into it and get more out of it. The generic services still have flexibility built into them for variety, so that every service is different, but it is variety within a framework.

In addition, we have developed several one-off services for particular occasions. But as no one attending those (bar the leader) knows what will be happening, they need extra-careful thought and extra-careful explanations before the start as well as clear guidance all the way through. Possible pitfalls need to be anticipated and prepared for.

vi. How often should we gather?

Wild church can be anything from a one-off event to a weekly gathering. You will need to work out what will work best for your context. I will say one thing: in terms of formation, it seems to me that eco-spirituality is ineffective if it is treated as one-off events. This is a slow spirituality. From the things I have said in this chapter, it should be clear that you need to attend to a place over a sustained period of time if such worship is really to have any formative effect. That does not mean meeting every week. It may, however, mean meeting every month, or every two months, or perhaps once a term. Any less than that is to risk turning it into a mere entertaining alternative for bored Christians. It is much too important for that.[43]

---

43. It is worth mentioning, in this context, our Sophia Course, a one-year journey of eco-spiritual formation. Those who take the plunge undertake to participate in six learning days across the year (which combine sessions on key biblical texts, important theological themes, input on ecological issues, creativity/contemplative sessions working in the garden, outdoor worship, and fellowship around food) with a daily rule of life, which includes daily prayer (with an eco-spiritual tilt) and a journey of learning to live more gently on the earth and of finding how we can bless creation.

12

Between Denial and Despair
Worship and Eco-Anxiety

1. The Rise of Eco-Anxiety

HUMAN SOCIETIES HAVE ALWAYS had a tendency to degrade their environments, but in recent centuries we have acquired the technology and established the economic systems to do it on a scale and at a rate that is without historical precedent. The consequences are multiple, serious, and worsening.

In a world confronted with many and multiplying environmental crises and losses, increasing numbers of people experience ecological grief, which may manifest as Kübler-Ross' so-called five "stages" of grief—denial, anger, bargaining, depression, and acceptance. Others add to them further elements, such as shock, pain, guilt, and loneliness. These are not linear stages: we don't all experience them all nor do we all experience them in a certain order. They are, rather, different aspects of the morphing condition of grief.

> In the *shock of discovery*, we may be simultaneously *horrified* at the truth, and in *denial*.

In *disbelief*, we may say things like: "This can't possibly be true. It's so awful, why have I never heard this before? Surely the government or the United Nations or the G7 are doing something about it? And we all know that activists are young and hot-headed...."

As the truth sinks in, as we learn that the scientists haven't got it wrong, we may begin to *grieve* for what has been lost, for what is being lost, for missed opportunities, and for future losses. We may grieve the lost perfection of a self-sustaining planet. We may grieve the future and present deaths of millions, both human and more-than-human, and the destruction of places and habitats.

We may *fear* the future, not necessarily for ourselves but for those who follow us. We may fear the pain and anguish of life on a planet which is several degrees hotter than is sustainable. We may fear violence, the chaos of population movements, climate apartheid, social and economic breakdown, perhaps the rise of dictatorships.

We may be *angry* that it has got this far, and that we have been led into climate and ecological catastrophe. We may *blame* big corporations, governments, systems, globalisation, politics. Anger and blame can be a way of coping with powerful feelings of *guilt* or can be a form of *denial*—we may say that we are not part of the problem, it's the government, industry, or our cultural history over which we have no control.

We may feel *guilty* that we have blindly or willfully accepted things we know to be wrong, unsustainable, and destructive. We may remember how many said for years that the science wasn't fixed, even though at the same time scientists and activists around the world were telling us clearly.

If we live in a wealthy country, we may feel *guilt* at our privileged lives, knowing that other countries are already experiencing climate and ecological chaos, and that their prime concern is survival. Or we may attempt to *blame* developing nations who are catching up in terms of material possessions, manufacturing, vehicles and pollution. We may say that it's not entirely our problem, that they need to change their behaviour.

We may alter our behaviour, recycle avidly, refuse to buy plastics. We may try to shop locally, grow vegetables, buy expensive ecological products. This can be a form of *bargaining*: if I go vegan, refuse to fly, recycle, etc., that will help. But we quickly realize this is a drop in the ocean. We can't and don't persuade everyone. Systems aren't changing. We look around and see things "getting worse."

We may feel *confusion* or *frustration,* when we realise that other people aren't even thinking about the problems or taking them seriously.

We may *despair*, waking daily in *depression* and with a sense that it is all too late, there is nothing any of us can do, that all our *efforts are in vain* in the face of unstoppable climate change and ecological collapse.

We may get *stuck*, right here, in despair. Or we may move rapidly between feelings of *depression, sadness, anger, blame, guilt and regret, and anxiety*. We may *lose sleep, or sleep too much*; find it *difficult to concentrate*, or *speak about nothing else*; have *physical symptoms of illness* but be told there is nothing wrong. Our anxiety may have been pathologised or medicalised. We may have been given anti-depressants; our friends or family may have lost patience.

We may feel desperately *lonely*. We may feel that we know no-one else who feels the same way, *that no-one cares*. We may risk becoming *burnt out* by urgency and the weight of the emotional load. We may feel a sense of *emptiness and pointlessness*. We carry on because we feel there's nothing else we can do.[1]

The data indicates that growing numbers of people, especially younger people, are struggling with eco-anxiety. The problem is that such anxiety is built on solid ground. We can't just dismiss it by clearing up the facts and demonstrating that things aren't really that bad. Generally speaking, things *are* that bad.

2. Unhelpful Responses to Our Ecological Crises

There are several common responses to ecological anxieties that are, on the whole, not constructive. I will mention three, represented by the fool, the hare, and the ostrich.

a) The Fool: Denial

Climate change denial comes in several forms. Some claim that the whole climate change story is a pernicious hoax, and that the climate is only experiencing one of its many temporary wobbles. This variety is increasingly

---

1. The extended quotation is from the Green Christian course on eco-anxiety, "Deep Waters," session 2. Used with permission. Green Christian is a grassroots, interchurch, creation care organization based in the UK. For more information, visit the Green Christian website: greenchristian.org.uk.

looking untenable, even to the denying communities themselves, so it seems to me to be slowly being replaced by other versions. One of these asserts that while the climate is changing, it's not a big deal. After all, we've faced climate changes in the past, and this is just another adjustment. Put on some sun cream and stop whining. Others argue that while the climate is changing, and presents real challenges, it is not doing so as a consequence of human action and so human societies don't need to modify their *modi operandi*; we can carry on living as we have done and just deal with the changing situation through our usual practices of technological innovation.

Despite the popularity of climate change denial in certain sections of the population, it's clear that most deniers are not such because they find the scientific arguments underpinning belief in human-influenced climate change unconvincing. It is true that they will often *claim* that the science doesn't support the scary warnings, but it seems to me that this is in large part a desperate grasping at straws to persuade themselves and others that their position is rational. Most climate change deniers are not remotely qualified to properly understand, let alone evaluate, the climate science. And most of them have probably never even tried. The underlying reasons for the denial are much more personal and ideological. For instance, the majority of Westerners have embraced consumer lifestyles in deep and existential ways. If climate scientists are correct, then we need to change the way that we live. *But we don't want to*. We grab at anything, no matter how flimsy, that will allow us to keep on living the way we desire. Climate change is *deeply inconvenient* to the lifestyles we have been socialized to crave and upon which our current economic systems depend. In a nutshell: we don't maintain those lifestyles because we reject climate change; we reject climate change because we want to maintain those lifestyles. One way or another, the science must be cut down to size so it can be ignored.

There is, however, no denying the fact that the *overwhelming majority* of scientists who specialize in climate (i.e., the ones who have a better idea what they are talking about than most of us) agree that:

- change is happening,
- it is significant,
- it is rapid,
- it will have a plethora of harmful impacts, and
- it is, in large part, a consequence of human activities.

Refusal to take the threat seriously leads to failure to address the issues that desperately need facing. That in turn exacerbates the problem, to the detriment of all. Denial is a pathway to disaster. A Christian should listen for the cry of Wisdom in the science, a call to heed her warnings or face the consequences. And in a wisdom worldview climate change denial is the pathway to the house of Dame Folly, who calls seductively to those passing by, promising much. "But little do they know that the dead are there, that her guests are deep in the realm of the dead" (Prov 9:18).

b) The Hare: Despair

The flip side of this is to take the data and the various scientific models seriously and to become overwhelmed. Looking with care at the science and then at the seeming inability of governments, businesses, and societies to make changes even remotely approaching the levels necessary can easily lead to despair. Like a hare transfixed by the lights of an oncoming car, we freeze and await our doom. Rather than motivating constructive action, despair leads to paralysis, and that's bad both for our mental health and for the environment.

c) The Ostrich: Ignoring

Another response, which may at first sight look like "denial," is the ostrich response.[2] Here one does not outright deny climate change, one simply refuses to speak or even think about the issue. Instead, the approach is to bury one's head in the sand and ignore the question entirely. This, however, is not to be confused with climate change denial. If anything, it is motivated by a fear that human-affected climate change *is* a horrible reality and that facing up to it will be too distressing. So as a coping mechanism one simply avoids the issue. And let me be very clear: sometimes, for one's psychological welfare, this is a necessary strategy. However, it is such only as a *temporary* "fix." This is not an approach that empowers anyone to make or advocate for the changes required to mitigate climate change. We might need to stop and rest here, but we should not seek to settle down.

3. Worship and a Christian Path Between Denial and Despair

What we need is a pathway between the inaction of denial and the paralysis of despair. This path must balance honesty and hope.

2. With apologies to actual ostriches, which do not do this.

- *Honesty* must look the reality of our current situation full in the face and recognize that things are bad and that they will get worse, even if we take radical action.
- *Hope* is what enables us to look beyond the current crisis to better possibilities and empowers us to push toward them.

This pathway is something of a tightrope walk. There is not some universally correct and static balance of honesty and hope that we can "get right" and then move forward with a permanently fixed equilibrium. Our situations—personally, locally, nationally, and globally—are dynamic, and keeping the right balance, whether as individuals or communities, requires constantly readjusting the relative weighting as we move forward. We may oscillate, sometimes focusing more on hope and at other times more on the bleakness of the situation. Yet we always hold both together. Without honesty, hope is naïve optimism that excuses inactivity. Without hope, honesty leads to despair and inaction. Holding both together in an ever-changing balance sensitive to our contexts can help us survive and motivate positive world-blessing action. And taking positive action and making a difference further inspires hope and clears a path away from crippling anxiety.

Notice that last phrase: it is a path away from *crippling* anxiety, the kind that paralyses us. It is *not* a path away from anxiety. Such is not our lot in this life. Grief and fear will remain, for they are fitting responses to the reality of our situations. But they can be transformed by hope into provocations to action. My belief is that the Christian spirituality offers a way to walk this tightrope.

a) Honesty: Confession, Intercession, and Lament

The kinds of faith encouraged in the Bible do not require people to pretend everything is OK when it is not OK. Such pretense is not faith, it is self-delusion. The story we sketched in Part I of this book marks out the present age in which we live as one characterized in part by sins and sufferings, great and small. Denying any of that is no part of faith as understood by the early Christ-followers. Quite the contrary. The story we inhabit requires that we recognize such things, and in biblical spirituality such acknowledgment initially takes the form of prayer. This is clear in three particular (and partially overlapping) modes of prayer: confession, intercession, and lament.

Part II: Inhabiting The Story

i. Confession

Confession of sin has been a feature of Jewish and Christian devotion, both private and public, from the very beginning. The point of such confession is not to shatter our sense of self-worth and keep us in our lowly place (though misshapen versions of confession can do precisely that). Rather, it is aimed at *restoration* and *transformation*. It is about becoming more like Christ.

Confession is hard work. It requires self-examination, on the part of individuals and groups, and vulnerability. It demands humility and a willingness to see our mistakes and to own them as culpable sin. It requires us to seek forgiveness—from God and from those against whom we have offended—and, whenever possible, to make restitution. Confession is part of a wider process directed towards positive change in our behaviors and attitudes.

When it comes to eco-spirituality there is much important work to be done in this realm. In the first instance, we need to be called to and guided in self-examination, individually and communally. We need to regularly reflect on how our everyday choices and actions are impacting the world around us and we need to acknowledge our culpability in their negative effects. We need to seek forgiveness.

In the modern world we are so deeply entangled in complex webs of nature-harming economic and social systems that the process of discerning the damage they cause (which is usually well hidden from plain sight) and finding ways to navigate the systems with godly wisdom is a lifelong voyage of learning and change. When it comes to eco-spirituality we can't just repent once and move on. Self-examination, confession of sin, and repentance need to be an integral and ongoing part of the change-journey. And this spiritual habit is precisely a way of holding together honesty and hope: vulnerable recognition of the sometimes-ugly truth, about ourselves and our communities, alongside the hope for forgiveness and positive change (see chapter 7).

One final matter. I said that confession of sin was directed both toward God and towards those against whom we have offended and that when possible restitution of some kind should be made. Yet when it comes to harm done to forests and rivers and animals and such like, surely confession and restitution are out of place. Am I seriously suggesting that it is appropriate to ask forgiveness from bees or woods, say, and to seek to make restitution to them? Actually, I *do* think that this would be a good spiritual practice. Even if you know that the bees and trees do not understand what you are saying or what you are doing, such a practice shapes *our* attitudes and behavior towards them. It helps us to see the world differently. It treats nonhuman creatures as valuable and as having suffered harm as a result of human actions (actions in which we ourselves have participated in one way or another) and it seeks to take steps towards righting the wrongs. It forms more thoughtful and considerate patterns of engaging with nonhuman creation. Personally, I think it would be very worthwhile for individuals and for communities, through their representatives, to "get over themselves" and to engage in such "quirkiness."

ii. Intercession

Another prominent part of Judaeo-Christian spirituality has been intercessory prayer. It goes without saying that if everything was as it should be there would be no need to ask God to bring deliverance. The very act of praying for salvation of some kind implies that the world is out of sorts and that it needs saving. Every time we ask God to act, we are simultaneously being encouraged to be honest about situations and to hold them before God with hope.

How does this relate to eco-spirituality? Praying for the health of the world, its environments, and the blessing of its diverse inhabitants ought to be a regular part of Christian worship. Praying for godly change in human use of the natural world is an acknowledgment that things are not as they should be nor as they could be and to seek divine help in redirecting human behaviors. Such a community practice recognizes the value of the thriving of the earth and both manifests and helps to form our priorities. Learning to pray for the world is to join with God's mission of blessing creation and to open our hearts to be a part of the answer to our own prayers.

iii. Lament

Alongside this is the practice of lament, crying out to God in grief, dismay, anguish, and anger. Laments bring our confusion, disappointment, loss, and anxiety about a current situation into the presence of God.

Let's be clear: lament is not some marginal aspect of biblical spirituality. Around a third of the book of Psalms is lament prayers, and one finds other laments spread across the Bible, both Old and New Testaments. Even Jesus laments while he is on the cross. After hours of suffering in silence, he cries out in a loud voice, "My God, my God, why have you forsaken me?" (Mark 15:33–34, quoting the opening of Psalm 22).

As lament is not so common in Christian worship, I will need to spend a little more time on it, beginning by clearing up a few misunderstandings.

First, lament is *not* irreverent. It can sometimes sound like it is. Here are prayers in which people do not merely express sorrows but can sometimes even direct their anger towards God, accusing God of failure or injustice. The book of Job is telling here. Job speaks very bluntly about his innocence and the injustice of his sufferings. He even wishes he could put God on trial. However, in the end of the book, while Job comes to realize that he spoke without really understanding (Job 42:1–6), God endorses Job's words and rejects the words of Job's "comforters," those who sought to defend God's honor from this complaining man! They spoke wrong. Job spoke right (42:7). More than that, Job's laments were compatible with the fear of God. It is not irrelevant that the Bible carefully preserved and gave such a prominent space to this kind of spirituality. In effect, this puts God's own stamp of approval on complaining against God. Remember, *even Jesus* prayed this way.

Second, lament is *not* faithless. Job's tormented prayers of complaint were, in a sense, *a refusal to let go of God* in the face of calamity. Lament insists on bringing confusion and anger and pain before God. Pay careful attention to the lament Jesus prayed: "My God, my God, why have you forsaken me?" God is still addressed as *"my* God." This is not an abandoning of faith. This is faith weeping.

Third, lament is *not* hopeless. You might think that people who pray the kinds of prayers found in some of the psalms have given up all hope. Not so. The very act of bringing their fear and grief to God is an act of hope for a future beyond the present suffering. Many of the lament psalms include expressions of hope in the swirling torrent of grief. Even the book of Lamentations, perhaps the bleakest book in the Bible, in which divine silence is heartbreakingly loud, offers glimpses of real hope for restoration (Lam 3:19–33; 4:22).[3]

How does this relate to eco-spirituality? Fairly simply. The grief we may feel at the ravaging of the earth is not to be set aside but embraced and brought into the presence of God. It needs to be a part of our personal and communal prayers.

While lament has always featured in individual Christian piety, it has often not been prominent in communal worship. In part, this is out of a concern that many of those present may not be "feeling" sorrow on the occasion of any particular gathering. So, rather than making people pray prayers that they are not "feeling," we avoid laments. Of course, exactly the same argument could be made of the joyful prayers that are regularly a part of communal worship. On any particular occasion many will be sorrowful and

---

3. On Lamentations and Christian spirituality, see Parry, *Lamentations*.

not able to "feel" the words of joy we ask them to pray. That doesn't stop us using them. Perhaps we believe that the joyful prayers are aspirational and that they can help to lift people out of sorrow. Maybe. However, teaching people how to lament well is an important part of Christian worship. If we do not provide folk with the language and patterns in which to lament, they may struggle to handle grief with Christian integrity. By our neglect of communal lament, we implicitly signal that such prayer is somehow "unfitting." It *isn't* unfitting. And environmental crises are perfect issues over which laments can be integrated into our worship. After all, the concerns raised affect *every* person in the gathering, either directly or indirectly, whether they know it or not. And the issues certainly affect countless millions of people across the world, as well as untold numbers of animal and plant species. If that is not a reason to lament, then we are a people with no compassion.

The act of communal lament is formative. It teaches values and ways of relating to the ruptures in our worlds. It provides the community permission to grieve. It gives us words when we may struggle to find words. It places the earth's troubles into a prayerful context so they can be held before God.

Lament can be either extempore and free-flowing or more structured and prepared. Context will affect which is most suitable. In communal gatherings it will often be more helpful to plan ahead for lamentation.[4] While that can sound contrived and fake, do not confuse planning and writing prayers of lament in advance with inauthenticity. All the psalms of lament in the Bible are poetic compositions. The heartbreaking poems in Lamentations 1–2 are even acrostics! Someone took a lot of time to craft them. Yet there is nothing fake about the pain they articulate. It is still raw. These poems bleed on the page in front of you. And because of the care taken in finding words to express the sorrow, they have proved to be an enduring help for countless generations of Jews and Christians ever since. Think yet again of Jesus on the cross. His cry of dereliction was not some extempore prayer. Rather, he reached for a long poetic composition, Psalm 22, and found words that perfectly captured how he felt. There is nothing of "performance" in Jesus' lament.

Here is an example of such a prayer, from Jessica Abell.

> Has God left creation?
> We stumble over the carcasses of earth in search of life.
> Abandoned, betrayed, and denied its goodness, we weep.
>   Lightless.

---

4. For those who need guidance and resources for eco-lament in churches, an excellent place to start is Anne and Jeffrey Rowthorn's *God's Good Earth in Crisis*.

> Hopeless.
>> Helpless.
>
> God, you once moved and lived and breathed in all things.
> God, you once walked in the Garden and consecrated creation.
> God, you once bound us all together in your covenant of salvation.
>
> But where is our help to be found
>> in this world clouded by sin?
> But how can we reach you, God,
>> as we choke on this poisoned air?
> But when can we eat this food,
>> emerging from toxic soil?
>
> All of your creation struggles to breathe,
>> to live and thrive.
> Our city's streets are slick with oil,
>> our walls with slime.
> Your birds falter.
>> Your deer stumble.
>> Your streams die.
>
> God, you have seen creation and called it good.
>> Save us now.
> God, you have made creation in your image.
>> Save us now.
> God, you have called us into your healing love always.
>> Save us now.
>
> God, you knock at our doors, begging entrance.
>> But we look away, we turn toward ourselves.
> God, you invite us down a different path.
>> But we go our own way, sure of our footing.
> God, you offer us abundance and plenty.
>> But we see only through eyes of fear and greed.
>
> God, be with us in our despair and hear us as we cry out to you.[5]

Alongside prayers of lament in worship gatherings, churches can also organize eco-vigils as safe spaces for local communities to come and express their lamentation over the climate crisis or other environmental degradations. Here there is less guided direction offered in how to express lament, but a protected and holy "space" is opened and guarded in which such feelings are respected and honored.

---

5. With thanks to Rev. Jessica Abell for permission to reproduce this prayer.

b) Hope: Gospel-Shaped Living

As we spelled out in Part I, hope is integral to the story of the cosmos that Christians tell, the story in which we live and move. God created the world for a purpose, with a destiny. Although sin throws a major spanner in the works, God has acted in Christ to bring creation to the goal for which it was made. Jesus is the Creator living among us as a creature. In his crucifixion, the Creator-creature dies *with* and *for* creation. In his resurrection he overcomes sin and death *as* a creature *for* creatures. That future of the world is *already a reality* in the body of the risen Lord, in his capacity as representative. His resurrection *is* the resurrection of the whole creation. Because of God's work in Jesus, the ultimate future of the cosmos is already accomplished and thus guaranteed.

However, it is crucial for any understanding of the New Testament and its mode of faith and spirituality that we grasp the ever-present tension between the "now" and the "not yet" in Christian understandings of the world. Allow me to recap. The basic apocalyptic worldview inherited by the early Jesus-followers was one in which history was divided into two ages: the present evil age and the age to come. The present world is marked by sin and death, but the age to come, the kingdom of God, will be characterized by life and peace in the Holy Spirit. The transition from the present sinful age to the coming kingdom age is marked by a radical divine act of judgment and resurrection from the dead. It was this divine act that many in Israel awaited and hoped for.

That basic picture was complicated by the coming of Christ. With Jesus, the sun started to rise, the new age began to dawn, the long hoped-for future was arriving. The kingdom of God, Jesus said, was arriving *now* in and through him. And his resurrection was the promised new life from the dead at the turn of the ages, the new creation—and it was becoming a reality *right here and now*.

Yet, the new creation of resurrection was restricted to Christ. *He* has been raised. *We* have not. Not yet. The New Testament is crystal clear on this matter. Because he is our representative, his resurrection is a *foretaste* of what the rest will experience in due course. It is a *promise*. It is like the first fruits gathered from the coming harvest, anticipating the full gathering yet to come. So for the followers of Jesus and for the rest of creation, the fullness of the resurrection and the kingdom lie still in the future.

In Christian thought this all makes the present moment somewhat perplexing. Salvation is both present and future, both "now" and "not yet." There is a tension between the present age and the coming age. We still live in a broken world, a world that crucified Jesus and that often crucifies others, the followers of Jesus included. However, a new era has started to seep into the present era, but only in glimmers and signs. The fullness still lies ahead and must be awaited in hope. This is precisely why hope is a core Christian virtue (1 Cor 13:13). It is built into the very heart of the Jesus-story we inhabit.

Precisely here, in Jesus of Nazareth, lies a key insight of Christian spirituality and the heart of my claim about the Christian middle path between denial and despair. The gospel proclamation of the Christ-community has always insisted on the importance of *holding together* the cross and the resurrection of Jesus, giving great weight to both.

If our story was the story of a cross but without a resurrection, it would be a tale of darkness without light. It would be a narrative of despair, terminating in a tomb. That is not the gospel.

If, however, our good news was all about new life with no cross, it would be little more than a naïve romanticism that turns a blind eye to the torments of the world.

Our gospel story has never been either of those things. It has always held the cross and the resurrection in tension, shifting its focus between the two. Sometimes, such as Holy Week, the cross is the focus, but never in such a way as to lose all sight of the coming resurrection. At Easter the focus shifts to the resurrection, but always careful to keep in mind that the risen Lord is the crucified Lord who still bears scars in his flesh.

From their first days, Christ-followers have always believed themselves to live lives characterized by *both* the cross *and* the resurrection. The story of Jesus interprets their own stories. As Christ's body, the church and its members carry their crosses and share in Christ's sufferings. At the same time, the church experiences anticipations of the resurrection age even now: they have been buried and raised with Christ in baptism and know something of freedom from sin's power, the Spirit of God has been poured out on them, and in their communities they experience an anticipation of the multi-ethnic unity of humanity transcending the divisions of this age. Yet all these anticipations are painfully partial and imperfect, as anyone who has ever been part of a church will know. Our full participation in Christ's resurrection is still very much in the future. If anything, the New Testament teaches that our present existence is marked most clearly by the sufferings of the cross; yes, we taste the powers of the age to come, but we only *taste* them and must continue looking forward with hopeful yearning for their coming fullness.

How does this relate to eco-spirituality? Like this:

- The message of the crucifixion is a refusal to paper over creation's damage. It will not allow us to pretend that everything is OK. It is a loud NO to denial.
- The message of the resurrection is a refusal to let sin and death have the final word. You cannot speak of the resurrection and reject hope. The empty tomb speaks, declaring, "In the end, all shall be well. If all is not well, it is not the end." It is a loud NO to despair.

Precisely because the church believes that the Jesus story is not merely a story about Jesus but is *also the story about all whom Jesus represents*—Israel, the nations, and the whole cosmos—this gospel narrative provides the framework for interpreting the world. Christians do not merely tell the story of Jesus—they see *their own* stories in relation to his. In baptism, their lives and identities are bound to his story: they die, are buried, and are raised with him. They are called to live the gospel in the shape of their own lives. And because the story ties death and resurrection so closely together, when times are dark, the gospel refuses to allow the eclipse of either honesty or hope.

It is primarily in worship that Christians learn to inhabit this gospel. Every act of Christian worship has the cross and resurrection of Jesus at its heart. Not only that but the entire Christian year is formed around the story of incarnation, death, and resurrection such that the very rhythms of time habituate our increasing indwelling of it. Lives slowly formed around that narrative are gradually orientated to the world in ways that enable wise traversing of the tightrope. And when we lose balance and start to fall off to the left or the right, the worship of the community helps us to gain our equilibrium again.[6] It is such a spirituality that enables resilience and empowers action for change.

4. Prophetic Acts of Hope

Allow me to take you back to Jerusalem around 2,600 years ago. And let me introduce a prophet: Jeremiah—a man with an unwelcome message—unwelcome by *him* as much as by his Judean audience. It was this: *Repent or you will face destruction at the hands of the Babylonian Empire.* But the

---

6. A word of warning: the gospel offers solid and ultimate hope, but it is not naïve hope. It does not rule out the possibility of massive catastrophes before the telos. It does not even rule out the possibility of human extinction. This is precisely because Jesus did not merely suffer—he *died*. His resurrection was on the other side of experiencing irreversible termination. Those who claim that God would never allow things to get that bad for the earth speak of things they cannot know.

people didn't listen, despite repeated warnings. And the time came when a line was crossed. Jeremiah's message changed. It was now: *It's too late. You've reached a tipping point. Even if you change your ways, you can't avert the coming catastrophe. Nonetheless, even now you can mitigate its impact. Surrender to Babylon or face annihilation.* Surrender to Babylon?! As you can imagine, this message was about as welcome in Jerusalem as a hornet in the underpants. It may not surprise you that Jeremiah was imprisoned for treason. . . . And outside the walls of the city the Babylonian army was laying siege to it. The doom Jeremiah had spoken of was approaching, inexorably. Yet even with disaster at the very gate, the king and the people remained in denial.

This situation reminds me in some ways of the message that scientists and environmentalists have been making for decades now: we can't carry on living the way we currently are, or we face catastrophe. Repent! In recent years the focus has been on climate change: we need to vastly reduce our carbon emissions, or we'll reach a point of no return.

A major scientific review based on over two hundred climate studies published in 2022 says that the world is on the brink of as many as sixteen disastrous tipping points.[7] Five of them might have already been passed when the report was written—including the collapse of Greenland's ice cap (with large sea level rises to come), the collapse of a key current in the north Atlantic (disrupting the rain billions of people depend on for food), and a melting of the permafrost (releasing vast amounts of carbon into the atmosphere, accelerating climate change). Imagine a tipping point as like when you're pushing a ball up a hill—there comes a moment, at the top, when even if you stop pushing the ball it'll continue rolling on, down the other side. According to the review, there's nothing we can do now to avert some of the consequences of our actions, for we've pushed certain balls over the top of their hills, setting into motion sequences of events that *will* play out. However, despite this, there's still time to mitigate their impact and to stop more tipping points being reached with other balls.

Yet, despite such information being widely and easily available, human societies across the globe, but most especially among the rich nations, still seem to be continuing apace with their destructive ways. Like King Zedekiah and the Jerusalemites of Jeremiah's day, besieged by Babylon's armies, *we too* bury our heads in the sand hoping to ignore what's going on, and some even, like Zedekiah, declare the message of doom to be "fake news."

Yet in the midst of this dark situation God sends a message of hope to the prophet: *redeem your cousin's field in Anathoth* (Jer 32). (Anathoth was

---

7. Carrington, "World on Bring of Five 'Disastrous' Climate Tipping Points."

Jeremiah's hometown, about three miles from Jerusalem.) Let me explain the situation: this was an agrarian society in which land wasn't only home but also the means of subsistence: growing crops, raising vegetables and legumes, planting trees for nuts and fruit, pasturing animals. One didn't sell land except in the most desperate of circumstances. What had happened was probably this: Hanamel, Jeremiah's cousin, had at some point in the past experienced economic pressure that had forced him to seek help. He had contracted a loan from a lender and had signed his family field over as collateral. But when his loan came due, he was unable to repay the lender. This meant the lender could take the field (which would be catastrophic for Hanamel and his family). So Hanamel appealed to his cousin Jeremiah to redeem the family field before the lender could take possession, thus keeping the field in the family. Jeremiah agreed and redeemed the field by contract and the payment of seventeen shekels to Hanamel so that he could pay off the lender.

So far so good. Now consider the wider context in which this family crisis took place: Judah and Jerusalem were facing inevitable destruction. Jeremiah *himself* had prophesied as much. The cities of Judah would be razed to the ground, with devastating consequences for decades to come. Jeremiah could see this doom fast approaching. *So, what's the point of buying this field to keep it in the family?* In the circumstances, it looks like a futile, pointless gesture, a waste of time. Yet it's precisely the prophetic action that God requires. It's a sign of *hope*. "For this is what YHWH Almighty, the God of Israel, says: 'Houses, fields and vineyards will again be bought in this land'" (Jer 32:15).

The point is *not* that catastrophe can be averted. It can't. The point is *not* that it won't be bad. It will be bad. The point is: *this is not the end of Jerusalem's story*. The point is: *there is hope beyond the seeming hopelessness*. The point is: *God is committed to his people and will not allow their story to end in annihilation*. Jeremiah's little act may *seem* futile, but it is a prophetic sign of hope for the future, because Jeremiah believed that there *was* a future beyond the coming disaster. God had promised it.

In our current environmental crises, the church should be walking in the footsteps of Jeremiah. On the one hand, we are to refuse the option of denial. Denial might make us *feel* better, but it's the road to hell. The church *must not* avert its gaze from environmental devastations. And what we see *should* distress us, as Jeremiah was distressed by his message.

On the other hand, and at the very same time, like Jeremiah, we are not those who despair and give up. We are Easter people. We are a people of incurable hope. We believe that the future of creation is in God's hands and so creation has a future, a good one. But just as resurrection lies on the other side of the cross, so too we must be prepared to face the dark before the dawn breaks. Such hope enables resistance. As William Sloane Coffin once put it: "hope criticizes what is, hopelessness rationalizes it. Hope resists, hopelessness adapts."[8]

Some decades back, the environmentalist message was: repent, change your ways or face disaster. But we're past that now. It's too late. The task is now to proclaim: we can't avert some of the coming crises, but we can change our ways to limit their impact.

That's a hard message to persuade people of when things still don't *look* super bleak in our daily lives, especially in wealthy nations, where we can insulate ourselves against the worst of the impact. Poorer nations don't have that luxury. Ask people in the Horn of Africa, where climate change is bringing increasing drought and famine on a scale not seen for many decades. Ask people in Pakistan, where climate change is similarly bringing increased heat and drought, but also extreme weather, and where sea level rises and melting glaciers in the Himalayas are contributing to devastating flooding. This is all made worse because the country lacks the resources to shield its people against the multiple impacts of such events. The church, like Jeremiah, needs to point to such catastrophes and help Westerners to see that *we* bear considerable responsibility for this situation.

In addition to calling for change, our task as Christian communities is also to perform a million little acts of prophetic hope, like Jeremiah's. His response to the coming darkness was to light a candle, to buy a field, to invest in the future of the land—because he trusted that it had one. Such acts are not trite trivializing deeds that pretend all is lovely when it isn't but acts that invest for the long-term future of the world. Acts that proclaim that there *is* a future for creation. And acts that *contribute towards* that future.

It is not in your power to save the world nor is it your responsibility. It is God's. Yes, God gives us freedom, even freedom to sin, and God may allow us to go so far as to crucify his world, *but* the God of the gospel, the God of Jesus Christ, determines its destiny. And its destiny is *resurrection*, not a tomb. *That* is the gospel. Our responsibility is to do the good that we can do, to participate in God's kingdom work through our own acts of audacious hope.

I will leave the final word with the great Christian author J. R. R. Tolkien:

"I wish it need not have happened in my time," said Frodo.

---

8. Coffin, *Passion for the Possible*, 88.

"So do I," said Gandalf, "and so do all who live to see such times. But that is not for them to decide. All we have to decide is what to do with the time that is given to us."[9]

---

9. Tolkien, *Fellowship of the Ring*, ch. 2, "Shadow of the Past."

B
Wise Living

13

Monastic Eco-Wisdom

ONE IMPORTANT STREAM IN the Christian tradition is monasticism and it provides a useful example of building a healthy, creation-attuned form of spiritual life.

Monasticism is probably to be traced back to second-century Syrian Christian ascetics[1] and especially to the fathers and mothers of the Egypt desert, beginning in the fourth century, men and women seeking God and battling the demonic in solitude, simplicity, and silence.[2] After the empire was Christianized in the fourth century, bearing witness through martyrdom became an unlikely fate and discipleship less demanding. Some, such as St. Anthony, felt the need to embrace a living martyrdom for Christ, "white martyrdom" (as opposed to "red martyrdom"). These spiritual seekers attracted followers and imitators, who wrote down some of their wisdom and perpetuated their practices. Many colonies of solitaries and ascetics sprang up in the desert. Here, silence was cultivated as a critical spiritual discipline. It was and is an intense and dedicated life. "To be a monk," writes Greg Peters, is at its core "to be single-minded toward God."[3]

---

1. On Syrian ascetics, see MacCulloch, *Silence*, 69–74. On even earlier roots for Christian monasticism, see Peters, *Story of Monasticism*, 1–20.

2. On the desert fathers and mothers, see Farag, *Balance of the Heart*. On the general history of monasticism, see Belisle, *Language of Silence*, and MacCulloch, *Silence*.

3. Peters, *Monkhood of All Believers*, 35.

In the fifth century, John Cassian brought his experiences of monasticism in Palestine and Egypt to Gaul, transplanting it into the West. The following century, in Italy, the landmark Rule of St. Benedict for community life was written. From the Benedictines all the branches of Western monasticism emerged over the coming centuries.

1. Monasticism and Ecology

Monasticism is not an environmental movement, and its focus is not on plants and animals and ecosystems. It is first and foremost a spirituality and discipleship movement. However, by seeking to live out the Christian story in their own lives, monks past and present have ended up creating patterns of life that have much to teach us about wise creation-sensitive living.

In the sixth century, St. Benedict (c. 480–c. 550), who was to become one of the founts of Western monasticism, lived close to the natural world. He'd turned his back on urban life in the degenerating Roman Empire and had gone to live as a hermit in a cave near Subiaco, Italy. In the three years he was there he learned to feed and clothe himself from the forest around him, and he would have come to appreciate his utter dependence upon the land. Like other hermits before and after him, Benedict developed a kind of friendship with animals, famously a raven, which used to turn up each day at his mealtimes and feed from his hand.[4] Might his years living in the cave have contributed to his comment in the Rule that "we believe that the divine presence is everywhere" (*RB* 19.1)? And might it have shaped his sense of the place of humanity in creation?

> After all, this was the man who spent considerable energy discussing the virtue of humility, a term derived from *humus*, the dark rich soil of the earth. To live into humility or *humus* suggested that the Christian and the monastic be rooted in the earth, *down* to the earth, not puffed up, not "above" others, not arrogant. Seeing Benedict *within* nature, rather than above it, allows one to see beasts, birds, and vegetation—God's creation—not as a mere backdrop but as primary actors with the young hermit and soon-to-be abbot.[5]

After the years as a hermit (and a failed spell as the abbot of a nearby monastery) Benedict set up his own small lakeside community in Subiaco, which he built up over twenty-five years. After that he settled at Monte

---

4. Gregory the Great, *Dialogues* II.8.3.
5. Torvend, *Monastic Ecological Wisdom*, 63.

Cassino, near Naples, and built a new monastery. It was here that he wrote his famous Rule (*regula*). A *regula* was a set of rules governing monastic life within a community. At the time of Benedict there were many different sets of such rules, often very long and severe. Benedict's Rule by contrast was short, humane, and moderate, and over time it gradually became the standard rule in Western monasteries.

Benedict's Rule makes *stability* a critical component for communities. A monastery and its monks are to be fixed in one place, not nomadic. Monks are to commit to live with a particular community. And that community is committed to the area in which it is located. Monasteries are to be self-sufficient. Thus, they were traditionally located near springs or rivers, for water, and produced all that they needed for food, clothing, and medicine. Such monastic communities inevitably become acutely aware how dependent they are on their environment. And the commitment to stability means that the monks cannot use up the resources of a place and move on. If their soil becomes depleted or their water source polluted it would be catastrophic, certainly in times gone by. Consequently, they come to appreciate how important it is to develop ways of living in a location that enables it to flourish. In this way, an ethic of *care* for the natural world around them is instilled. Such a life requires the community to come to know, in an intimate way, the particularities of the natural world around the monastery. It is, in a real sense, a partner in their lives. In Benedict's day, this was in stark contrast to the cities of the Roman Empire, which were gobbling up natural resources to their own detriment.[6] We might say that "Benedict can be regarded as patron saint of those who believe that true conservation means not only protecting nature against human misbehavior but also developing human activities which favor a creative, harmonious relationship between [humanity] and nature."[7]

Another important element in monastic life is that there is *no private ownership* in the community. The lands and water around them are not owned by any individuals. The logic is that the earth does not belong to humans but to God (Ps 24:1). Participating in the fruit of the land is shared among them and so too is responsibility for its care.

A further core aspect of monastic spirituality is *simplicity* of life. Benedict made the following a requirement for his monks: "in all matters frugality is the rule" (RB 39.10). He encouraged moderation (*moderatio*), a middle path between the extremes of excess and deprivation, of having too much or

---

6. On the Roman practices of degrading environments and the consequences, see Burroughs, *Creation's Slavery and Liberation*, ch. 2; Torvend, *Monastic Ecological Wisdom*, ch. 1.

7. René Dubos (1974), quoted in Torvend, *Monastic Ecological Wisdom*, 73.

too little. Monks should not take more than necessary, and resources should be distributed as they are needed. Greed and overconsumption and pointless waste are considered spiritually decadent. St. Paul would have agreed:

> But godliness with contentment is great gain. For we brought nothing into the world, and we can take nothing out of it. But if we have food and clothing, we will be content with that. Those who want to get rich fall into temptation and a trap and into many foolish and harmful desires that plunge people into ruin and destruction. For the love of money is a root of all kinds of evil. Some people, eager for money, have wandered from the faith and pierced themselves with many griefs. (1 Tim 6:6–10)

This path of simplicity is essential for the health of the soul, but it is also essential for maintaining a balance of life that does not exhaust the land on which the community depends.

The life of a monk is governed by a daily rhythm of prayer, work, rest, and study (especially *lectio divina*). The day is divided up by sunrise and sunset and seven times of communal prayer are spread across the day: "From the rising of the sun to its setting, the name of the LORD is to be praised" (Ps 113:3).

Day and Night		Hours	Communal Prayer
			Lauds (at first light)
Daytime		6 AM	**Prime** (first hour)
		7 AM	
		8 AM	
		9 AM	**Terce** (third hour)
		10 AM	
		11 AM	
		12 PM	**Sext** sixth hour)
		1 PM	
		2 PM	
		3 PM	**None** (ninth hour)
		4 PM	
		5 PM	

Nighttime	First vigil (watch) of the night	6 PM	**Vespers**
		7 PM	
		8 PM	
	Second vigil of the night	9 PM	**Compline** (just prior to bed)
		10 PM	
		11 PM	
	Third vigil of the night	12 AM	
		1 AM	**Vigils** (during third watch)
		2 AM	
	Fourth vigil of the night	3 AM	
		4 AM	
		5 AM	

The daily pattern of prayer, governed by the natural rhythm of light and dark, is interspersed with work—four to five hours a day, which includes, among other things, working outdoors tending plants and animals or working in hospitality. This work is also understood to be an act of service to God, a mode of worship. The skill is in learning to "practice the presence of God," as the Carmelite Brother Lawrence famously put it in the seventeenth century, in the everyday tasks of life.

The monastic rhythm is also attuned to the natural cycle of the week and the liturgical rhythms of the year (which synchronize in various ways with nature's annual rhythms). This is a shape of life that fosters a Christian spirituality tuned into creation, one in which caring for creation is a spiritual duty and joy.

Finally, the practice of silence is developed within monastic communities, and it too plays an important role in forming a healthy eco-spirituality. As I develop this idea at some length in Appendix 1, I will say no more about it here.

In 1967 Lynn White argued that "[b]y destroying pagan animism, Christianity made it possible to exploit nature in a mood of indifference."[8] That claim is unfair. Of course, one can find Christians who abused their environments, but one can say exactly the same about ancient pagans. After all, the pagan Rome Empire that Christianity replaced had a notably poor environmental track record. The point here is that those who followed the Christian path most devoutly in the past were those who forged habits of life that were deeply respectful of the natural world. Those who did not live that way were arguably not fully inhabiting the Christian story.

8. White Jr., "Historical Roots," 1205.

2. Monasticism for the Rest of Us

Most of us can't become monastics. We have families, jobs, and a range of other life commitments. That, however, does not mean that there are not valuable lessons for all Christians in the monastic way. Greg Peters speaks helpfully of "the monkhood of all believers." Not everyone can or should be a monk, but every Christian can and should develop a monkish aspect to their lives, capturing that single-minded pursuit of God at the heart of monastic life. After all, the way of the monk is really a radical attempt to live the baptized life, and that is something to which *all* Christians are called.[9]

a) Asceticism

The monastic way is often referred to as ascetic, from the Greek *askēsis*, a word referring to the training required to develop a skill. It speaks to the discipline and self-control required in the pursuit of God and the development of virtues. Greg Peters defines it thus: "asceticism, as an essential component of spiritual growth, is the voluntary abstention from food and drink, sleep, wealth, sexual activity, and so on (for a period of time or permanently), for the purpose of maintaining inner attentiveness to God and achieving union with God."[10] The intention of the abstention is, in part, to gain self-control over our desires so that they do not control us. Such discipline underpins the formation of a life that is liberated from the seductive and mesmerizing power of all that glitters. And that is more ecologically important than we may think. "[W]hat asceticism is ultimately about is the correction of the chaotic desire and moral disorder within us so that we can perceive and welcome the world as God does. Asceticism is the discipline and art that, at its best, enables us to contemplate the beauty that radiates throughout creation."[11] As Thomas Merton helpfully puts it, "We do not detach ourselves from things, in order to attach ourselves to God, but rather we become detached *from ourselves* in order to see and use all things in and for God."[12]

We live in a consumer culture. Our economy works by constantly selling us things. Some of those things are things that we need, but many of them are not. That's why advertisers are constantly bombarding us with the message that we really do want—no, we *need*—this, that, or the other. Go on,

---

9. Peters, *Monkhood of All Believers*, ch. 3.
10. Peters, *Monkhood of All Believers*, 93.
11. Wirzba, *From Nature to Creation*, 88.
12. Merton, *New Seeds of Contemplation*, 21.

be a devil. Treat yourself. You're worth it. Get rid of that old coat—for goodness sake, it's over two years old! Buy a new one! That cell phone is so last year! You don't want this chocolate bar? C'mon, buy one, get one free! You'd be saving money, dude! Things that until recently were considered luxuries quickly become "necessities." All day, every day, we are being groomed into compliant consumers. We are becoming *Homo consumericus* (consumerist human), a creature very much lacking the vaunted wisdom (*sapientia*) of the so-called *Homo sapiens*. How so? Because this new consumer living is *literally* costing the earth. There are more than enough resources for the number of human beings on the planet. The main problem is not the size of the population, it is, in large part, the hugely expensive lifestyles we now expect as our "right."[13] This planet cannot afford to subsidize our extravagant living.

The challenge is that choosing to be different is not easy, for individuals, let alone societies! Our mindsets have been formed—or more accurately, *de*formed—around consumption. We are addicts. Even when we know about the impact of our lifestyles on the earth, we often choose to turn a blind eye and to follow our wayward hearts. That is as true for governments and businesses as it is for individuals. And the modern world is very skilled at shielding us from the consequences of our consumer choices, making such willful blindness a very real possibility for us. We often silently agree together to keep that kind of stuff out of sight as much as possible.

Change will only come if we learn new habits of perceiving and of living and that will require some education, some honesty, some courage, and *sustained discipline*. Training your brain into new patterns of thought and action is akin to learning a musical instrument. It takes time, effort, and staying power. In other words, we need to practice ascesis. That is not easy, and it will require both a motivating vision and a supporting community. Such a vision is something that Christianity can offer, and such a community is what the church must become if we are to be re-formed such that we can offer an alternative way of being in the world.

---

13. I am wary of those Westerners who blame environmental crises on the size of the global population. It is true that the world cannot sustain such a population *if everyone lives the way we in the West do*. But it's hard not to suspect that underneath it all is the assumption that we Westerners must maintain our lifestyles, and to do that we need to either keep global population numbers low or make sure the rest of the world don't live as well as we do. In fact, it is *we* who need to change.

b) Simplicity

The monastic path of simplicity, the Benedictine path between too little and too much, is of considerable importance for our modern world of excess. That is the case at both the macro- and the micro-scale.

At the macro-level, the recent work of economists like Kate Raworth resonates very deeply. Raworth's "doughnut economics" imagines a different road for the world's economies. The idea that economies are judged successful when they achieve year-on-year growth ad infinitum is taken as an unchallengeable "truth" by most economists, businesses, politicians, and journalists in the Western world. Yet it is deeply problematic at numerous levels, not the least of which is that it has led to *mind-bogglingly vast* wealth inequalities (which is never a good way forward for societies) and it is degrading the very planet upon which we depend for our lives, such that we are, in effect, committing suicide in slow motion. Raworth and other economists like her say that we need to abandon the idea that growth is *the* measure of economic health. Of course, there's a fundamental and positive place for growth in economies, especially for societies with considerable poverty. But as with living beings, there comes a time when we are fully grown. To continue growing after that is not healthy, it is a sign of sickness.

Raworth proposes a vision in which the goal of economies is meeting a wide range of human needs without it costing the earth. She presents her vision as a doughnut (see below).[14]

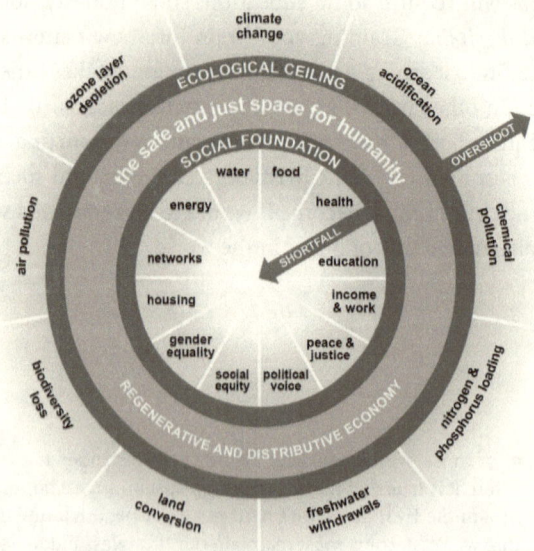

14. Doughnut (economic model). Reproduced under Wiki Commons license.

The outer circle of the doughnut shows the nine planetary boundaries that, if they are exceeded, threaten the environment we depend on. These boundaries map out the limits within which we can safely exist. (Current data indicates that we have already crossed six of the nine, with a seventh close to being crossed!) A healthy economy will imagine and implement ways of living that keep us thriving *within the safe limits*.

The inner circle of the doughnut shows twelve social dimensions that are indicators of a healthy society. An economy is a successful one if it keeps people from falling beneath the minimal threshold in these areas. The "wealth" of a community is not simply a measure of its finances. In this approach, social justice is integral to any healthy economy.

In the modern West we have already achieved hitherto unknown prosperity and now have more than enough material goods and wealth to keep everyone from falling below the threshold of the inner ring. What the West needs now is not unending growth but rather learning to live better together with the wealth we have generated. This is what Katherine Trebeck and Jeremy Williams call "the economics of arrival." They write: "Arrival is about adequacy, being able to meet basic needs. It is primarily a material notion, a matter of having the resources to deliver a good life."[15] And the West *has arrived*. Obviously not every individual, but we have enough now collectively to find ways to create societies in which no individuals fall below the thresholds. That is the task.

This is a holistic vision of *oikonomika* (economics) that is very much on the same wavelength as the theological picture presented in this book. To my thinking, an economics along these lines is a *wisdom* eco-nomics, a discernment of the nature of creation, the house (*oikos*) we are "managing" (from *nomos*, law, principle) for the health of humanity and of all its other inhabitants.

Making it a reality is no mean feat (understatement of the century), but it begins with imagining new ways of doing things, of thinking them through carefully together, and of implementing them on small scales and increasingly on wider scales.

The small scales are where the eco-spirituality of the church comes in. This is because the monastic path of moderation is an essential life-skill for the kind of shifts that we need to make. It is not just some quirky pathway for the super-holy. *All* Christians need to learn how to be content, indeed happy, with having all our needs met. Constantly hungering for more, bigger, better, newer, trendier is bad for us, bad for others, and bad for the planet. Learning to be content and to find joy in having enough is a key

---

15. Trebeck and Williams, *Economics of Arrival*, 5.

spiritual quality. Individual Christians need to pursue that mindset and communities of Christians need to foster it. This requires intentionality and ascesis. In this way, the church can model a different, a better, attitude to material wealth and social values. And in our current context that would be a prophetic sign indeed—an act of gospel witness.

c) A Rule of Life

An important supporting structure in the practice of ascesis and the re-forming of the mind and heart is developing a new daily rhythm of work, rest, and worship. And a rule of life can provide such a structure. Obviously, trying to pray the hours in the traditional monastic way (see above) is completely unrealistic for most people. But some regular pattern of daily prayer, Bible reading, and ecological living *is* realistic for many Christians and, with community support and self-discipline, achievable. We would need to work out a rule of life that fits the life God has called us to. Some people will need to work out a bespoke rule for themselves. Others will be part of a community that seeks to develop a rule together that they hold each other accountable to. For most of us the latter is the better way, as the former risks the traditional fate of a New Year's resolution: a solid start with good intentions rapidly followed by amnesia. Being part of a group in which there is mutual accountability and mutual support makes following a rule of life much more sustainable.

Let's just imagine what such an eco-spiritual rule of life might look like. It would involve a commitment to things such as the following:

- Some kind of daily practice of prayer and Scripture reading that follows a weekly rhythm. It may involve a traditional "daily office" (i.e., a formal morning and evening prayer as set out within a specific tradition) or perhaps a mix of devotional practices. Some care would be taken to bring out the creation emphases in such devotions.

- Gathering weekly for communal Christian worship, preferably on the first day of the week[16] and ideally gathering on fixed occasions (weekly, monthly, or at key seasonal and liturgical times) for outdoor worship.

---

16. For Christians, Sunday, not Monday, is the first day of the week. The shift towards making Monday the first day is a move toward building our lives around work. Sunday is the first day of creation in Genesis 1 and it is also the first day of the new creation—the eighth day, resurrection day. Eco-spirituality encourages us to take both time and the symbolism of time seriously, and so maintaining the traditional day of Christian gathering on a Sunday, whenever possible, is to be encouraged.

Again, care would be taken to shape such worship in creation-attuned ways.

- The practice of living respectfully towards nonhuman creation, by embarking and continuing on a path to reduce the negative impact of our lifestyles on the world and its inhabitants and by actively seeking the blessing of creation. For individuals that can be worked out in a wide range of ways.
- The practice of simplicity and moderation in life. This will be especially challenging.
- Ongoing learning, both about Scripture and about the natural world and ecological issues.
- The practice of hospitality (another traditional core of monasticism) and the service of others.

I have kept this general. Specific groups will need to decide what would work best for them. My point here is very simple: embracing a rule of life is one of the best ways of embedding eco-spirituality in our lives. What I am advocating for in this book is, as mentioned previously, a slow spirituality that takes a lifetime to grow into. It is not something that one-off events can bring about, even if they are fabulous. That is mere titillation. Formation needs support, direction, and training over time to really have an impact. For that, a rule of life is more than a decoration or the icing on the cake. It is a key part of the support structure that helps us to grow right.[17]

---

17. In this context, I should mention The Sophia Course. See 195n43.

14

Philo-Sophia

The Way of Wisdom and Lifelong Learning

A SPIRITUALITY IS A way of living in the world, and that includes the ways we seek to *know* the world. A *Wisdom*-shaped spirituality cannot but be interested in such matters. This chapter does not seek to answer any specific questions about the world but rather to consider how Christian eco-spirituality informs our dispositions towards understanding it.

1. Philosophy as a Way of Life

Nowadays we sometimes think of philosophy as clever people pondering difficult and puzzling questions, and in our more cynical moods we might think of this as simply playing intellectual games. Sometimes modern philosophy is exactly that. In the ancient world, it was not so. Philosophy literally means "the love of wisdom" and it was fundamentally concerned with *how to live a worthwhile human life.* To do that was thought to require some grasp of what a human being is and what kind of life is good for a human being.[1] And that inevitably leads to careful reflection on a whole range of matters, traditionally falling into four domains:

1. What is the nature of reality? (metaphysics)

1. Hadot, *What Is Ancient Philosophy?*

2. How can we know truth? (epistemology)
3. How should we live? (ethics)
4. How should we organize life together? (politics)

Wisdom for life required attention to such questions because the answers we give to them will have profound implications for how we live. Philosophers were not people who sat in ivory towers thinking hard about things that don't matter—they were deeply invested in discovering and modeling "the good life." And their followers were not simply attracted by entertaining ideas, they were following a pattern of life, one that they hoped would develop them as human beings and help them to become good.

There are reasons for thinking that Jesus would have been understood in his context to be a philosopher[2] and understandably the movement he inspired was originally known as "The Way."[3] In the second and third century prominent adherents to Christianity very clearly saw their movement as a philosophical path, like other such paths.[4] It taught answers to the big four questions above and schooled people in ways of living in the light of them. Indeed, if you read Part I of this book you should already have some general sense of the kind of answers it provided.

In what follows I am going to address the question of wisdom more generally in Christian spirituality before zooming in on eco-spirituality.

2. The Pursuit of Wisdom as a Way of Life

Chapters 1–9 of Proverbs, which introduce the collections of proverbs found in the rest of the book, place great stress on the centrality of the pursuit of wisdom. Indeed, it is the core pursuit in a person's life.

For Israel's wisdom traditions, the search for Sophia involved various important strands, most notably:

a) Listening to the wisdom of the community

b) Listening to divine revelation

c) Listening to experience

---

2. See Pennington, *Jesus the Great Philosopher*; Napier, *Soul Whisperer*.

3. Acts 9:2; 19:9, 23; 22:4; 24:14, 22.

4. E.g., Justin Martyr, *Dialogue with Trypho*; *1 Apology*; *2 Apology*; Tatian, *Address to the Greeks*; Athenagoras, *Embassy*. See, e.g., Karlowicz, *Socrates and Other Saints*.

a) Traditional, Communal Wisdom

Communities that have existed over long periods of time build up a lot of accumulated wisdom. It is passed on to children by parents and other teachers. That wisdom is often distilled into memorable sayings and stories and proverbs. The book of Proverbs, which gathers oral wisdom accumulated over centuries, teaches young men—yes, Proverbs was originally written for young men living in a patriarchal society—to pay close attention to the instruction of their parents and teachers.[5] To take one example at random: "Hear my son, your father's instruction, and forsake not your mother's teaching, for they are a graceful garland for your head and pendants for your neck" (1:8-9).

Now the Israelite wisdom teachers are well aware that communal wisdom is not infallible and that its insights don't apply in all situations, but part of learning wisdom is learning to discern when a teaching does and doesn't apply in any particular context. A classic illustration is Proverbs 26:4-5, which places two incompatible proverbs side by side. "Do not answer a fool according to his folly, or you yourself will be just like him" and "Answer a fool according to his folly, or he will be wise in his own eyes." So which one is true? Which one is wise? The point is that students are being taught that the general insights of proverbs are not applicable in all situations. Both teachings are wise when applied appropriately and both are folly if applied in the wrong situation (26:7, 9). Learning wisdom is not about simply repeating traditional insights and woodenly replicating them—that is what fools do. It's learning to discern which ones are *fitting* here and now and *how* they are fitting (15:23). There's no mathematical formula for discernment. And wisdom, while drawing respectfully on the insights of the tradition, is always accountable to the nuances of the particular situation.

b) Revelation and Wisdom

The Torah was not considered a mere community insight but was received by the people as *divine revelation*. Consequently, its authority in ancient Judaism was immense and its wisdom was taken as given. Nonetheless, it did need interpretation. Exactly what specific teachings *meant* and how they were to be *applied* in concrete situations required much study and insight and discussion to discern, for it is not always obvious. We see that process

---

5. For a thorough exploration of how the moral vision of Proverbs does and does not translate into the modern world, see Sandoval, *Moral Vision of Proverbs*. I don't follow Sandoval in all his views, but he makes a solid case for the view that Proverbs teaches a virtue ethic.

of interpretation taking place within the Torah itself. For example, compare the laws given at Sinai in Exodus with their equivalents in Deuteronomy—we can see some modifications to adapt to changing circumstances. And the books of the Hebrew Bible indicate ongoing reflection on the law and its application. This developed into various schools of interpretation within Second Temple Judaism (diverse Jewish interpretative traditions continue to this day), with Jesus himself offering his own interpretations of the law as an alternative to those offered by other Jewish teachers.[6] For followers of Jesus, he is the interpreter of the Torah par excellence (being himself the enfleshment of the very Wisdom made manifest in the law). But reading the Torah in the light of Christ still requires ongoing interpretation, and always will. My point is that while the Torah is wise, its interpretation and application in new contexts are not straightforward and reading it well requires great wisdom. (The same can be said, by extension, to the teachings of the Christian Scriptures more generally.)

c) Experience and Wisdom

Israel's wisdom tradition also placed great store in experience. Indeed, a lot of the wisdom contained in its traditional proverbs is a condensation of insight gained from countless experiences distilled into short, memorable, general truths. E.g., "Pride goes before destruction, and a haughty spirit before a fall" (Prov 16:18). And paradigmatic models of wise people, like Solomon, were thought to have acquired great understanding of plants and animals and astronomy and human nature and such like through observation and careful understanding of what was observed (1 Kgs 3:16–28; 4:33–34; Wis 7:17–22). You can't be wise without looking at the world.

Transposing this discussion into Christian terms: the pursuit of Wisdom will involve an ongoing listening to the traditional insight of the historic church community, to the teachings of the Scriptures, and to actual experiences of the world, both our own experiences and those of others (including those of beyond our own traditions). The conversation between these will be a dynamic and ceaseless back-and-forth.

The pursuit of wisdom is understood as *an always-unfinished task*. One mark of folly is that one rejects correction, closing oneself off to learning, whereas the wise are those who welcome constructive correction (Prov 9:7–9). In the world of Israelite wisdom, the wise person is not the person

---

6. Jesus did not reject the teachings of the Torah but sought to interpret them through the lens of what he considered to be their heart: love for God and neighbor (Matt 22:36–40).

who has arrived at his or her destination but the one who is on the road towards it. It is a lifelong voyage marked by a love for and chasing after Sophia, for that is what marks us out as *ever open to learning* (Prov 12:1). Thus, Jesus Ben Sirach ends his advice to students with saying that he is still, after a lifetime of seeking, looking for Woman Wisdom (Sir 51:13–22). It is a path that involves much finding along the way, but never a completion. "Before the temple, I asked for her, and *I will search for her until the end*" (Sir 51:2). The reason for this is that wisdom is not something that one *possesses*, as such. She is only found *in the pursuit*, for that is the attitude of the heart that is open and receptive.

So there are certain intellectual virtues that are fitting for Christian wisdom seekers:

- *The fear of YHWH*. This is foundational for the book of Proverbs, which claims it to be "the *beginning* of wisdom." In fact, "the fear of YHWH" is so central to Proverbs that it is the climax of the opening paragraph (1:7), tops and tails chapters 1–9, the introductory section of the book (1:7 and 9:10), and recurs throughout the text.[7] This is a distinctively Jewish (and Christian) theological intellectual virtue, for YHWH is not God understood generically but as *the covenant God of Israel*, the God revealed in their story. The "fear" of YHWH is a *respect* and *reverence* for YHWH. Why is this the foundation for Israelite wisdom? Because this God is the ultimate Source of all wisdom, the giver of wisdom. The pursuit of wisdom is, ultimately, the pursuit of God.

- *Wonder*. Socrates famously said that philosophy begins with wonder, an astonishment in the face of the world and oneself. Those who start off by thinking they know everything do not seek understanding and will be rewarded by not receiving it.

- *Humility* (derived from the word *humus*, earth) is an orientation of the receptive, teachable heart.

- *Love*. Christian philosopher Esther Meek argues that true knowing in all spheres of knowledge requires an orientation of love towards what one seeks to know.[8] Her approach, which she calls "covenant epistemology," is very much on the same wavelength of the eco-spirituality I am recommending in this book.

---

7. Prov 1:7, 29; 2:5; 8:13; 9:10; 10:27; 14:2, 26, 27; 15:16, 33; 16:6; 19:23; 22:4; 23:17; 25:12; 28:14; 31:30.

8. See Meek, *Loving to Know*. For short, accessible account see Meek, *Little Manual for Knowing*.

The wise will seek to cultivate such fear, wonder, humility, and love, ever learning to see more clearly and to better understand, ever open to correction and to new insight.

3. All Wisdom Is God's Wisdom

No person or group has a monopoly on wisdom and those who seek Wisdom are open to find her wherever she pitches her tent. For biblical authors this meant *a discerning openness* to find truth and insight outside their own tradition. Let me give a few illustrations of this. Israelite religion was unique in certain very important ways, but it was not *utterly* unique. It contained many overlaps with the pagan religions of its neighbors.

- There are numerous laws given by God to Moses that have parallels in older law collections from the surrounding nations. For example, various laws in the law code of Hammurabi (king of Babylon, c. 1755 BCE) are very similar to those found in the much later Book of the Covenant (Exod 20:19—23:33) in the Torah.
- There are numerous aspects of Israel's God-given pattern of worship that have parallels in older patterns found in the surrounding nations. For example, temples, sacrifices, priests, and prayers are ubiquitous in the ancient Near East and long predated Israel.
- The central motif of Israel's relationship with God—the covenant—was based on the widespread pattern of ancient Near Eastern covenant treaties.
- There are stories in the inspired Torah that have older equivalents from other nations, most famously the story of a worldwide flood and survivors in an ark (compare Genesis 6–9 with the Epic of Gilgamesh and the Epic of Atrahasis).
- There are parallels found in many of the social and political arrangements in Israel and outside of it. Indeed, the Hebrew Bible is very clear that the institution of the monarchy itself was based on the political model of the nations around Israel (1 Sam 8).
- All sorts of cosmological ideas found in the Hebrew Bible have parallels in pagan nations surrounding them. For example, the idea that the sky was a solid dome or that the world was created out of the sea.
- The wisdom traditions in Israel form part of a much older international wisdom movement and Israel's wise were open to appropriating insights from sages elsewhere. For instance, Proverbs 22:17—24:34 very

likely draws on the much older Egyptian Teachings of Amenemope. Here are a couple of examples: compare "Don't cheat your neighbor by moving the ancient boundary markers; don't take the land of defenseless orphans" (Prov 23:10–11) with "Do not remove the boundary stone of the cultivated land; nor throw down the boundary of the widow" (Amenemope VII.12); compare "For wealth certainly makes itself wings; like an eagle that flies toward the heavens" (Prov 23:10) with "They [dishonest riches] make themselves wings like geese, and fly to heaven" (Amenemope X.5).

Of course, Israel was also distinctive in numerous ways, which marked it out from its neighbors. And these distinctives were very important. The gift of the Torah did, they felt, mark them out as recipients of a higher gift of divine wisdom than any other nation and served as a sieve to help in their evaluation of wisdom from elsewhere.

Ancient Israel displayed what we might think of as a *discerning openness* to wisdom found beyond its borders. By openness I mean that there is an orientation to discovering truth from other cultures and traditions and to embrace and incorporate helpful insights. Nonetheless, it is a *discerning* openness. Biblical authors did not think all religious beliefs and practices were equally true or equally valid. They were not full-blown cultural relativists. They very clearly rejected a range of ideas and practices from surrounding religions, and those that they appropriated they reinterpreted within their own religious worldview.

The New Testament displays the same attitude. We can see the influence of certain Greco-Roman ideas in early Christian beliefs and practices, but these were always subject to modification in light of the gospel story, for Christ was the incarnation and definitive revelation of Wisdom herself. Christ is the plumb line against which all claims to wisdom are measured. As an example, the majority of scholars argue that we can discern certain Hellenistic ideas informing the massively influential opening to John's Gospel (1:1–18). Most significantly, the idea of the Divine Logos ("the Word") is one that bears a striking resemblance to ideas found in Greco-Roman thought. But John doesn't simply take it and drop it into his Gospel. He blends it with the Jewish traditions about Wisdom and about the powerful and active word of God, both found in the Hebrew Bible. So John's Logos is at once deeply grounded in the Hebraic biblical tradition while simultaneously being enriched by the pagan Logos traditions. But while *enriched* by pagan philosophy, John's rendering of it is not pagan. One finds similar instances of influence in Paul and Hebrews, both of which likely draw on Middle Platonism and stoicism, but in distinctive Jewish and biblical ways.

That attitude of discerning openness marked the story of Christian thought thereafter. The church fathers were unapologetic about the wisdom they found in pagans such as Socrates and Plato, the stoics, and others. Socrates was even described as a "saint" and a "Christian before Christ." The influence of the Platonic tradition in particular on Christianity is well charted. However, it was always a *discerning* appropriation, with the gospel calling the shots. Aspects of Greek wisdom that did not fit the gospel were dropped like hot rocks and this led to certain important innovations within the Western philosophical tradition by Christian thinkers. That essential orientation towards learning from wisdom beyond the Christian tradition can be instanced throughout church history.

Underneath all of this lies a theological worldview in which the world is created through God's Logos (Word/Reason) and as such it is a cosmos manifesting logos (patterned order), which can be discerned by human logos (reason). With such a view of reality one would *expect* to find insight and wisdom everywhere. And if one is looking for Wisdom then one will seek her *wherever* she is found. All truth is God's truth; all wisdom is God's wisdom. It doesn't matter where she is discovered.

Humility and modesty are essential in this pursuit. After all, we are all finite, so all human wisdom is fallible and limited. Furthermore, from the perspective of a Christian worldview, this is a world profoundly affected by sin, and that means that any human wisdom is tainted and distorted. And those two truths apply to *Christian* attempts to find wisdom too. The church gets it wrong. Quite often! That's why Christianity should always be self-critical and why the journey towards truth remains ongoing. Wisdom requires nothing less.

4. The Ecological Implications

All this has several significant implications for wisdom-focused Christian eco-spirituality.

a) Learning from Our Own Story

First off, we listen to and learn from the history of *our own* community—the church—and its Scriptures. There is no neutral "view from nowhere" on the world. We have to think about things, at least in the first instance, from where we stand. Thus, those of us who are Christians must seek to explore the ecological implications of our own story of the world. Part I of this book was my attempt to sketch one angle on that story.

This emphasis on exploring our own Christian tradition is not because Christianity claims to have the whole truth about reality, obviously it doesn't, but it's because we do think that some critical, albeit only fuzzily grasped, truths about reality have been *revealed* to us in Christ by the Spirit. If we did not think that those Christian claims were true, why would we bother with Christianity at all? And if we say we believe Christian truth claims then we need to take them very seriously and explore their implications.

b) Learning from beyond our own tradition

Second, we seek to learn ecological wisdom from sources beyond our story.

i. Science

> Sometimes people ask if religion and science are not opposed to one another. They are: in the sense that the thumb and fingers of my hands are opposed to one another. It is an opposition by means of which anything can be grasped.
>
> —Sir William Bragg[9]

Scripture and the tradition both teach the importance of observation and experience in learning about the world, and this leads us to take the empirical study of the world very seriously, and that inevitably includes the various sciences. Indeed, modern empirical science was born and flourished in Christian cultures, facilitated by Christian theological beliefs, and Christians were key pioneers in its development. From a theological perspective, "[t]he beauty of the world is the co-operation of divine wisdom in creation.... The object of science is the presence of Wisdom in the universe."[10] Anyone today who wants to hear Wisdom on ecological issues cannot ignore her voice in the work of scientists. (That should go without saying, yet sadly it cannot.)

The contributions of the sciences to better understanding the biology and ecology of the earth, to discerning various challenges to its ecosystems, and to offering creative solutions are well established. Indeed, at this point one is so overwhelmed with things one could say that it is impossible to know where to start. Thankfully, it is not the purpose of this book to explore any of them, so much as it is to indicate their important place within a holistic Christian approach to living well in creation. No Christian analysis

---

9. Cited in Grant, *Life and Work*, 43.

10. Simone Weil, *Notebooks*, 122, 124, quoted in Clark, *How to Think About the Earth*, 120.

of any ecological issue or proposed solution should try to ignore scientific work in the area; and in this way we will find that we share much common ground with people of all faiths and none when it comes to matters of environmental concern.

ii. Non-Christian spiritual traditions

Another source of eco-spiritual wisdom will be non-Christian religious and spiritual traditions. Here the great world religions all have wisdom to impart, as do some recent spiritualities, especially those neo-paganisms with a nature orientation, like Druidism and Wicca.[11]

We need to appreciate that a basic Christian theological story will inform the worldview through which we make sense of the world around us. Through those "glasses" we also try to understand and evaluate claims about the world made by others, those who see it through the lenses of different worldviews (whether secular or religious). To the extent that those other perspectives are genuinely incompatible with a Christian perspective, we will be strongly inclined to reject them, at least where they conflict. To take an extreme example, consider someone who claims that there is no God, that the universe has no meaning, purpose, or value beyond any we choose to project onto it. Apart from the fact that such a philosophy (if genuinely embraced) is a potential disaster for environmentalism, a Christian will not take the "it's 'true' for its adherents but not 'true' for us" approach. That is the pathway to abandoning the idea of truth altogether. Rather, a Christian will consider the no-God view to be straightforwardly false. Why? Obviously, because it's incompatible with a view they believe to be true. However, even the person who embraces a no-God-or-meaning position may still have profoundly valuable things to teach Christians about creation care. There is always truth and insight to find. There is always good reason to listen to and learn from others. And most worldviews are not as incompatible with

---

11. I say "recent" because the paganisms found in the West today, Druidism and Wicca included, are not straightforward revivals of ancient paganisms nor directly descended from them. They are, rather, a very diverse and ever-changing range of modern spiritualities that draw some inspiration from ancient paganisms (some symbols, some vocabulary, some ideas, some myths, some ritual actions) and blend them with modern ideas, sensibilities, and praxis. See Hutton, *Triumph of the Moon*. Much the same can be said about "Celtic Christianity"—it too is largely a modern spirituality and is unlike ancient British Christianity in many ways, but it draws some inspiration from selected elements of that olde religion. See Meek, *Quest for Celtic Christianity*. I say this not as a criticism of "Celtic Christianity"—which I love—but simply as a call to self-awareness and historical integrity.

Christian perspectives as this one, leaving a lot more scope for real mutual learning.

I would suggest that dialogue between people from different religious traditions is more likely to be constructive when those engaged in the discussions have both a respect for the "other" (even if disagreeing over certain matters) and at the same time an informed sense of their own identity and heritage, of their community's beliefs and practices and history.

With that said, what might Christians learn from other spiritual traditions about creation care? Well, many of the eco-theological ideas that I've set out in this book find analogues in other religious faiths. For instance, notions of divine transcendence of creation and immanence within creation, of the cosmos having a divine origin, of the sacred nature of created reality, of a holy duty to respect and care for the world. Christians will find much overlap between their own theology and ethics and that of non-Christian faiths, even amid differences. But more than that, there will be aspects of the teaching of non-Christian religions and worldviews from which Christians can discern fresh wisdom that they themselves have overlooked or underemphasized. Let me give a couple of quick examples.

First, consider the orientation of animism, a view found among numerous Indigenous peoples, past and present. For animists, features of the world around us, even so-called nonliving things, are regarded and treated as in some sense persons. This has not been a typical belief or practice for Christians. Indeed, many Christians have seen it as a strength of their religion that it rejects such a "primitive" view of the world. However, animism is being taken more seriously today by anthropologists and some ecologists, and this has prompted several biblical scholars to notice various animist-like ideas in the Bible. I have discussed some of that material in this book. Some theologians too have realized that animism is not an inherent threat to orthodox Christian theology, and this opens the door for more reflection and discovery. My point here is that, had it not been for listening more carefully to non-Christian spiritualities, modern Christian thinkers may never have been able to modify the interpretative glasses through which they were reading their Scripture and thinking their faith. Attending to animism more closely is starting to open fresh possibilities for an eco-sensitive Christian faith (Christianimism?) that nonetheless remains true to its own sacred text and traditions. That rethinking process is only just beginning and must, of course, be undertaken with discernment and wisdom.

Second, consider the range of traditions in which the earth is considered a goddess. Those traditions are generally treated with great caution by Christians, for reasons to do with idolatry, of worshipping creation rather than the Creator. Nonetheless, can't Christians avoid idolatry while at the same time learning positive insights from such earth-goddess spiritualities? Allow me to make a few sweeping and explorative orientations (with apologies for the supreme superficiality of this discussion). First off, speaking of the earth as a goddess is to consider our planet *as a single being*. That can be very valuable. Here I think about the way that in the 1970s scientist James Lovelock famously used the ancient Greek earth goddess Gaia as a metaphor for speaking of the way that earth's systems are interlocking and interwoven into a single, complex, self-regulating, life-sustaining system. Many Christians freaked out when Lovelock spoke of Gaia, as though the idea was inherently anti-Christian. Whatever its scientific merits (which are not for me to adjudicate), it was nothing of the sort. It is true that Christians do not typically speak of the earth as a single living entity, composed of many living entities, but the idea is not incompatible with their faith. The Bible itself treats the promised land as a living whole composed of other living wholes. Scripture also addresses the heavens and the earth as distinct entities. It even sometimes treats the sun, moon, and stars as gods, created by YHWH, the God of gods. To see the earth as in some sense a single, complex creature (even if only metaphorically) does not require abandoning the distinct identities of the individual parts. It simply helps us to locate ourselves within a much vaster web of being in which wholes are more than the sum of their parts. Secondly, to speak of the earth as a goddess is to attempt to speak of it as sacred, as holy, as worthy of honor.[12] That too is not incompatible with orthodox Christianity so long as the goddess in question is regarded as *a creature of God*, albeit an exalted one, who *worships God* along with all other creatures. Third, while Christians would regard Worship (capital W) of an earth goddess as idolatry, they would not need to regard respect for her, honoring her, thanking her, and such like as idolatrous. After all, we don't consider such things to be a problem when directed towards humans who bless us. The issue, for Christians, should come down to how her divinity is understood in relation to the Triune God[13] and how our in-

---

12. And I should point out that neo-pagans who celebrate an earth goddess are not required to believe that the earth is *literally* a goddess, a sentient being. There is a lot of space within modern paganism for flexibility over how such language is interpreted. I should also point out that talk of the earth as a goddess can be seen, from a Christian perspective, as a way of trying to understand the sense of the presence of Divine Wisdom in the world. If that is so, while we will consider it conceptually inadequate, embracing immanence while losing transcendence, we can still recognize it as a response to a genuine awareness of God's presence and a sincere attempt to respond to it. Furthermore, while we will reject aspects of the conceptualization, we can still learn from other aspects of it.

13. I.e., she is not a competitor to YHWH, but a beautiful creature of YHWH.

teractions with her are enfolded within our relation to the Creator.[14] Great care is needed here, to avoid the pitfalls of idolatry, but I see no inherent reason why those of us who are Christians can't find Sophianic insights in earth-goddess spiritualities, insights that can inform our own Christian faith and praxis. Our dependence on the sacred earth, our Mother, is *utterly fundamental*. Exploring ways of more deeply appreciating that dependence and practicing respect, honor, and gratitude for (and even to) the sacred earth in religious contexts can be spiritually formative in a healthy way and is something about which Christians have much still to learn.

Exactly the same points could be made about relatively smaller creatures, such as rivers and forests, which can be fruitfully reimagined as living wholes—spirits or souls or gods. In some more-than-trivial (though not easy to clarify) sense, rivers, oceans, marshes, and forests are not simply an assemblage of parts, like a machine, but exist as vibrant, dynamic, emergent "beings"; they do not merely *contain* living things, they themselves *are* living things (perhaps somewhat akin to a superorganism, like a hive of bees, but on a grander scale and in a more species-diverse mode). Finding ways of perceiving them as alive—even poetic, imaginistic, and mythic ways—could, if done intelligently, help us in developing healthier, more respectful ways of interacting with them.[15] (Now I'll just sit back, relax, and wait for the furious reviews.) 😌

c) Remaining Open to Correction

Third, all ecological wisdom is provisional and subject to correction. Take the sciences. Working scientists are acutely aware of the provisional nature of their work and the fact that it is always subject to revision or correction or refutation. If only this was better appreciated by the public, we could avoid those scenarios in which a Christian rejects scientific claims about climate change with the argument that "Climate scientists predicted that such and such would happen by this date, and it hasn't happened. Which just goes to prove how so-called 'science' can't be trusted on this matter." This superficial dismissal of scientific work (only deployed, I should note, when the science is inconvenient) is not the path to wisdom.

The provisionality of scientific analyses and predictions applies too to scientific proposals for solutions to ecological problems. Well-meaning and well-informed attempts to solve problems can have unintended

---

14. I.e., that we recognize that all the goods we receive from her are, as with all the goods we receive from other creatures, ultimately goods we are receiving from YHWH.

15. An idea beautifully explored by Robert MacFarlane in *Is a River Alive?*

consequences that can sometimes make matters worse. This is the fragility, the vulnerability, the risk of goodness. The ability to recognize that the well-intentioned solution is not working is part of the necessary orientation of wisdom lovers. If we are so committed to our "solutions" that we refuse to see when they don't work, then we need to ask ourselves whether care for the environment is really what is motivating the actions.

It is also the case that real-life environmental questions are bound up in very complex ways in webs of competing needs and that sometimes the only solutions are compromises of various kinds. Knowing the best compromises to make, for the optimal long-term outcome for as many as possible, is not at all straightforward and requires wisdom and humility and courage. It is an area in which it is easy to make mistakes or in which solutions that work at one stage cease to become the best way forward. Vigilance, humility, and the ability to make course corrections are essential.

Christian eco-theology is also subject to correction. We may think that we know that the Bible teaches something, but we are not infallible readers of Scripture. Our interpretations may be inappropriate for all sorts of reasons, and we need to remain open to correction if more plausible interpretations appear. Of course, adjudicating these things is not always easy. In this, as in everything, we need wisdom, and the pursuit if wisdom is never complete.

> Blessed are those who find wisdom,
>   those who gain understanding,
> for she is more profitable than silver
>   and yields better returns than gold.
> She is more precious than rubies;
>   nothing you desire can compare with her. (Prov 3:13–15)

15

Conclusion

Baptism and the Art of Living Gently on the Earth

1. Go in Peace...

Go in peace to love and serve the Lord.
In the name of Christ, amen.

EVERY TRADITIONAL ACT OF Christian worship concludes with a blessing on the people before they are sent out into the world to serve Christ. This is a very important part of the service. It signals that "church" isn't something we do on a Sunday before leaving it behind for the rest of the week to enter some God-less, neutral space. There is no such space, as far as Christians are concerned, for the earth is the Lord's and everything in it. Church is, first and foremost, not somewhere we go nor an event we attend; it is, rather, *who we are*. And daily life is not the Jesus-free zone in our lifescapes but the space in which we live out our Jesus-defined identity. Sent out, blessed and commissioned, we leave from our gatherings in order to live as the body of Christ, to be his hands and feet, in our day-to-day lives. And what that amounts to, as I said right back at the very start of this book, is living the baptized life.

2. Living Out Our Baptism

Baptism is the initiation ritual through which the Spirit unites individuals to Christ, incorporating them into the community of the church. The symbolism of the ritual is multilayered, but the heart of it is focused on the paschal narrative of Jesus' death and resurrection. Jesus the Messiah, our representative, died and was buried in the tomb, but was then raised to eternal life by God. Baptism is about having our individual lives and stories joined to Jesus and his story. In the New Testament period, and often to this day, the candidate was baptized by full immersion in water. As they are submerged under the water, they are symbolically buried with Christ, their old life dead. Then, as they are lifted out from the water, they are raised with Christ into new life. Baptism is thereby the ritual marker of a sharp break between an old life and a new life (Rom 6:1–14).

The person who has been baptized has been made one with Christ and from that point on the shape of Christ's story is determinative for the shape of their own. When I was at school I used to love the three-legged race, in which one child's left leg is tied to the right leg of another child, before releasing them to run. The only way to do it well is to get in synch and to run as one. In baptism we are tied to Christ, as it were, and we need to learn to synchronize the patterns of our running with his. And the gospel is that pattern.[1] That's why I said that Christian spirituality is, in essence, nothing more (nor less) that living out our baptism in the power of the Spirit.

In the New Testament epistles, the steps of such baptismal spirituality are set out in terms of two movements: (a) the old life is taken off, set aside, or put to death and (b) the new life is put on, taken up, lived out. Here is one example from Colossians 3:

> Since, then, you have been raised with Christ, set your hearts on things above, where Christ is, seated at the right hand of God. . . . For you died, and your life is now hidden with Christ in God. . . . *Put to death*, therefore, *whatever is earthly in you*: sexual immorality, impurity, lust, evil desires and greed, which is idolatry. Because of these, the wrath of God is coming. You used to walk in these ways, in the life you once lived. But now you must also *rid yourselves* of all such things as these: anger, rage, malice, slander, and filthy language from your lips. Do not lie to each other, since you have *taken off your old self with its practices* and have *put on the new self*, which is being renewed in knowledge in the image of its Creator. Here there is no gentile or

---

1. See especially Gorman, *Cruciformity*.

Jew, circumcised or uncircumcised, barbarian, Scythian, slave or free, but Christ is all, and is in all.

Living out our baptism is a matter of identifying and turning away from the vices that mark a human life governed by sin and of putting on (with the Spirit's help) the virtues that characterize a human life lived in righteousness.

Now here's something obvious but worth noting: all the exhortations in the New Testament letters to set aside a sinful pattern of living and to adopt a Christlike pattern of living, all the appeals to live out the meaning of baptism, are addressed to already-baptized Christ-believers. Baptism marks a turning point of a voyage towards righteousness, but it is not the end of the journey. Becoming like Christ is a lifelong adventure of entering ever deeper into the meaning of one's baptism.

What does any of this have to do with eco-spirituality? Yeah, you guessed it—everything.

3. Living Gently on the Earth

a) Sin and the Environment

In this book I have argued that, in a Christian eco-vision, human beings are called to live in harmony with the rest of creation, in relationships of reciprocal blessing. Failure to do so is sin, which causes harm both to those sinned against and to the sinners. Christ was revealed to defeat sin (Rom 6:1–14), to undo the devil's work (1 John 3:8), and to defeat the demonic principalities and powers that operate in human societies (Col 2:15). However we interpret "satan" and "the powers" (whether literal, symbolic, or something in between), there can be no doubt, in terms of Christian theology, that to the extent that modern societies strut the earth in environmentally insane ways they are vehicles of demonic influence and sin. (Which is not to say that there is not much that is also good and to be affirmed in such societies.) Environmental carelessness is an aspect of human social, economic, and political life that marks it as what John's Gospel calls "the world"—by which he means not "God's good creation" but "human society in rebellion against God."

Christians need to recover the language of sin when considering ecological issues. At its heart, to speak of sin is to speak of the ways that things are not right with the world, in particular, the ways in which human actions contribute to the damage within creation. It is a fundamentally relational concept that indicates fractures in the connections within and between both individuals and communities. It also indicates breaks in our human relationship with the environment we inhabit and the nonhuman creatures we share it with. In its essence, we might say that sin is *a failure to love*—failure to love the world, failure to love those who share it with us, failure to love God.

There is more to sin, however, than a mere recognition that things are askew. Sin is a *theological* concept. To speak of sin is to view the harm done within creation *in the light of its relation to God*. As such, sin-talk highlights the way in which damage to creation is, amongst other things, an offense against God. It is not that God is directly harmed by our sins—that would be impossible. Rather, sin is an offense against creatures and *precisely for that reason* is an attack on their Creator. That's why, when responding to sin, things need to be put right *both* with creatures *and* with God.

Creation—from the subatomic level right up to the universe as a whole—is essentially a complex, dynamic web of relationships, reflecting its Triune Creator. In such a world, sin too, while focused on human beings, is complex and entangled. Think about it. We are deeply entwined with the lives of other humans, the societies of which we are a part, and the natural environment in which we live. We are parts of complicated webs of connection and our actions have reverberations near and far across the webscapes we inhabit. Sin and evil are not merely located in individuals but are also dynamically dispersed across these webs. So we find ourselves enfolded into sin-infected systems—social, cultural, political, economic—that we are inevitable participants in. Those systems long preceded us as individuals and will outlast us. We didn't choose to be born into the worlds we inhabit—we find ourselves "thrown" into them and, to one degree or another, they both shape and misshape us as we grow. We come to participate in the world's sin, often to benefit from it, and to perpetuate it. Sin is much more complicated and messier than straightforward individual acts of transgression, such as stealing.[2]

Taking things a step further, theologian Rebecca Copeland speaks of "sin that both involves and exceeds individual agency in causing unintentional, communal, and intergenerational harms."[3] Global warming is a

2. The Bible thus sometimes speaks of sin not merely as a flaw within us but also as a power in the world that transcends and stands outside of our individual lives and that seeks to imprison and oppress us. It is like a prowling beast waiting to pounce on us (Gen 4:7). It is like an oppressive ruler who seeks to make us his slaves (Rom 6–7). Other times Scripture speaks of "principalities and powers" that rule the human world and misdirect it (Eph 6:12). Theologians often talk in this regard of "structural sin and evil"—sin embedded in the ways that society is organized, entrenching patterns that perpetuate injustice.

3. Copeland, *Entangled Being*, 45–46.

classic case of such "unoriginal sin." All of us participate in activities that increase the amount of CO_2 in the atmosphere, facilitating global warming. However, our sin here is *unintentional*. We are not *seeking* to create global warming. Indeed, we *don't want* global warming. All that we are seeking is to live comfortable lives—to drive to work, to fly on holiday, to cook lunch, to heat our home, to light our streets. However, those actions—because of the way they are entangled in complex social, economic, and environmental webs—have the effect of generating global warming, which is causing very real and increasing harm. For most people in the middle-distant past this was also a sin performed in *ignorance* as most people were unaware of the damaging impact of their lifestyles. The sin is *communal* in that it is not something that I as an individual am doing alone, but I am a participant in a communal way of life that, for all its many benefits, is having catastrophic effects. Furthermore, the sin is *intergenerational* in that the harm takes places over a long period of time, beginning prior to my arrival on the scene and extended after I leave. And if our ignorance of the sin mitigates our culpability to varying degrees, once the reality of the harm we are doing becomes known, as is now the case with global warming, to deliberately ignore that reality and continue to pursue our harmful practices, often very aggressively, makes us much more culpable and is a striking display of the sheer *stupidity* of sin, driven in this case by ethical vices such as greed, laziness, and fear.

All this means that it's not easy to live "in the world" (as we must) at the same time as not being "of the world." That is the case with environmental sins as much as anything else. At one level, there are many powerful players who have a deeply vested economic interest in keeping our focus off the harm that is being caused to habitats, animals, the climate, and to numerous poorer human communities. Instead, they point us to the many wonderful goods and luxuries that are on offer, and they seek to make us depend on them. They persuade us that the world cannot be imagined any other way. And when environmental concerns are raised, many businesses have engaged in "green washing," giving the impression that they are being responsible in their practices when the sober truth is very different.

There are countless examples in our day-to-day lives in which the harm we are actively involved with is hidden from us. Take banks, many of which invest *vast* amounts of the money we deposit with them in the fossil fuel industry. Yet customers would have to go out of their way to find out about this. Or consider our food. When we go to the supermarket, we are simply choosing from an ever-expanding range of delicious goods. There is often nothing to make us think that this activity is anything other than an utterly neutral exercise of our consumer choice. And we understandably rejoice at the selection of products, especially when we can have them at cheaper prices. In reality, the production, processing, and transportation of this selection of foods has a wide range of impacts, often negative, on the environment and the creatures (human and nonhuman) that inhabit it. This is kept out of the shopper's sight and mind, and to uncover it often requires time and effort. The same applies to our transport and the energy we use to power our modern lives, and many other mundane issues.

It's easy to blame the businesses that have vested interests in sweeping their dirty laundry under the carpet or the governments that fear that they will not be reelected unless they water down the unpopular measures they know need taking to steer us away from a cliff edge. We like to lay the blame elsewhere. The honest truth, and the other side of the coin, is that we are often more than happy to go along with this deception. We like our consumer lives. We like our cheap fuel with the new vistas opened up for us for work and holidays. We like to eat lots of meat and to do so cheaply (which requires the industrialization of meat production—with huge ethical and environmental consequences following in its wake). We like the energy-consuming devices that fill our homes. Increasingly, we come to see all of this as a "necessity," even a "right." We are complicit, to varying degrees and for differing reasons, in this sin and in sweeping it out of sight. "Each one of us—in very different proportions depending on whether we are rich or poor, influential or impoverished, wasteful or ascetic—each of us is at once an innocent victim, and evildoing sinner, and an exterminating angel."[4]

b) Environmental Sin and Baptism

To use the language of sin is valuable, for Christians, because it underlines the *gravity* of issue. It pulls the rug from under attempts to trivialize the acts in question. It also implies the need for the sinful situation to be rectified—so the language is intended to expose harms and to motivate positive change. In that sense, weird as it seems, talk of sin is "good news" because it points towards the hope of change and redemption.

Living out our baptism involves leaning to live "in the world" while not being "of the world." And that means that going with the flow is not an option. We need, as individuals and church communities, to seek wisdom to discern the structural sins we are wrapped up in and to take steps to address them.

The responses the Bible seeks from people in relation to sin are: (a) confession; (b) repentance; (c) restitution. These three belong together and

---

4. Latour, *If We Lose the Earth, We Lose Our Souls*, 64.

none is complete without the others. Furthermore, they track with the baptismal pattern of taking off the old pattern of life, like a dirty set of clothing, and then putting on a new pattern, formed in the image of Christ.

i. Take off...

The Holy Spirit desires to work in the community of faith exposing sin *as sin*, by shining a light on our deeds and convicting us of wrong (John 16:18). This is not in order to make us feel terrible (though we may feel terrible) nor to condemn us but to enable healing transformation. The first step is always to recognize our sin for what it is and to confess it as such, to God and to those against whom we have sinned. Without such acknowledgment we remain trapped in the vicious cycle of self-deception and harm. In terms of taking off the garments of the old self, one first needs to *recognize* the garments that need removing.

The second step is to take action to remove those garments. This is repentance. The Hebrew word for repentance is *tᵉšûbâ*, which means to "return" or "turn"—it is about a reorientation in our way of living. The Greek word for repentance is *metanoia*, which means to change one's mind, to change one's way of *thinking* in relation to some matter, for that is what lies beneath changing one's way of *acting* in relation to it.

The third step is the work of repair and restitution (e.g., Exod 21:1, 3–6, 14; Luke 19:8–9). Many harms cannot be undone or can only be partially undone. Nonetheless, serious work of restitution still needs to be undertaken to mitigate the harm. Such repair needs to be appropriate and a serious attempt at putting things right. What that looks like in practice will vary enormously depending on the matter at hand.

What all this means for living the baptized life in our modern world with its many ecological traumas is that we need to engage in serious and sustained self-examination, as individuals and communities, to uncover and face up to the harms that we participate in. We need to confess them as sin, to take active steps to turn from them, and to take appropriate action to effect repair. None of this is quick. None of this is easy. Sometimes we can only partially extricate ourselves from the systems of harm. Nonetheless, it is a long pathway that we have to pursue if we are to live the gospel.

Furthermore, it is not something any one individual can do alone. It requires a community of people who are committed to getting educated on contemporary environmental issues and the ways in which we are all implicated in the damage being caused—a community committed to exploring practical ways of living more gently on the earth, in our lives as individuals, as churches, and as a wider society.[5] That is not an optional extra for Christians who feel so inclined. It is a matter of living the baptized life.

ii. Put on . . .

"Taking off" means stepping away from activities that inflict damage and taking steps to heal the harm done. "Putting on" means embracing virtues and practices that facilitate the blessing of creation. And in doing this we discover that in giving we receive, and in blessing we ourselves are blessed. This is the gospel path.

There are countless ways in which Christ's followers can engage in such positive, creation-blessing work and my task here is merely to flag up the fact that, from the perspective of Christian spirituality, such work is gospel work; such work is mission; such work is spirituality.

c) Environmental Mission and Baptism

I want to end by returning to the story of Noah's ark. For the early church the account of the great flood and the ark could serve as an image (or "type") of baptism. The foundation text for this way of interpreting the Noah story is found in 1 Peter 3:20–21, where Peter writes of "the days of Noah while the ark was being built. In it only a few people, eight in all, were saved through water, and this water symbolizes baptism that now saves you also." Entering the ark, says Peter, is like being united to Christ in baptism, passing through the waters of death and then out the other side into new creation. But once we start to think about Noah's ark in that light, we could be forgiven for wondering about the animals and birds. After all, the presence of mating pairs from every species is a prominent feature of the story. Although animals are not baptized by the church, they too are carried through "in Christ the Ark" along with "baptized" humans (Noah and company) into the new creation. The salvation of the humans is here linked to the salvation of the nonhumans. Translated into Christian terms, the baptism of the humans is not just for the humans but is linked to a wider, creation-embracing mission of salvation. We're in this boat together.

---

5. Here there are many resources available, but a good place to start is Ruth Valerio's little book *L Is for Lifestyle*. It is full of practical and achievable ideas for changes we can make in our everyday lives.

Noah's Ark by Edward Hicks, 1846[6]

4. And the Blessing . . .

Deep peace of the running wave to you.
Deep peace of the flowing air to you.
Deep peace of the quiet earth to you.
Deep peace of the shining stars to you.
Deep peace of the gentle night to you.
Moon and stars pour their healing light on you.
Deep peace of Christ, of Christ the light of the world to you.
Deep peace of Christ to you.

And may the blessing of God,
of God's Wisdom,
and God's Spirit,
be with you and remain with you always.

Amen

---

6. Philadelphia Museum of Art. Public domain. Reproduced under Creative Commons license.

Appendix

The Sound of Silence

SILENCE AS A SPIRITUAL practice within the Christian tradition arose from the creative confluence of two streams—one Hebrew, one Greek. Christian theology and practice as we know it emerged from that creative commingling.

1. Biblical Silence

Silence in the mode of the contemplative devotional practices so integral to Christian monasticism is not a core aspect of biblical spirituality. Nevertheless, the seeds of the practice can be found within the Bible—seeds that, watered with Athenian rain, produced a tree that continues to provide shade for seekers.

Biblical spirituality can be loud and certainly values the importance of words. And silence can sometimes be a negative thing: the numbed silence of those reeling from catastrophic events (Lam 2:10; Job 2:13),[1] say, or the humiliating speechlessness of simply not knowing what to do in a situation (Ps 137:1-4), or the refusal to speak out when righteousness demands speech (Rom 10:14c).

---

1. Which is not so much negative as a psychological coping strategy.

However, Scripture also recognizes the role of solitary prayer, most clearly in the life of Jesus,[2] and of inaudible, inarticulate, prayer, classically in the prayer of Hannah (1 Sam 1:12–15). More than that, there is also good silence in the Bible:

(a) *Silence as the correct posture of the learner.* Job speaks of the time when "men listened to me and waited and kept silence for my counsel" (Job 29:21).[3] Silence was the mode of open receptivity appropriate to students,[4] never more so than before God: "Teach me, and I will be silent," says Job to God.[5] The admonition in 1 Timothy 2:11 to "let a woman learn quietly with all submissiveness" is similarly a call to be students harkening to God. This quiet orientation of openness to God remains essential to the contemplative silence of the later Christian tradition. For instance, Thomas Merton: "My life is a listening; His is a speaking. My salvation is to hear and respond. For this, my life must be silent. Hence, my silence is my salvation."[6]

(b) *Penitential silence*, either individual (Lam 3:28) or corporate (Mic 7:16). This too retains a place within contemporary practice.

(c) *Silence as trust in God*, ceasing one's own efforts and waiting on YHWH. Paradigmatically, Moses, addressing Israel at the Red Sea: "YHWH will fight for you, and you have only to be silent" (Exod 14:14). Psalmic texts advocate for such a stance too: "Be still and know that I am God" (Ps 46:10); "For God alone my soul waits in silence; from him comes my salvation" (Ps 62:1); This is a restful, waiting silence. "By waiting and by calm you shall be saved, in quiet (*hašqēṭ*) and in trust shall be your strength" (Isa 30:15). Again, this resting, trusting quietness of spirit, abandoning oneself to God, is an integral part of contemplative

---

2. See Matt 14:13; Mark 1:12–13, 35; Luke 5:16; 6:12–13; 9:18; 11:1–2; John 6:15. He advocated it for his followers too (Matt 6:6; 17:1–2; Mark 6:31–32). Other biblical figures spent time alone with God, e.g., Moses (Exod 33:7, 11), Elijah (Exod 19:9ff), Paul (Gal 1:15–17).

3. Elihu expects the same of Job: "Pay attention, O Job, listen to me; be silent, and I will speak . . . be silent, and I will teach you wisdom" (Job 33:31, 33; cf. Deut 27:9; Acts 15:12). Conversely, those who babble and mock should not expect an audience to respond with silent receptivity (Job 11:3; cf. Eccl 9:17).

4. Thus, in the wisdom tradition the start of the journey from folly to wisdom is to stop talking (Prov 30:32).

5. Job 6:24.

6. Merton, *Choosing to Love the World*, 124.

silence in the later tradition. Contemplation is "a locus of surrender for a life of surrender."[7]

(d) *Silent contemplation on divine truth.* This inner meditation "in the heart" on divine words or acts is a common theme in Scripture, especially in terms of meditating on divine *tôrâ* (instruction) (Ps 1:2). Consider a NT instance: following the events surrounding the birth of her son, we read, "But Mary treasured up all these things, pondering them in her heart" (Luke 2:19).[8] The silence of the *meditatio* moment within lectio divina grows from this biblical seed.[9]

(e) *Meeting God in silence.* Elijah's encounter with YHWH on Mount Sinai was famously unexpected in that it was not in a blazing theophany of the kind Israel had experienced at that mountain. Rather God met him in a *qôl d^emāmâ daqqâ*—literally, a voice/sound of thin silence, or as the NRSV renders it "a sound of sheer silence."[10] This is one of several key texts reappropriated in fresh ways in later contemplative spirituality.

(f) *Silent worship.* Psalm 65:1 is an interesting though ambiguous text in that it opens with, literally, "To you silence is praise, God in Zion."[11] This is echoed in St Ephrem: "The highest form of praise is silence."[12] Perhaps we might hold this alongside the silent witness of the astral bodies to God in Psalm 19:1-4.

(g) *Silence before the awe-inspiring divine presence:* "Be silent before YHWH God! For the day of YHWH is near" (Zeph 1:7). Again: "But YHWH is in his holy temple; let the earth keep silence before him" (Hab 2:20). Psalm 131 seems to suggest a humble silence in the majestic divine presence: "O YHWH, my heart is not lifted up; my eyes are not raised too high; I do not occupy myself with things too great and too marvelous for me. But *I have calmed and quieted my soul*, like a weaned child with its mother." Perhaps the clearest advice along these lines is that of Qohelet: "Guard your steps when you go to the house of God. To draw near to

---

7. Belisle, *Language of Silence*, 21.

8. Cf. Luke 9:36.

9. See Pennington, *Lectio Divina*; Hall, *Too Deep for Words*.

10. 1 Kgs 19:12. Other translators go with "a still small voice" (KJV, ASV), "the soft whisper of a voice" (GNB), "a gentle whisper" (TLB, NIV), "a low whisper" (ESV), "a gentle breeze" (CEV), "the sound of a gentle blowing" (Amplified), "a sound. Thin. Quiet." (CEB).

11. Translators usually ignore the word *dumîyâ* (silence) and render verse 1 "Praise is due to you, O God, in Zion."

12. Ephrem was a fourth-century Syrian deacon. Quoted in Ross, *Silence*, 93.

listen is better than to offer the sacrifice of fools, for they do not know that they are doing evil. Be not rash with your mouth, nor let your heart be hasty to utter a word before God, for God is in heaven and you are on earth. Therefore, let your words be few" (Eccl 5:1–2).

2. Silence and the Classical Synthesis

This final silence—i.e., in the presence of divine majesty—was particularly influential in the development of the practice of contemplative silence, especially as the doctrine of divine reality was explored in the categories of Greek philosophical ontology. God is Creator, the source of all being. As such, God in Godself is *beyond the categories of created being*—beyond concepts, beyond language, beyond thought. Our words only gesture in the direction of the truth of God and cannot pin God down like a butterfly in a case. To try to *capture* God in an image, even a verbal one, is to create an idol. This approach was an outcome of the synthesis of Hebrew and Hellenistic thought. Many schools of Greek philosophy had come, under the influence of Platonism, to understand God as both utterly transcendent and profoundly immanent and therefore developed the so-called *via negativa* ("the negative way") and the practice of silence. Christians adopted and adapted this philosophy, reshaping it around Jesus and the biblical texts. Here, as a sixteenth-century Anglican representative, is Richard Hooker: "Dangerous it were for the feeble brain of man to wade far into the doings of the Most High; whom . . . our soundest knowledge is to know that we know him not as indeed he is, neither can know him: *our safest eloquence concerning him is silence*, when we *confess without confession* that his glory is inexplicable, his greatness above our capacity and reach."[13]

3. The Story of Christian Silence

A major thread in the Christian devotional practice of silence is the monastic tradition, in which solitude and silence became a main path to knowing God, toward stripping away all our illusions and knowing the Deity in "learned ignorance"—in "unknowing."

In the early days of monasticism, the desert fathers and mothers cultivated silence as a critical spiritual discipline.[14] It became central to all forms

---

13. Hooker, *Laws of Ecclesiastical Polity* I.i.2 (italics added).

14. E.g., Arsenius 2, 25; Agathon 15, 16; Bessarion 10; Evagrius 1, 3; Zeno 8; Theodore of Pherme 6; Theophilus the Archbishop 2; John the Dwarf 20; Isidore of Pelusia

of monasticism thereafter. In the West, the Rule of St. Benedict for community life devoted the sixth chapter to silence. From the Benedictines all the branches of Western monasticism emerged over the coming centuries, as "Western monks . . . made silence their specialty."[15]

In the fourteenth-century East, silence took on a new form in hesychasm (from *hēsychia*, silence), which linked silence with contemplation of icons, attuned to the divine Light that shines through them. Another characteristic practice is the repetitive use of the Jesus Prayer (see later) in contemplation. Hesychasm had a huge impact on the shape of Orthodox spirituality, and its practices gradually seeped into the Western church too.

The heart of the matter was *knowing God*. Contemplatives of many varieties came to speak of two ways in which one can know the Divine: a lower way (*ratio inferior*), which engages discursive rationality, logical thought, words that divide and categorize reality, and a higher way (*ratio superior*), which takes the road of silence to grasp (or be grasped by) truth too deep for words. Hear Isaac of Nineveh: "If you love the truth, love silence. This will make you illumined in God . . . and deliver you from the illusions of ignorance. Silence unites you to God himself."[16]

4. Silence: Individual and Communal

Silence is not everything, but it is important. "A brother said to Abba Poemen, 'Is it better to speak or to be silent?' The old man said to him, 'The man who speaks for God does well; but he who is silent for God's sake also does well.'"[17] A biblically shaped approach to silence will see it as having a place within the spiritual ecosystem. There is "a time to keep silence and a time to speak" (Eccl 3:7)—a time when speaking is inappropriate (Job 13:5; Prov 11:12; 17:28) and a time when if we try to keep silent "the very stones would cry out" (Luke 19:40). Heaven itself is pictured as full of the noise of praise, but also as having spaces for silence (Rev 8:1). Wisdom is in discerning the times for silence.

Furthermore, silence is a discipline for navigating Western culture well. It connects us with the God who *walked* with God's people across the

---

1; Isaac, Priest of Cells 2; Carion 1; Macarius the Great 33; Moses 3; Poemen 37, 42, 45, 47, 78, 79, 84, 147, 150, 168, 173, 187; Sisoes 30, 42; Felix 1; Psenthaisios 1. All can be found in Ward, trans., *Sayings of the Desert Fathers*.

15. MacCulloch, *Silence*, 95.
16. Isaac the Syrian, *Ascetical Homilies*, 64.
17. Poemen 147 in Ward, *Sayings of the Desert Fathers*, 158.

wilderness—the one David Runcorn calls "the three-mile-an-hour God."[18] Silence teaches us to resist the huge cultural pressures for instant gratification and to learn the biblical virtue of patient waiting on the Lord. It can even, as Rowan Williams observes, help with the pull of consumerism: "the contemplative who knows how to enter into the silence and stillness of things is, above all, the one who knows how to resist fashion and power, to stand in God while the world turns."[19] Living at God's speed requires us to slow down and to pay attention to the world, to ourselves, to God, and to resist an achievement-orientated lifestyle, instead embracing what is seemingly a "use-less" activity, a "royal waste of time."[20] Such foolish wisdom!

a) Silence in Individual Spirituality

Contemplation is a slow spirituality, "a process of learning to pay attention, to concentrate, to attend.... It is not just a matter of keeping our tongues still but much more of achieving a state of alert stillness in mind and heart."[21] Learning silent meditative prayer takes time and is not easy. "There are few who are willing to belong completely to such silence, to let it soak into their bones, to breathe nothing but silence, or to feed on silence, and to turn the very substance of their life into a living and vigilant silence."[22] However, the tradition has distilled certain tried and tested practices that aid the journey.

First, *attend to the body*, for humans are psycho-physical unities, and a still body can aid the stilling of the mind:[23]

- Adopt a comfortable sitting position, sitting upright, feet flat on the floor.
- Relax your body, releasing the tension.
- Breathe in a regular, deliberate, and calm way.

How we think about our breathing helps, once more reminding us of the importance and spirituality of our embodiment.

> For starters, don't call it a cage,
> corralling the breath. Savvy fingertips

18. Runcorn, *Silence*, 9.
19. Quoted in Ross, *Writing the Icon of the Heart*, 40.
20. This phrase is that of Marva Dawn, speaking of worship.
21. Main, *Word into Silence*, 3, 7. On silence, see also Longley, *Conversations with Silence*.
22. Merton, *Dialogues with Silence*, 1.
23. See Laird, *Into the Silent Land*, 32–34.

mutely Braille two dozen ribs,
each commandeering its own space
24–7, salaaming and shifting,
then rising. *Selah-h-h-h* . . .

Next, re-envision those lungs
as an inner atlas:
one hundred routes
funneling
into branch lines,
cloverleafs,
cul de sacs.
Wild as papyrus, they might be
a psalter. A Rorschach. A centerfold.

Or call them dual panniers
flanking a breastbone,
an albino koi kissing a mirror,
all lips and flared silk.

Now, boneless as a cat at rest,
inhabit that next inhale, discerning
how spacious a backbone can be,
freeing shoulders to roll, the head to loll
and lift, floating into place: the body
aligned, alight, a home for the holy.

—"Next Breath, Best Breath," Laurie Klein[24]

    Breathing reminds us of our utter dependence on that which is "not us if we are to exist, it recollects our non-self-sufficiency, our creatureliness." In the words of French philosopher Jean-Louis Chrétien, "Breathing is the perpetual refutation of solipsism[25] in action, and of any thesis according to which our life is self-sufficient, or would moreover attempt to be so. At every moment, we depend on the ambient air, and if we can cease eating for a few weeks, or even drinking for a few days, our apnea cannot last for more than a few moments."[26] Let your breathing remind you of your need and the gift of being that you receive.

    Second, *attend to the mind*. The major initial difficulty with silence is quieting the mind, which can experience thoughts like popcorns on a griddle. John Cassian recommended meditating on a short verse over and

---

24. In Klein, *Where the Sky Opens*, 8. Used with permission.
25. The belief that nothing exists apart from yourself.
26. Chrétien, *Ten Meditations*, 1.

over to stop distractions.[27] This practice was picked up by St. Benedict[28] and thence in the monastic tradition. The spiritual discipline of *lectio divina*, sacred reading, emerged from it.

We could think of lectio divina as a way of prayerfully reading Scripture. It involves four "moments":

- Read (*lectio*): in which we read a short passage (usually a biblical passage) aloud.

- Reflect (*meditatio*): in which we take time to ponder the text, listening for a "word" from the Lord. Does any phrase or word stand out? Silently chew it over in your mind, ruminating on it like a cow chewing the cud.

- Respond (*oratio*): in which we return that which we have received in our meditative listening back to God in prayer.

- Rest (*contemplatio*): in which we silently and contemplatively rest in the presence of God.

There are plenty of books on the ancient practice of lectio divina,[29] so I will say no more, except for one thing: that it can fuel Christian eco-spirituality very easily if creation texts from Scripture are taken as the subjects. It is a great way of allowing such passages to penetrate more deeply into the soul and to form us. In outdoor worship one could, on occasion, use a lectio on a creation text in the slot for the talk. And one could easily devote sessions of outdoor prayer to lectio.

The idea of contemplating a text was often distilled down further to a single prayer word,[30] known in the West as a *formula*[31] (though now often referred to as a "mantra" or a "sacred word"). It is usually suggested that we pick a single formula (e.g., "Jesus" or "Spirit" or "Sophia") and pray it over and over, each day. It is best to *pray it in rhythm with one's breathing*. John Main sees the aim in beginning meditation to be repeating the mantra for the full duration of the meditation, without interruption, while remaining calm and undistracted.[32] The word brings the mind back from distractions

---

27. Cassian, *Conferences*, 10.10.
28. *Rule of St Benedict* 42.6, 13; 73.14.
29. E.g., Hall, *Too Deep for Words*; Pennington, *Lection Divina*.
30. *Cloud of Unknowing*, ch. 39 speaks of it as praying in a "little word" as opposed to praying with "many words."
31. Latin for "a small pattern" or rule/method/principle.
32. Main, *Word into Silence*, 14–15.

to silence, creating openness to God in our "deep mind." What is sometimes called "centering prayer" is a version of this practice.[33]

A similar form of contemplative practice, but with a slightly longer prayer, is the well-known "Jesus Prayer." This exists in various forms but is usually known in something like the following form: "Lord Jesus Christ, Son of God, have mercy on me, a sinner." This is prayed repeatedly and reflectively, much like the "mantra" mentioned above.

The basic version of the Jesus Prayer that I use in pursuit of a contemplative eco-spirituality is the following: *"Lord Jesus Christ, Wisdom of God, have mercy on me"* (and in the penitential seasons of Advent and Lent I add *"a sinner"*). I have a couple of different patterns of breath with the prayer, but the one I have found most useful is:

Out-breath:	Lord Jesus Christ, Wisdom of God	[pause]
In-breath:	Have mercy on me (a sinner)	[pause]

(If starting on an "out" breath" seems back to front, the reason I do it that way is so that I feel myself *receiving* mercy as I receive the new breath.) Alternatively, one could gradually reduce the prayer as follows:

In-breath:	Lord Jesus Christ	[pause]
Out-breath:	Wisdom of God	[pause]
In-breath:	Have mercy on me	[pause]
Out-breath:	(a sinner)	[pause]

After a set period moving into:

In-breath:	Jesus	[pause]
Out-breath:	Wisdom	[pause]
In-breath:	mercy	[pause]
Out-breath:	(sinner)	[pause]

Then to

In-breath:	Jesus	[pause]
Out-breath:		[pause]

Finally moving into simply breathing, mind still and open to God. "This silence is not the absence of noise; it is the vast interior landscape that invites us to stillness."[34] And in stillness we simply *behold*.

Critical to remember is that these are *not techniques*. Technique aims to control. God cannot be manipulated. Rather, "We enter a land of silence

33. For an excellent introduction, see Boyer, *Centering Prayer for Everyone*.
34. Ross, *Writing the Icon of the Heart*, xvii.

by the silence of surrender, and there is no map of the silence that is surrender. There are skills, however, by which we learn to dispose ourselves to surrender and thus to discover this uncharted land."[35] Silence is an openness to sheer grace: "It is not something we can attain alone, by intellectual effort. . . . It is not a kind of self-hypnosis, resulting from concentrating on our own inner spiritual being. It is not the fruit of our own efforts. It is the gift of God; . . . the natural life in us has been completed, elevated, transformed and fulfilled in Christ by the Holy Spirit."[36]

We should also appreciate that such practice aims not at seeking to *acquire* something from God but at realizing what God has *already* given us in Christ.[37] We aim to grasp (*not* to bring about) our existing "differencing union" with God achieved in Christ: we are like a sponge in the ocean—*in* the ocean, *filled with* the ocean, yet *not* itself the ocean.[38]

In terms of teaching individuals to practice silence, especially with an eco-spiritual tilt, the above advice is invaluable. One might also encourage people to explore silence in other ways:

- Silent, meditative walks.[39]

- Paying close and sustained attention to a single item in nature, e.g., a flower.

- Listening to the eloquent "sound of silence" from creation, the "music" of the patterns we see around us.[40]

- Silently contemplating an artwork with a creation focus. This is sometimes known as *visio divina* (divine vision).[41]

- Focusing attention through touching an item (e.g., a wooden holding cross, a stone, a feather, water).

- Sitting silently, spending some time noticing your surroundings using different senses, one at a time: Look—slowly, carefully. Listen. Smell. Use your touch and taste to explore the natural world. This is a simple exercise in attention. You can then turn your focus from what

---

35. Laird, *Into the Silent Land*, 3.
36. Merton, *New Seeds of Contemplation*, 4–5.
37. This is a major emphasis of Thomas Merton. See *New Seeds of Contemplation*.
38. Laird, *Into the Silent Land*, 17.
39. For an introduction to walking meditation, see Boyer, *Centering Prayer for Everyone*, 34–35.
40. See Merton's beautiful reflections on God in creation in *New Seeds of Contemplation*, ch. 5.
41. For an introduction, see Boyer, *Centering Prayer for Everyone*, 28–33.

is around you to your own body: What do you feel in each part of your body? Notice yourself as embodied. Then, finally, you can move into the wordless stillness of contemplative prayer.

Much of this is really a contemplative form of *invitation* and *hospitality*—of welcoming the unexpected guest in nature and embracing her, actively attending to her, and in doing so perhaps discovering that we are entertaining angels, and ultimately the Divine.

b) Silence in Communal Spirituality

Worship leaders do well to remember that *silence speaks*. William Desmond's comments on the silence in the theater are pertinent here:

> Wordings need not be confined to vocalized utterances. Nothing need be said for something to be said. An actor stands there and simply by being there is a transformation of the space of the between in the direction of communicative possibility. An accomplished actor will know how to hold the silence, and hold it not so much as silence but as a way of being in communication, both with other players and those who watch.[42]

In communal worship, silence is best experienced if some empathetic guidance is given on how to make the most of it: in our noisy culture, uncomfortable with quiet, we need to help normalize communal silence, removing its awkwardness.[43] This means doing it regularly and gently guiding congregants in it.[44] If more than a cursory pause is used, such silences can become powerful moments of openness.

The tone of a silence will depend on its context. We might think of silence having a shape, determined by what is around it. For instance:

- At the start, the leader can guide the people into a stillness before God, setting aside distractions—silence as preparing to face the divine.

- Before confession or after confession—silence for reflection on one's own conduct.

- After the Bible reading or sermon—silence for pondering and individual application.

---

42. Desmond, *Gift of Beauty*, 258.
43. Runcorn, *Silence*, 8.
44. Which may include indicating how long a particular silence will last.

- In intercessions—silence allowing individuals space to hold up to God situations on their minds.
- Space for wordless lament, introduced by a sensitive prayer, after news of a communal tragedy.
- In open times of listening to the Spirit for charismatic "words" or "pictures"—silence as receptive openness.
- After the Eucharist—silence for restful, contemplative engagement.

The practice of silence makes it easier for us to be grasped afresh by a sense of the *mystery* at the heart of creation, which solicits our sense of *wonder*. In 1819, John Keats was among many who worried that modern empirical natural philosophy (i.e., science), for all its many merits, was "disenchanting" the world:

> There was an awful rainbow once in heaven:
> We know her woof, her texture; she is given
> In the dull catalogue of common things.
> Philosophy will clip an Angel's wings,
> Conquer all mysteries by rule and line,
> Empty the haunted air, and gnomic mine—
> Unweave a rainbow[.][45]

We need help to "reenchant" the world, to perceive the integration of the material and the spiritual. Not to reject the countless insights into it granted us by the sciences, which should be welcomed with much gratitude, but to appreciate that the truth of the world is always infinitely *more* than science can speak. It needs metaphysics, it needs poetry, it needs art, it needs prayer, and in the end, it needs silence.

We live in a culture that to its own detriment fears and avoids silence. Churches need leaders with the courage to nurture counter-cultural spaces for silence, helping us resist the unbroken soundscapes we hide behind.

---

45. From Keats' poem, "Lamia." For an excellent study of learning from the Romantic movement for a path to re-enchant the world, see Yost, *Romantic Life*.

The Sound of Silence

Sources Cited

Adams, Marilyn McCord. *Horrendous Evils and the Goodness of God*. Ithaca, NY: Cornell University Press, 1999.
Angela of Foligno. *The Book of the Blessed Angela of Foligno*. In *Angela of Foligno: Complete Works*, translated by Paul Lachance, 123–318. Classics of Western Spirituality. New York: Paulist, 1993.
Aquinas, Thomas. *Summa theologiae*. Translated by the Fathers of the English Dominican Province. 2nd ed. 22 vols. London: Burns, Oates & Washbourne, 1912.
Balthasar, Hans Urs von. *Prayer*. Translated by A. V. Littledale. London: SPCK, 1961.
Barrett Browning, Elizabeth. *Aurora Leigh* (1856), Book Seven. https://www.gutenberg.org/ebooks/56621.
Bauckham, Richard. *The Bible and Ecology: Rediscovering the Community of Creation*. London: Darton, Longman and Todd, 2010.
Belousek, Darrin W. Snyder. "God the Creator in the Wisdom of Solomon: A Theological Commentary." Unpublished paper, 2015. https://www.academia.edu/15912414/God_the_Creator_in_the_Wisdom_of_Solomon_A_Theological_Commentary.
Belisle, Peter Damien. *The Language of Silence: The Changing Face of Monastic Solitude*. London: Darton, Longman and Todd, 2003.
Benedict. *The Rule of Saint Benedict*. Online: http://www.osb.org/rb/text/toc.html.
Berry, Wendell. "How to Be a Poet." https://www.poetryfoundation.org/poetrymagazine/poems/41087/how-to-be-a-poet.
———. *It All Turns on Affection: The Jefferson Lecture and Other Essays*. New York: Counterpoint, 2012.
Blake, William. *The Marriage of Heaven and Hell* (1790). https://blakearchive.org/work/mhh.
Bonaventure. *The Works of Bonaventure, Volume II, The Breviloquium*. Translated by José de Vicck. Paterson, NJ: St. Anthony's Guild, 1963.
Bowen, Nancy R. "God and Wisdom: The Power of Relationship." Paper given at the Oxford Institute of Methodist Theological Studies, August 1997.
Boyer, Lindsay. *Centering Prayer for Everyone*. Eugene, OR: Cascade, 2020.
Brookins, Timothy A. *Rediscovering the Wisdom of the Corinthians: Paul, Stoicism, and Spiritual Hierarchy*. Grand Rapids: Eerdmans, 2024.

Brown, William P. *Seeing the Psalms: A Theology of Metaphor.* Louisville: Westminster John Knox, 2002.

Burroughs, Presian Renee. *Creation's Slavery and Liberation: Paul's Letter to Rome in the Face of Imperial and Industrial Agriculture.* Eugene, OR: Cascade, 2022.

Calvin, John. *Calvin's Commentaries, Volume 6, Psalms 93–150.* Grand Rapids: Baker, 1989.

Carrington, Damian. "World on Brink of Five 'Disastrous' Climate Tipping Points, Study Finds." *The Guardian*, September 8, 2022. https://www.theguardian.com/environment/2022/sep/08/world-on-brink-five-climate-tipping-points-study-finds.

Cassian, John. *The Conferences of John Cassian.* Translation and notes by Edgar C. S. Gibson. Online: http://www.osb.org/lectio/cassian/conf/index.html.

Chesterton, G. K. *Collected Works, Volume 1.* San Francisco: Ignatius, 1986.

Chrétien, Jean-Louis. *Ten Meditations for Catching and Losing One's Breath.* Translated by Steven DeLay. Kalos. Eugene, OR: Cascade, 2024.

Christie, Douglas. *The Blue Sapphire of the Mind: Notes for a Contemplative Ecology.* New York: Oxford University Press, 2012.

Clark, Stephen R. L. *How to Think About the Earth: Philosophical and Theological Models for Ecology.* London: Mowbray, 1993.

Cocksedge, Simon, Samuel Double, and Nicholas Alan Worssam. *Seeing Differently: Franciscans and Creation.* Norwich, UK: Canterbury, 2021.

Coffin, William Sloane. *A Passion for the Possible: A Message to U.S. Churches.* 2nd ed. Louisville: Westminster John Knox, 2004.

Copeland, Rebecca L. *Entangled Being: Unoriginal Sin and Entangled Problems.* Waco, TX: Baylor University Press, 2024.

Darragh, Neil. *At Home in the Earth.* Auckland: Accent, 2000.

Davidson, Richard M. "Proverbs 8 and the Place of Christ in the Trinity." *Journal of the Adventist Society* 17.1 (2006) 33–54.

Davis, Ellen F. "The Pain of Seeing Clearly: Prophetic Views of the Created Order." In *Biblical Prophecy: Perspectives for Contemporary Ministry, Interpretation: Resources for the Use of Scripture in the Church*, 83–110. Louisville: Westminster John Knox, 2014.

———. *Scripture, Culture, and Agriculture: An Agrarian Reading of the Bible.* Cambridge: Cambridge University Press, 2009.

Davison, Andrew. *Astrobiology and Christian Doctrine: Exploring the Implications of Life in the Universe.* Cambridge: Cambridge University Press, 2023.

Desmond, William. *The Gift of Beauty.* Veritas. Eugene, OR: Cascade, 2018.

Douglas, Sally. *Early Church Understandings of Jesus as the Female Divine: The Scandal of the Scandal of Particularity.* LNTS 557. London: T&T Clark, 2016.

———. *Jesus Sophia: Returning to Woman Wisdom in the Bible, Practice, and Prayer.* Eugene, OR: Cascade, 2023.

Dowling, Maurice. "Proverbs 8:22–31 in the Christology of the Early Church." *IBS* 24 (2002) 99–117.

Ducharmie, Jamie. "7 Surprising Health Benefits of Gratitude" *Time Magazine*, November 20, 2017. http://time.com/5026174/health-benefits-of-gratitude/.

Dunn, James D. G. *Christology in the Making: A New Testament Inquiry into the Origins of the Doctrine of the Incarnation.* London: SCM, 1980.

Edwards, Denis. "Experience of Word and Spirit in the Natural World." In *The Nature of Things: Rediscovering the Spiritual in God's Creation*, edited by Graham Buxton and Norman Habel, 13–26. Eugene, OR: Pickwick, 2016.

———. *How God Acts: Creation, Redemption, and Special Divine Action*. Theology and the Sciences. Minneapolis: Fortress, 2010.

Farag, Lois. *Balance of the Heart: Desert Spirituality for Twenty-First Century Christians*. Eugene, OR: Cascade, 2012.

Garvey, Jon. *God's Good Earth: The Case for an Unfallen Creation*. Eugene, OR: Cascade, 2019.

Gorman, Michael J. *Cruciformity: Paul's Narrative Spirituality of the Cross*. Grand Rapids: Eerdmans, 2001.

Gottwald, Norman K. *The Hebrew Bible in Its Social World and Ours*. Atlanta: Scholars, 1993.

Grant, Kerr. *The Life and Work of Sir William Bragg*. Brisbane: University of Queensland Press, 1952.

Green Christian. "Deep Waters" course. https://greenchristian.org.uk/deep-waters-a-project-of-borrowed-time/.

Greeves, Tom, Sue Andrew, and Chris Chapman. *The Three Hares: A Curiosity Worth Regarding*. South Molton, UK: Skerryvore 2016.

Grumett, David. *The Bible and Farm Animal Welfare*. Eugene, OR: Cascade, 2024.

Haarsma, Loren. *When Did Sin Begin? Human Evolution and the Doctrine of Original Sin*. Grand Rapids: Baker Academic, 2021.

Hadot, Pierre. *What Is Ancient Philosophy?* Cambridge: Harvard University Press, 2004.

Hall, Thelma. *Too Deep for Words: Rediscovering Lectio Divina*. Mahwah, NJ: Paulist, 1988.

Hanby, Michael. *No God, No Science: Theology, Cosmology, Biology*. Oxford: Wiley-Blackwell, 2013.

Harrison, Peter. "Subduing the Earth: Genesis 1, Early Modern Science, and the Exploitation of Nature." *Journal of Religion* 79 (1999) 86–109.

Hartropp, Andrew. *What Is Economic Justice? Biblical and Secular Perspectives Contrasted*. PTM. Milton Keynes, UK: Paternoster, 2008.

Hayes, Zachary. *The Gift of Being: A Theology of Creation*. Collegeville, MN: Liturgical, 2001.

Hodson, Martin J., and Margot H. Hodson. *The Ethics of Environmental Management: Does Stewardship Lead Us Down a Blind Alley?* Bramcote, UK: Grove, 2024.

Hooker, Richard. *Laws of Ecclesiastical Polity*. Volume 1. 7th ed. Arranged by John Keble. Oxford: Clarendon, 1888.

Holland, Tom. *Dominion: The Making of the Western Mind*. New York: Little, Brown, 2019.

Hopkins, Gerard Manly. "God's Grandeur" (1877). https://www.poetryfoundation.org/poems/44395/gods-grandeur.

Houston, Walter J. *Justice for the Poor? Social Justice in the Old Testament in Concept and Practice*. Eugene, OR: Cascade, 2020.

Hughson, Thomas. *Neanderthal Religion? Theology in Dialogue with Archaeology*. Eugene, OR: Pickwick, 2024.

Hutton, Ronald. *The Triumph of the Moon: A History of Modern Pagan Witchcraft*. Oxford: Oxford University Press, 1995.

Ingold, Tim. *Being Alive: Essays in Movement, Knowledge and Description*. London: Routledge, 2011.
Isaac the Syrian. *Ascetical Homilies of Isaac the Syrian*. Boston: Holy Transfiguration Monastery, 1984.
Joerstad, Mari. *The Hebrew Bible and Environmental Ethics*. New York: Cambridge University Press, 2019.
Johnson, Elizabeth A. *Ask the Beasts: Darwin and the Love of God*. London: Bloomsbury Continuum, 2015.
Juza, Ryan P. *The New Testament and the Future of the Cosmos*. Eugene, OR: Pickwick, 2020.
Karlowicz, Dariusz. *Socrates and Other Saints: Early Christian Understandings of Reason and Philosophy*. Kalos. Eugene, OR: Cascade, 2017.
Klein, Laurie. *Where the Sky Opens: A Partial Cosmography*. Poiema Poetry. Eugene, OR: Cascade, 2015.
Kringlebotten, Kjetil. *Liturgy, Theurgy, and Active Participation: On Theurgic Participation in God*. Eugene, OR: Cascade, 2023.
Laird, Martin. *Into the Silent Land: The Practice of Contemplation*. London: Darton, Longman and Todd, 2006.
Latour, Bruno. *If We Lose the Earth, We Lose Our Souls*. Cambridge: Polity, 2024.
LeFebvre, Michael. *The Liturgy of Creation: Understanding Calendars in Old Testament Context*. Downers Grove, IL: IVP Academic, 2019.
Lenzi, Alan. "Proverbs 8:22–31: Three Perspectives on Its Composition." *Journal of Biblical Literature* 125.4 (2006) 687–714.
Lewis, C. S. "The Alliterative Metre." In *Selected Literary Essays*, edited by Walter Hooper, 15–26. Cambridge: Cambridge University Press, 1980.
———. *The Last Battle*. 1956. Reprint, London: HarperCollins, 2009.
———. *The Voyage of the Dawn Treader*. 1952. Reprint, London: Collins, 1995.
Lodahl, Michael. "Wisdom's Invitation." In *Matthew Matters: The Yoke of Wisdom and the Church of Tomorrow*, 1–16. Didsbury Lectures series. Eugene, OR: Cascade, 2021.
Longley, Sally. *Conversations with Silence: Rosetta Stone of the Soul*. Eugene, OR: Cascade, 2021.
Lucas, Hannah J. *Sensing the Sacred: Recovering a Mystagogical Vision of Knowledge and Salvation*. Veritas. Eugene, OR: Cascade, 2023.
Lynch, Matthew J. *Flood and Fury: Old Testament Violence and the Shalom of God*. Downers Grove, IL: IVP Academic, 2023.
MacCulloch, Diarmaid. *Silence: A Christian History*. New York, Viking, 2013.
MacFarlane, Robert. *Is a River Alive?* London: Penguin, 2025.
MacIntyre, Alasdair. *After Virtue: A Study in Moral Theory*. 3rd ed. Notre Dame: University of Notre Dame Press, 2007.
Macquarrie, John. *The Humility of God*. Louisville: Westminster John Knox, 1978.
Main, John. *Words into Silence: A Manual for Christian Meditation*. Norwich, UK: Canterbury, 2006.
Mann, Mark. "The Church Fathers and Two Books Theology." Biologos, November 4, 2012. https://biologos.org/articles/the-church-fathers-and-two-books-theology.
Mayhew-Smith, Nick, with Sarah Brush. *Landscape Liturgies: Outdoor Worship Resources from the Christian Tradition*. Norwich, UK: Canterbury, 2021.

McFarland, Ian A. *From Nothing: A Theology of Creation*. Louisville: Westminster John Knox, 2014.

Meek, Donald E. *The Quest for Celtic Christianity*. Edinburgh: Handsel, 2000.

Meek, Esther Lightcap. *A Little Manual for Knowing*. Eugene, OR: Cascade, 2014.

———. *Loving to Know: Covenant Epistemology*. Eugene, OR: Cascade, 2011.

Merton, Thomas. *Choosing to Love the World: On Contemplation*. Boulder, CO: Sounds True, 2008.

———. *Dialogues with Silence: Prayers and Drawings*. New York: Harper Collins, 2001.

———. *New Seeds of Contemplation*. 1961. Reprint, New York: New Direction, 2007.

Middleton, J. Richard. *A New Heaven and a New Earth: Reclaiming Biblical Eschatology*. Grand Rapids: Baker Academic, 2014.

Moltmann, Jürgen. *God in Creation: A New Theology of Creation and the Spirit of God*. Minneapolis: Fortress, 1993.

Moo, Douglas J., and Jonathan A. Moo. *Creation Care: A Biblical Theology of the Natural World*. Grand Rapids: Zondervan, 2018.

Moriarty, John. *Serious Sounds*. Dublin: Lilliput, 2007.

Morris, Henry. "The Fall, the Curse, and Evolution." *Back to Genesis* 112a (April 1998). https://www.icr.org.

Murphy, Roland E. *Proverbs*. WBC 22. Nashville: Thomas Nelson, 1998.

Napier, Daniel Austin. *Soul Whisperer: Jesus' Way Among the Philosophers*. Eugene, OR: Cascade, 2023.

Niehaus, Jeffrey J. *Righteousness*. 3 vols. Eugene, OR: Pickwick, 2023–24.

Nixon, Rob. *Slow Violence and the Environmentalism of the Poor*. Cambridge: Harvard University Press, 2011.

Parker, Theodore. *Ten Sermons of Religion*. New York: Charles S. Frances and Co., 1853.

Parry, Robin A. *The Biblical Cosmos: A Pilgrim's Guide to the Weird and Wonderful World of the Bible*. Eugene, OR: Cascade, 2014.

———. "Creation Out of Nothing. Part 5: Is It Biblical?" YouTube video, 5:05. https://www.youtube.com/watch?v=d6G2MjB1K4I&t=117s.

———. "Did Noah's Flood Happen? Theological Reflections." Parts 1–2. Theological Scribbles (blog). https://theologicalscribbles.blogspot.com/search?q=Did+Noah%27s+Flood+Happen%3F+Theological+Reflections.

———. *Lamentations*. Two Horizons. Grand Rapids: Eerdmans, 2010.

Pennington, Jonathan T. *Jesus the Great Philosopher: Rediscovering the Wisdom Needed for the Good Life*. Grand Rapids: Brazos, 2020.

Pennington, M. Basil. *Lectio Divina: Renewing the Ancient Practice of Praying the Scriptures*. Redwood City, CA: PublishDrive, 1998.

Perdue, Leo G. *Wisdom and Creation: The Theology of Wisdom Literature*. 1994. Reprint, Eugene, OR: Wipf and Stock, 2009.

Peters, Greg. *The Monkhood of All Believers: The Monastic Foundation of Christian Spirituality*. Grand Rapids: Baker Academic, 2018.

———. *The Story of Monasticism: Retrieving an Ancient Tradition for Contemporary Spirituality*. Grand Rapids: Baker Academic, 2015.

Polkinghorne, John. *Science and the Trinity: The Christian Encounter with Reality*. New Haven: Yale University Press, 2004.

Raworth, Kate. *Doughnut Economics: Seven Ways to Think Like a 21st-Century Economist*. With a new afterword. New York: Random House Business, 2018.

Reyburn, Duncan B. *The Roots of the World: The Remarkable Prescience of G. K. Chesterton*. Veritas. Eugene, OR: Cascade, 2025.

Richter, Sandra L. *Stewards of Eden: What Scripture Says About the Environment and Why It Matters*. Downers Grove, IL: IVP Academic, 2020.

Ringgren, Helmer. *Word and Wisdom: Studies in the Hypostatization of Divine Qualities and Function in the Ancient Near East*. Lund: Ohlssons, 1947.

Roberts, Robert C. *Virtue Ethics in Christian Perspective*. Cascade Companions. Eugene, OR: Cascade, 2024.

Ross, Maggie. *Silence: A Users Guide. Volume 1: Process*. Eugene, OR: Cascade, 2014.

———. *Writing the Icon of the Heart: In Silence Beholding*. Eugene, OR: Cascade, 2013.

Rowthorn, Anne, and Jeffrey Rawthorn, eds. *God's Good Earth in Crisis: Liturgies of Lament*. Eugene, OR: Cascade, 2024.

Runcorn, David. *Silence*. Bramcote, UK: Grove, 1986.

Russell, Norman, trans. *The Lives of the Desert Fathers: The Historia Monachorum in Aegypto*. Cistercian Studies 34. Piffard, NY: Cistercian, 1981.

Sandoval, Timothy J. *The Moral Vision of Proverbs: A Virtue Oriented Approach to Wisdom*. Grand Rapids: Baker Academic, 2024.

Santmire, Paul. "A Supremely Natural God: Fragments of a Christian Spirituality of Nature." In *The Nature of Things: Rediscovering the Spiritual in God's Creation*, edited by Graham Buxton and Norman Habel, 27–40. Eugene, OR: Pickwick, 2016.

Schroer, Silvia. *Wisdom Has Built Her House: Studies on the Figure of Sophia in the Bible*. Translated by L. M. Maloney and W. McDonough. Collegeville, MN: Liturgical, 2000.

Scott, Carol, and Caitlin Gilson Smith. *Luminous Darkness: The Passion of the Last Words*. Kalos. Eugene, OR: Cascade, 2025.

Scott, Martin. *Sophia and the Johannine Jesus*. JSNTSupp 71. Sheffield, UK: Sheffield Academic, 1992.

Scott, R. B. Y. *Proverbs, Ecclesiastes*. Anchor Bible 18. Garden City, NY: Doubleday, 1965.

Soulen, R. Kendall. *The Divine Name(s) and the Holy Trinity: Volume 1, Distinguishing the Voices*. Louisville: Westminster John Knox, 2011.

Southgate, Christopher. *The Groaning of Creation: God, Evolution, and the Problem of Evil*. Louisville: Westminster John Knox, 2008.

Srokosz, Meric, and Rebecca Watson. *Blue Planet, Blue God: The Bible and the Sea*. London: SCM, 2017.

Stanley, Bruce. *Forest Church: A Field Guide to Nature Connection for Groups and Individuals*. N.p.: Mystic Christ, 2020.

Stovell, Beth M., and David J. Fuller. *The Book of the Twelve*. Cascade Companions. Eugene, OR: Cascade, 2022.

Sutterfield, Ragan. *The Art of Being a Creature: Meditations on Humus and Humility*. Eugene, OR: Cascade, 2024.

Taylor, Michael Dominic. *The Foundations of Nature: Metaphysics of Gift for an Integral Ecological Ethic*. Veritas. Eugene, OR: Cascade, 2020.

Terrien. Samuel. "Wisdom in the Psalter." In *In Search of Wisdom*, edited by L. G. Perdue and W. J. Wiseman, 51–72. Louisville: Westminster John Knox, 1993.

Theokritoff, Elizabeth. *Living in God's Creation*. Crestwood, NY: SVS, 2009.

Thomas, Ryan. "אל קנה ארץ: Creator, Begetter, or Owner of the Earth?" *Ugarit-Forschungen* 48 (2017) 451–521.
Thompson, Francis. "To a Snowflake." https://poets.org/poem/snowflake.
Tolkien, J. R. R. *The Fellowship of the Ring.* London: George Allen & Unwin, 1954.
Torvend, Samuel. *Monastic Ecological Wisdom: A Living Tradition.* Collegeville, MN: Liturgical, 2023.
Trebeck, Katherine, and Jeremy Williams. *The Economics of Arrival: Ideas for a Grown-Up Economy.* Bristol: Policy, 2019.
Valerio, Ruth. *L Is for Lifestyle: Christian Living That Doesn't Cost the Earth.* 2nd ed. Nottingham, UK: IVP, 2019.
Van Leeuwen, Raymond C. "Cosmos, Temple, House: Building and Wisdom in Ancient Mesopotamia and Israel." In *From the Foundations to the Crenellations*, edited by Mark Boda and Jamie Novotny, 399–421. Münster: Ugarit Verlag, 2010.
Ward, Benedicta, trans. *The Sayings of the Desert Fathers. The Alphabetical Collection.* London: Mowbray, 1975.
Weil, Simone. *Notebooks.* Volume 1. Translated by A. Wills. London: Routledge, 1956.
Wenham, Gordon J. "Sanctuary Symbolism in the Garden of Eden." *Proceedings of the World Congress of Jewish Studies* 9 (1981) 19–26.
White, Lynn, Jr. "The Historical Roots of Our Ecological Crisis." *Science* 155 (March 1967) 1203–7.
Wiederkehr, Macrina. *A Tree Full of Angels: Seeing the Holy in the Ordinary.* London: HarperCollins, 1990.
Wiggins, Steve. *Weathering the Psalms: A Meteorotheological Survey.* Eugene, OR: Cascade, 2014.
Wilkinson, Loren. *Circles and the Cross: Cosmos, Consciousness, Christ, and the Human Place in Creation.* Eugene, OR: Cascade, 2023.
Wirzba, Norman. *From Nature to Creation: A Christian Vision for Understanding and Loving Our World.* Grand Rapids: Baker Academic, 2015.
Wright, Paul H. *Understanding the Ecology of the Bible: An Introductory Atlas.* Jerusalem: Carta, 2018.
Yost, D. Andrew. *The Romantic Life: Five Strategies to Re-Enchant the World.* Eugene, OR: Cascade, 2022.

www.ingramcontent.com/pod-product-compliance
Lightning Source LLC
Chambersburg PA
CBHW022000220426
43663CB00007B/902